ULRIKE OTTINGER

OTHER BOOKS BY LAURENCE A. RICKELS PUBLISHED BY
THE UNIVERSITY OF MINNESOTA PRESS

Acting Out in Groups
The Case of California
The Devil Notebooks
Nazi Psychoanalysis
    Volume I. Only Psychoanalysis Won the War
    Volume II. Crypto-Fetishism
    Volume III. Psy Fi
The Vampire Lectures

ULRIKE OTTINGER
THE AUTOBIOGRAPHY OF ART CINEMA

LAURENCE A. RICKELS

UNIVERSITY OF MINNESOTA PRESS
MINNEAPOLIS · LONDON

Photographs copyright 2008 by Ulrike Ottinger

Copyright 2008 by the Regents of the University of Minnesota

All rights reserved. No part of this publication may be reproduced, stored in a retrieval system, or transmitted, in any form or by any means, electronic, mechanical, photocopying, recording, or otherwise, without the prior written permission of the publisher.

Published by the University of Minnesota Press
111 Third Avenue South, Suite 290
Minneapolis, MN 55401-2520
http://www.upress.umn.edu

Library of Congress Cataloging-in-Publication Data
Rickels, Laurence A.
   Ulrike Ottinger : the autobiography of art cinema / Laurence A. Rickels.
   p. cm.
   Includes bibliographic references.
   ISBN 978-0-8166-5330-0 (hc : alk. paper) — ISBN 978-0-8166-5331-7 (pb : alk. paper)
   1. Ottinger, Ulrike, 1942—Criticism and interpretation. I. Title.
   PN1998.3.O855R53 2008
   791.43023'3092—dc22
                                                                      2008012866

Printed in the United States of America on acid-free paper

The University of Minnesota is an equal-opportunity educator and employer.

15 14 13 12 11 10 09 08   10 9 8 7 6 5 4 3 2 1

It has always been rather ridiculous that she who is good friends with all the world and can know them and they can know her, has always been the admired of the precious. But she always says some day they, anybody, will find out that she is of interest to them, she and her writing. And she always consoles herself that the newspapers are always interested. They always say, she says, that my writing is appalling but they always quote it and what is more, they quote it correctly, and those they say they admire they do not quote. This at some of her most bitter moments has been a consolation. My sentences do get under their skin, only they do not know that they do, she has often said.

—Gertrude Stein, *The Autobiography of Alice B. Toklas*

CONTENTS

ACKNOWLEDGMENTS — viii
A NOTE ON THE PHOTOGRAPHS — ix
PREFACE — xi

INTRODUCTION: ART/CINEMA, ART/JOURNALISM — 1

1. BOUNCING BIO — 16
Laocoon and Sons
Berlin Fever — Wolf Vostell
The Infatuation of the Blue Sailors

2. SATANIC ARTS — 24
Madame X: An Absolute Ruler

3. BETWEEN MEDIA — 42
Ticket of No Return

4. HIT AND MISS — 65
Freak Orlando

5. OPERATION ART — 90
The Image of Dorian Gray in the Yellow Press

6. THE ART OF EVERYDAY LIFE — 115
China: The Arts — Everyday Life
Superbia
Usinimage

7. JOHANNA'S ARK; OR, DOCUMENTARY FILM'S   123
COVENANT WITH ART CINEMA
Johanna d'Arc of Mongolia

8. REAL TIME TRAVEL   137
Taiga

9. I WAS THERE   150
Countdown
Exil Shanghai

10. CURTAINS   166
Das Verlobungsfest im Feenreich

11. MY LAST INTERVIEW WITH ULRIKE OTTINGER   171
Southeast Passage
Ester
The Exemplar
Twelve Chairs

12. TOTEM TABOO   185
"Totem"

13. GOING APE   191
Prater

WORKS CITED   197

ACKNOWLEDGMENTS

This book was made possible by the generous cooperation of Ulrike Ottinger. The German Academic Exchange Service (DAAD) supported my on-location work in Ottinger's at-home archives.

I thank Ulrike Ottinger as well as her partner, Katharina Sykora, for hours and hours of hospitality and good company.

A NOTE ON THE PHOTOGRAPHS

Between the covers of this study, I have selected not film stills but photographs that Ottinger took "in the context" of each film (this is the formulation that was used in identifying the photographs on display at the David Zwirner Gallery in 2000). The correct setting of the compass for the voyage setting sail into Ottinger's work, into her way of seeing, is the unstoppable abundance of Ottinger's image language. "Her works are expeditions into an unknown visual territory, in a world of reflections and transformations, beauty and dreams, fears and visions, but also of the precise documentary gaze. Out of the montage of the independently existing filmic components next to one another there emerge sculptural, theatrical, and unorthodox images of great suggestive power. In these compositions there is a quality of perception that sharpens the capacity for making distinctions and that separates out in a differentiated manner content from its representation" (Franke, 51).

If I have just the same been selective in the number of illustrations this study reproduces, choosing those with the greatest cathexis in my exploration of her work, then I am relieved of a certain duty by the availability of Ottinger's Web site, a miniaturization (which, as Freud points out, holds interchangeable places with magnification) of an entire alternate world. Click in to it before or while you read this book: www.ulrikeottinger.com.

Finally, Ottinger's substantial volume, *Bildarchive*, which appeared in 2006 (at the same time as the English-language version, *Image Archive*), thoroughly documents her photographic work in a format to have and to hold.

The Mongolian princess (in the context of Johanna d'Arc of Mongolia).

PREFACE

This study was hosted and supported by a series of international art-world figures and venues. Diana Thater invited me to organize a mini retrospective of the films of Ulrike Ottinger at Art Center College of Design in Pasadena. My introductory remarks at those screenings gave me first formulations of my readings of *Freak Orlando, Dorian Gray im Spiegel der Boulevardpresse (The Image of Dorian Gray in the Yellow Press),* and *Johanna d'Arc of Mongolia.* I introduced Thater to this work; one introduction deserving another, she in turn introduced David Zwirner to Ottinger's image language, which was at that time an unknown quality in the art world. And yet there was inevitably a déjà vu effect along for these introductions. One of the major art stars of the 1990s, Matthew Barney, had during the period of Ottinger's missingness established himself with video and film works that at first sight share the Ottinger look of her 1970s and 1980s fictional films.

Eva Meyer, our friend in common, first introduced me to Ulrike Ottinger in summer 1990 in Berlin. Ottinger was finishing up postproduction work on *Countdown,* for which Meyer had composed the intertitle texts. Self-reflexivity is, precisely, next to impossible to keep up with. But let me point out, for now, that my title's attribution of "autobiography" to Ottinger's medium is also dedicated to Meyer's book *Die Autobiographie der Schrift* (The Autobiography of Writing), a study that, in addition to its mascot status here, will become part of the genealogical argument on these pages. Why autobiography? This is how I prefer to address the marginalized subject, as the subject of the margin. It skirts, for one, the assimilationist model of integration of what was left or kept on the outside within the existing network of central subject concepts, institutions, and related guilty assumptions. Our assumption for now, until we are well on our way through the genealogy of the autobiographical subject of technology, is that artists on the margin tell their stories via the autobiographies they let roll of the media, often techno media, in which they work. As we will see, this necessarily involves a kind of ghostwriting on the walls of crypts. This at

The Berlin Wall is falling (from a series of photographs taken in preparation for Countdown*).*

once theoretical and autobiographical impulse, which will also be addressed as technofeminist, belongs to a genealogy of media. Sabine Perthold summarizes the coordinates and conditions that we must explore in these memoirs: "Myths, metamorphoses, and media stand at the center of Ottinger's film work" (106). Psychoanalysis supplements the connection Frieda Grafe expertly draws (in a series of brilliant essays we will be consulting on these pages) between the film medium's self-presentation in Ottinger's films and myth formation. It is through the endopsychic status of media-technological and archaeological or funereal delusions (which thus open up, in their alternating alterations, inside views of the psychic *apparatus*) that we can, through Freud's interpretation of myth in *The Psychopathology of Everyday Life,* complete if not the picture then at least a frame of this thought experiment: "I believe that a large part of the mythological view of the world, which extends a long way into the most modern religions, *is nothing but psychology projected into the external world.* The obscure recognition (the endopsychic perception, as it were) of psychical factors and relations in the unconscious is mirrored—it is difficult to express it in other terms, and here the analogy with paranoia must come to our aid—in the construction of a *supernatural* reality, which is destined to be changed back once more by science into the psychology of the unconscious" (258–59).

Back in Berlin, summer of 1990, I was entrusted on the spot with the translation of the *Countdown* texts, which included extensive citations from Walter Benjamin. Since the translation had to be a rush job, I had no recourse to extant English-language versions, and found myself rendering some very difficult pieces of writing into English from scratch. The relationship of translation is always immediately binding. We became fast friends, in the best sense, in October 1992 when I hosted her stay in Santa Barbara during her regents' lectureship at the University of California. In February 1993, *Artforum International* published an interview I conducted with her during her visit. In the interview, "Real Time Travel," we discuss her newest film at the time, *Taiga*, which had its U.S. pre-premier on the Santa Barbara campus, and we look forward to her next project, her first fictional film in several years, "Diamond Dance." On the basis of this interview, Kaja Silverman proposed to me (and to Ottinger) that I should write the study of Ottinger's films that she was going to write but that she felt she no longer could, since in the meantime her method or model, which had proved a close fit with the earlier films, was out of sync with the oeuvre as it had developed or changed, with the oeuvre "as a whole" or "in progress."

Mongolian nomad photographed while making the documentary film Taiga.

The fit, Silverman did admit, with a film like *Bildnis einer Trinkerin: aller jamais retour (Ticket of No Return)* was subsequently a feature of her 1996 book, *The Threshold of the Visible World*. I agreed to take on the challenge, with the proviso that I would first need to bring to completion long-term writing projects in which I was yet engaged. The delay proved fortuitous; it doubles or documents the interminable deferral imposed on what would have been (or, hopefully, will still be) Ottinger's largest-scale film project to date.

"Diamond Dance," the film Ottinger was ready to make in 1992, was welcomed to the development hell of the 1990s. The relays and delays of this work's pitching and tossed-out journey through the studios could serve as allegory of the end of art cinema in the 1990s, an end at least in the terms of art cinema's former capacity to offer a functional alternative to mainstream movies made in Hollywood. This impasse is the material or historical condition of an era coming to an end. Thus, to conclude my own documentary moment, in reading Ottinger's work, I am in the position of the melancholy brooder who struggles to preserve by breaking for a difference that's already history.

"Diamond Dance" addresses the ultimate traffic wreck at the intersections of transfer; it juxtaposes the Shoah and the AIDS crisis within a melting plot featuring the international diamond business, the underworld of Mickey Marx, and a musical mix of klezmer and jazz. "I have a screenplay in big format with a photographic storyboard. It is a montage of photographs taken over twelve years of visits to New York" (Ottinger, in Kremski, 57). From a 1994 prospectus in English: "'Diamond Dance' follows the fortunes of four Jewish families in New York: a distinguished dynasty of Forty-seventh Street diamond merchants; three Yiddish aunts in Brighton Beach and their young nephew, a recent Russian immigrant; the Sheepshead Bay clan of a Russian gangster; and the traumatized Lady in the Buick convertible, whose son is an ailing gay psychoanalyst. Love and greed, clan loyalty, and unscrupulous ambition link these families in the frantic search for two fabulous, ancient diamonds, known as the Baghdad Gemini. The story builds with the tension of a thriller to a poignant climax that reveals both the diamonds' whereabouts and the Lady's dark secret." The story assigns interchangeable places to the Shoah and AIDS within one household or economy. This double occupancy is in turn set against the history of a family that for generations has been involved in the international diamond business. The primal networking across long distance that first appeared worldwide through the development of the diamond trade, a line of work historically associated with the Jews, placed the Jewish people early on at the forefront of technological relations, and thus on the horizon of the uncanny. But Ottinger's aim is to find the pulse of the upbeat with "a touching and funny saga of wandering diamonds and wandering Jews, a rich drama about intrigue, honor, unlikely love, loss, and the need for healing." The prospectus gives a summary:

> "Diamond Dance" is a love letter to New York's Jewish communities, a film that captures the throbbing pulse and syncopated rhythms of the city's Russian immigrant, underworld, business, and gay subcultures. We watch as the young Daniel Diamantstein is initiated into the fascinating world of Jewish diamond merchants and their age-old code of honor. We discover how the boy called Amerikanerle, recently arrived from Odessa and anxious to assimilate, betrays the trust of his Yiddish aunts, involves Daniel in an unscrupulous deal, and falls into the clutches of a notorious Jewish gangster. We see the Jewish underworld wheeling and dealing at a lavish party that the mobster throws at his Fire Island mansion; the party culminates in frenzied jam sessions of jazz and klezmer. Meanwhile, we follow Daniel on a trip through the changing and melancholy landscape of Fire Island's gay community, to meet David Weinstein, a very special client. At the Diamantstein family's wild Purim party, a masked singer recounts Daniel's escapades and misfortunes. His Aunt Jacinta, a famous Yiddish vocalist, offers her own musical commentary: "What a shlemozzel!"

When we got together in New York in the summer of 2000 for the opening of Ottinger's show at the David Zwirner Gallery, we spent a day in Brighton Beach. While she took picture after picture, she explained how changed the neighborhood was compared to the time when she first conceived the film. Knowing the original versions of the screenplay very well by then, I could see that a different genre of Russian immigrant, more Moscow disco than old Europe, had added another layer of cultural styling to the look and history of the environs of Coney Island. This newer layering look, together with epistemic changes brought about through the introduction of new AIDS drugs by the mid-1990s, would require an altered form for the juxtapositions she originally planned at the end of the 1980s.

Ottinger raised more money for "Diamond Dance" than for all her other films put together. But because she did not want to forgo shooting in and around New York City, she needed to be able to afford to work with a union cast and crew. Overhead costs that could add up with the delay of just one day in the shooting schedule could break the bank of her ample but finite budget. The film was not realizable in the 1990s because, lacking Hollywood backing, Ottinger lacked the only insurance or guarantee available that she would be able to film (and finish filming) in New York. After a series of near misses with independent studios, the European and East Asian backers began pulling out. A representative of one of the German foundations that had given Ottinger money encouraged her (verbally) to return the funds, apply again, and then the foundation could give her an even larger grant. Ottinger did as she was told: her new application was rejected. It was no surprise to Ottinger that German support for experimental or art films was history. But whatever hopes she held for the newly deregularized Hollywood of independent studios could also only keep disappointments.

Since then, Ottinger was able to make the fiction film *Zwölf Stühle (The Twelve Chairs),* in which she follows Russian stage actors on documentary location throughout the former Soviet Union. *The Twelve Chairs* is also the title of a Ukrainian novel from the 1920s. Transposing the plotlines of the quest for a dispersed inheritance to the current situation of the former Soviet Union, Ottinger conceived a fiction film she would make by traveling with her crew to the coordinates dotting the narrative, thereby mixing the literary text and screenplay with the attributes of her documentary filmmaking. Thus she was finally able to make another fiction film as stowaway in the format and budget of a documentary production. Ottinger discussed with me her plans for *The Twelve Chairs* in an interview titled "My Last Interview with Ulrike Ottinger," which we worked on for a special issue of *Alphabet City*. At the time of the interview she had not yet obtained funding, and therefore requested that I not give away any specifics. *Alphabet City* decided to excise the record of her hesitation, but I give it here because it responds to the chill factory of Hollywood excretion (and digestion) of "Diamond Dance":

> I try to avoid discussing or introducing new projects, the ideas behind and in them, before it is certain that the film will be made. I'll gladly tell you everything about the project. I only ask you to leave out the details when you publish the interview. I'm not at all the anxious type in these matters. But I learned my lesson with "Diamond Dance." In order to obtain major studio funding a screenplay is forwarded to so many different offices and readers. I haven't abandoned "Diamond Dance," I think it is a fascinating theme and will be a great film. But just as the system of screenplay writing today is not that there is one author but that forty people work on one screenplay, so there are so many carriers of the ideas that it becomes impossible over time to reconstruct what came from where or whom. Screenplays that are not filmed right away but are passed around a great deal end up being used a bit like open quarries from which anyone is free to break away a piece and use it, of course not in the way I would have filmed it, but one sees exactly where the ideas came from.

INTRODUCTION
ART/CINEMA, ART/JOURNALISM

Can art cinema in fact be assumed to be the subject of this autobiography? While Andrea Weiss places her discussion of Ottinger's work in a chapter titled "Women's 'Art' Cinema and Its Lesbian Potential," she characterizes Ottinger's films as rejecting and parodying the conventions of art cinema (128). In part, these are conventions that form a certain sexist continuity shot between art cinema and its public enemy number one, Hollywood. Weiss writes: "Ottinger's films intersect with several non-classical cinema practices, including art cinema, surrealism, and ethnographic cinema. She works in documentary as well as fiction, and her films combine, or at times juxtapose, formal strategies from both genres" (129). But this excess of interests and investments that would count art cinema among other distinct types of film production is precisely the access once afforded by art cinema. That Ottinger pushes collage or montage to the outer limits in her filmmaking is a consequence of and tribute to the culture of art cinema, one that I would be hard-pressed to distinguish from avant-garde cinema, which Weiss, in her next chapter heading, calls "Transgressive Cinema." Ottinger belongs to a film culture in which both Federico Fellini and Jonas Mekas would feel right at home and set their spell. In 2000, in the original version of her essay "Stationenkino" ("Cinema of Stations"), Ottinger placed her work in the auteur category—after all, she only produces, directs, and works the camera for all her movies—and freely associated the work thus with certain films by Rainer Werner Fassbinder, one film in particular by Hiroshi Shimizo, and just about every film by Erich von Strohheim and Robert Altman.

In 1982 Ottinger confided to Monika Treut what her way of seeing was up against: "I believe that is connected with visual habits that were not so circumscribed ten or fifteen years ago. In the meantime cinema must fit the pattern of TV dramaturgy. People are less and less willing to accept other forms. . . . I believe that my only chance is to be more radical the more uniform the others get. If you

The Kalinka Sisters depart on the Trans-Mongolian Express (in the context of Johanna d'Arc of Mongolia).

receive money for film production, a good attitude is expected in return—in the sense of conformity. If one just the same becomes even more radical, I believe that at some point it's just over. I'm really curious how much longer they will let me work" (in Treut, "Gespräch mit Ulrike Ottinger").

The postwar German political imperative of social critique that prayed to the lip service of the equation drawn (out of context) between aestheticization (of politics) and fascism, preyed, under this cover, on what was genuinely new in the arts. But what if all that protest was just one more way Walter Benjamin was to be exiled from his corpus? In the name of what was turned into a slogan, ideologues tried to place an embargo on the life-styling of homoeroticism and fetishism, among other border states falling between the cracks of the no contest between official and anti-official psyches.

Within the allegedly New German Cinema of social critique and extended representation, the taboo on "aestheticization" or formal innovation meant, for example, that whatever brand-new voices were being introduced for the first time were in fact swallowed up and ventriloquized. The extension of basic coverage to the overlooked or silenced cannot but leave intact (and undisclosed) the conceptual and discursive frame-ups of the same old histories of their exclusion. "We seem to be getting a somewhat slanted view of German cinema," Annette

Kuhn wrote in the 1980s, "a view that emphasizes its realistic, naturalistic qualities, its reworkings of established fictional genres such as melodrama. Its engagement with recent German history. That kind of commitment to verisimilitude and narrative transparency is absent from work by Ulrike Ottinger" (74).

In the meantime, the era of art cinema is over. Where it left off we find only simulacra of—inoculations against—the shock of what's new injected by independent films into the Hollywood mainstream. If art cinema is thus dated, indeed "history," it was also all along unmistakably art. While Chantal Ackerman had for many years found supporting representation in the art world, Ottinger, who is otherwise Ackerman's colleague as the only other woman director worldwide whose ongoing work deserves the designation *art cinema,* was overlooked. An overview of Ottinger's photographic work at the David Zwirner Gallery in New York in the summer of 2000 made the first move against this trend of forgetting. The oversight of Ottinger during the 1990s was in part the result of Ottinger's misunderstood turn to, or rather inclusion of, documentary filmmaking, and in equal parts it belonged to the good repression of headlines, which while serving the short-term memory of certain associations—as feminist, gay and lesbian, and, more recently, Jewish film—also guarantee, in time, long-term memory loss. Ottinger's missingness from the art world was, however, symptomatized by this same world's 1990s celebration of Matthew Barney's works, which are indeed examples of "art" cinema, but only to the extent that they have been designed for art-gallery viewing and are for sale, just like video art, as works in editions. Surprise! The first review of Ottinger's New York show referred to the Berlin filmmaker as Matthew Barney's "precursor" (Youens).

If I would just the same characterize Ottinger's work and sensibility as German-Jewish, it is not to nominate another contender for the throw-on label, but to underscore instead the near-extinction quality of the worlds (for example, those of old Europe and of art cinema itself) her cinema allegorically revalorizes and sustains. In 2000 Ottinger reflected on the case of Peter Lorre both within and outside his post-World-War-II German film *Der Verlorene,* in which Lorre plays a doctor in a displaced persons' camp who during the Third Reich had been physician and scientist involved in military research. "With this film German postwar history is shown with a precision that is possible only for the victim who plays the perpetrator who knows that he is guilty. Lorre thus interwove within the film in exciting ways his own history as actor and his hard times as emigrant. The film diagnoses what would remain Lorre's fate from that point onward: there was no longer a place for him" ("Peter Lorre: Der Verlorene," 18).

The missing cultural context for Ottinger's films belongs to another Europe that once hit high points of cosmopolitan development in the mix and meeting of irretrievably different cultural backgrounds in transit, in translation, in the big between of overlapping languages. To evoke this setting, in *Johanna d'Arc of Mongolia,* for example, the figures on the train are both castoffs from the postwar world of opposition in the place of loss, evacuation, displacement, and the spirits of the Europe that was a condemned site when national socialism took center stage. The move to a third world of the other is another framing and displacement—which concerns the move as well into a documentary medium, which Ottinger set aside as dedicated to "this" other, dedicated as at once futural and historical—around this European loss. Otttinger's dazzling juxtapositions (piracy and feminism, alcoholism and social conscience, American-Jewish show biz and Mongolian feudalism—to rapidly gloss over several examples) invite us to enter fully the excavation sites of lost cultures, all of them bearing reference to the long-gone Europe (in which German Judaism represented a triumph of centuries of cultural development), and dig with her all the adjacent areas too, the sidelines and asides that prove to be on the inside of the missing subject of culture.

Since 1974 Ottinger has produced a unique body of cinematic work at the intersection between (or internal to both) art cinema fictional film and post-

Jewish gravestones recycled (in 1996) as boundary markers for garden plots on the outskirts of Shanghai. Ottinger was not documenting desecration but rather a form of living on.

modern documentary film. At the same time, she has amassed a photographic oeuvre that, beginning in 2000, gained her the reception and support of the international art world. This monograph thus doubles as documentation of art cinema's demise in the recent past, and its subsequent survival as art via the documentary film genre. One part commemoration, the other part an affirmation of Ottinger's upbeat substitution for the loss of art cinema (and with it, what she likes to refer to as the old Europe) in what we call a world of difference, namely her documentary encounters with the other on the margins of big-screen culture: She was the first Western filmmaker to film in Mongolia.

The term *art cinema* separates what it cannot merge together, and thereby refers to a backup position of art cinema as art, the status or lying-in-state of its living on. Let the splitting of that which has been conjoined in art cinema announce a recontextualization, in this autobiography, of Ottinger's cinema, with regard to the art world (or word) that in the 1990s entered my own writing.

My first invitations to contribute essays to exhibition catalogs brought me before the biggest challenge for a writer who would rather not make the jump cut to journalism. How to write about contemporary art and artists? Each commissioned essay was my opportunity to encounter yet another artist and body of work. In the 1990s, then, I began opening up my discourse to meet the artist as other on what was and was no longer my turf. I revved up my discourse, accelerating outward but still inside it, spinning out digressions that overlapped with the recognizable or conceivable trajectories binding the works to or through their reception. For a writer (in contrast to a journalist) to reply to the work of the artist as other (in other words, as contemporary, as colleague, as friend) means, as it still literally does in *Hamlet,* to "replicate"—to reply to the full extent that he also replicates his corpus alongside or around the work of the other.

When you approach the contemporary artist, a veil of opinions or beliefs will muffle your tread, your breathing. In time, journalism, it seems, gets subsumed by sociohistorical context, and a pathway of writing and reading separates out and occupies the foreground. But when it comes to contemporary art, journalism leads the way and has the day, its day. In turn, one of the burdens placed upon the artist engaged in the necessary but impossible process of inventing the receiving line along which she can cosign her work, in addition to the related material conditions of art production such as long-term physical or mental illness and uninterrupted poverty, is journalism's intervention in the reception that can be the better half (in union or in divorce) of an artist's production. It cannot be overlooked that the press offers instant archivization of ephemeral acts and interventions that otherwise lack the backing of a canon, tradition, or institution. Just when the contemporary artist wonders if she's being shunned yet, the news that she has started passing reviews (again) cannot but be a welcome step in the direction hardest to follow for the contemporary writer who would write about, to, with her work.

By addressing its own conditions of production—the close quarters it must occupy/cathect with journalism—this study in a sense subsumes Karl Kraus's project of correctional rereading of the journalistic phrase. Through what psychotherapy refers to as a "paradoxical intervention," one can ask journalism to occupy the place of first contact with the other, to be possessed thereby like a veritable medium. In this way this study aims to work with and through journalism's monopolization and displacement of the encounter with the other, the future, the uncontrollable time to come. If the attempt is thus made to enable what the press represses to make ghost appearances between the lines, then this study is also operating in a manner inspired by Ottinger's film *The Image of Dorian Gray in the Yellow Press*. A guiding image for my celebration of Ottinger's work between and along the lines of its reception is brought to us by the scene of the press ball that is decked out with all that fits the fine print. The interior is covered—walls, ceilings, columns—with palimpsests of pages, headlines, clippings of articles. Even the champagne glasses the guests raise on the intake are made of newspaper, thereby raised to the power of collage.

If the veil of journalism that automatically drops between the writer and the contemporary artist cannot be peeled away, then "peal" the veil, let its press of opinion, belief, appreciation, rejection ring out, up, in a "first contact" with the other that it displaces, conceals, but by which it must also be impressed, however ephemeral and mumbling the traces.

Whatever art may be, it is constituted, received, and signed for in the office of the other. Whoever the artist, he or she is engaged in the invention of this other, the one who is to come, unsummoned, uncited, and uncontrolled, after-the-fact and affirmed, without reservation, without confirmation. This is the last stand and understanding of a difference between your regular psycho, say, and the artist. Paramount among artists' issues is the all-out effort to invent a reception for the body of work.

Journalism is not restricted to whatever the newspapers and magazines are currently backing. Already in the 1920s, Benjamin could refer to the crisis in art criticism (in his *Ursprung des deutschen Trauerspiels [Origin of the German Mourning Play]*) as the impasse resulting from the loss of a thread of distinction in the tradition (between allegory and symbol) that had been filled up by spinning instead, out of the symbol alone, the loop of received notions, barring any encounter whatsoever with work, word, or world. Benjamin did not assign this art-critical immunity to reading as an exclusive to the extracurricular or extra-academic activities of journalism. Is academic criticism by and large distinguishable from journalism, and if so, is the distinction to its credit? To provide us

The Press Ball (in the context of The Image of Dorian Gray in the Yellow Press).

with the measure of the hopelessness of this situation, in which no "opposition" already out there is sworn to protect our writing, Karl Kraus dismissed academics as "failed journalists." Indeed, academia issues its own basic self-coverage as journalism with bad digestion; by overextending dated debates into standards of history always to be revisited on the way to (in the way of) encountering the works of artists identifiable as female and gay, for example, a discipline's regard for itself proves to be a straightforward case of censorship. If there is going to be a difference, it will be between writing and journalism.

At what point does criticism become journalism, at what other point is it writing? According to Freud, our psychic constitution remains a declaration of dependence upon an inside-out institution of broadcasting that records and plays back both parental guidance and public opinion (*SE* 14: 96–98). The psyche must abandon body-based "primary narcissism," and either advance to the stage of "secondary narcissism," where the bodily proportions of self-love (or mother love) are replaced by relations of power, or prepare for the psychotic break. Through the ego's relations with its own mastery, a certain relationship to primary narcissism is nevertheless preserved in the perfect tense and tension of self-criticism or self-esteem.

There is therefore a bottom line to Freud's account of how primary narcissism survives itself by going into the business of public broadcasting. The only

Tabea Blumenschein applying makeup, with Ulrike Ottinger taking pictures (with her Retina camera). Beginning in the late 1960s, when Ottinger first met Blumenschein in Constance, Ottinger engaged in constant photographic studies of Blumenschein's metamorphic talent and inclination. This photographic relationship and body of work parallels and subtends the fiction films from Laocoon and Sons *through* Ticket of No Return. *Although the photographic relationship eventually came to an end, the rehearsal body of work is an ongoing influence in Ottinger's films.*

standard of criticism is self-criticism. Only criticism that comes to or out of its own body of work—and thus is always adding on and referring to its ongoing work of reformulation, even or especially while writing about something outside itself, something else—can be considered critical writing.

And journalism? It is criticism that can only refer beyond itself by default, by virtue of its complete inability to refer to itself. The journal or newspaper deadline, the only line that's given in journalistic criticism, all alone generates the immaculate assumptions of the journalist and his sense of audience. Critical writing, in contrast, is materialist to the extent that it accumulates its body of reformulation in the space of tension between its own self-reference and the emergency contacts it must nevertheless make with what lies outside. The constitutive push and pull in critical writing thus lies between the "closure" of the system within which it is destined to complete itself and that same system's inability to generate all its terms out of itself.

Journalism takes sides, on the side always "opposite" art and writing. Art and writing find each other in their between-ness, the difference whereby they can "be two" or doubles together, but still beside themselves.

Developmentally speaking, journalism is adolescent, and often doubles as acting out. Art and writing also pass through these phases or phrases—without, moreover, ever simply leaving them behind. Journalism begins, over and again, with the journal entries jotted down by the teenager trying to contain the new-found interiority and energy of insight. Adolescence can be defined as the crisis brought on by insights and opinions that are premature with regard to the teen's ability to give them a body and thus absorb and metabolize their shock value.

If we can define the "Teen Age" together with its journal-ism as that overloading tension arising and arousing between the prematurity of our capacity for insight and our ability at the same time to give the flash of intellectual or "spiritual" energy some kind of body or any kind of staying power, then we must also reconsider journalism as part and portrait of the artist as a young psyche.

Not to graduate from the mirror stage of journal writing commits you to the suicide drive. Every journal entry can function as the final line and dating of

Early metamorphosis of Tabea Blumenschein at the time of Ottinger's first fiction films.

suicidal ideation. Surviving the shock of insights means making the transfer from the utter unprotectedness of the short attention span into the longer-term infrastructures of self-criticism and corpus-building.

The Teen Age of journalism is not extraneous to the workings of art or of writing. But while "work" always requires, in addition, the input of a superego, journalism is exclusively egoic, standing thus, as it goes into the overtime of non-development, on the one-sided side of an impulse Freud called the death drive, the impulse to charge full circuit—ASAP—back into a state of quiescence.

Between journalism's lines and deadlines of repress release a certain adolescent linguistic metabolism can therefore be found still working overtime to sustain, survive, or preserve the first contact with what's coming at you, at the intersection between technology and the unconscious. It is up to the press, to the teen at heart, to pick up and make a first impression of reception, and displace (while holding the place of, in the history or archive of reception) first contact. Under pressure to meet the press more than halfway in a receiving era the artist also opens and tries to guide you through, Ottinger too projected her

Tabea Blumenschein as fantasy pasha, early 1970s, Berlin.

voice across the interview medium, in which just the same there remains an outside chance of getting at an intraview, too. From the pileup of morning-after reviews that hang on Ottinger's images and every word, now in the afterglow of art appreciation, now in the post-art funk of disappointment, I have worked to locate (even as unlocatable, which is still a location) the reception of Ottinger's work as it accrues to the work, as it is allegorized in the work in advance, as it advances. In making a montage rather than a history out of the journalism that cannot be avoided in the encounter with the contemporary artist, this autobiography makes a performative commitment both to itself and to Ottinger's way of seeing. Waltraud Liebl affirms the Ottinger way in constative terms: "Ottinger's work is determined by the principle of collage (and in this regard one can see a connection with surrealism). She doesn't present narrative cinema, but demands instead of her viewer a special kind of associative watching and listening" (29).

The tap, tap, tapping sounds of the spirits who communicated with the Fox sisters remained within earshot of the new medium of telegraphy. But that the newspapers regularly published séance reports or stories also belongs to the double influence of the telegraphs that were tap, tap, tapping press coverage across ever-longer distances. The press, from around the middle of the nineteenth century through the turn of the next century, was perfectly congruent with all the séance-medium activity that spread across the same wires that advanced the public, published sphere toward globalization. There must to this day remain a delegation of this meeting of mediums in journalism. The Christianization that necessarily accompanies mediatization works overtime to obscure any remnants by the force of its mission impossible to declare or define that the ghost is clear. That is why it is important to read and mark those deposits within mediatization—with the press at the front of the line—that are inevitably, irretrievably without redemption value. Or, on the upbeat, it is equally important to enter round-the-world, round-the-clock reception of communications with the good spirits and unhappy ghosts making up as they go along with the mass-media Sensurround. In turn we can affirm that without the ghosts in media technologization, absent and accounted for, there can be no outer space of reception, no future, no bottom line.

Once more around the blockage in Ottinger's main medium: In "American Psychos: The End of Art Cinema in the 1990s," I tried to parallel-track the cessation of art cinema and the demise of the *Psycho* legacy in horror films via the 1990s phenomenon of 1980s New York art stars making "independent" mainstream films about the psychotic break we get for our own survival. The literal-mindedness of artist as film director equaling art cinema in the 1990s, plus the full participation of these films in Hollywood's knitting together of another middlebrow genre out of slasher or splatter B-movies, could be set up as self-evidence of a certain end that was in sight, on screen, and as silent contrast to the films that were no longer being made, including, notably, Ottinger's "Diamond Dance."

The independent studios that passed on "Diamond Dance" bankrolled these "artist films." I give this reference—to "American Psychos"—just for the shame of it. The title of my article (of war) referred in its first part to Bret Easton Ellis's 1991 alle-gory of the 1980s, *American Psycho*. In the novel, art is labeled, identified, and identified with inside the memento-mori still life of commodities that has the psycho surrounded. "Spooky photographs by Cindy Sherman" (279) and a "huge Julian Schnabel" (351) spark recognition within a melancholic retention span set to short-circuit or flare up murderously. What slasher consumerism served up on a splatter in the 1980s was the "still alive" of identification's origin in trauma. American psycho's favorite film is Brian De Palma's 1985 *Body Double*. De Palma was going to be a surgeon, just like his father before him. Then, after watching Alfred Hitchcock's movies, he just had to switch to the other medium of cutting. But De Palma's signature "remakes" of Hitchcock were signed in the blood that had flowed inward down cuts unseen in the original horror. Cinema, as in the sequel treatments of the *Psycho* effect that were all the B-movie rage until the end of the 1980s, can be a medium of metabolization or healing, and that means it has all the limitations of an institution organized around therapeutic closure. Cinema could have been the other place of tension between analysis and therapy, the tension span associated with the psychoanalytic frame. But that was optioned out in the development hell of the 1990s, in the time it took for the declaration of independents to deregularize the industry. Now there is no alternative whatsoever to the Hollywood standard, at once liberalized and internalized as independence. In Europe, maybe two or three art cinema directors survived the 1990s. A vestigial version of art cinema is still being made, but only on the installation plan of the art-gallery world. So much of this artwork seems, moreover, linked to and separated from the era of art cinema by short-term memory loss, a loss that like every good plagiarism or incorporation, nevertheless also commemorates by default what gets swallowed whole and in bit parts.

In the 1980s, the last stand-up show of resistance in Hollywood (but only because to be overlooked and tax-written-off was its industry lot) was horror. Then films like *Silence of the Lambs* (1991) forced even the horror genre into the middlebrow-beat that industry types, even or especially the independents, are sworn to police—I mean please. In other words, the intellectual freedom enjoyed by slasher and splatter pictures from the 1960s through the 1980s was by the 1990s already irretrievably compromised and forsaken.

I thus deposit here in the opening of this book my perverse critical fantasy (or allegory): The movies that were directed in the 1990s by New York art stars of the decade before—David Salle's *Search and Destroy* (1995), Robert Longo's *Johnny Mnemonic* (1995), Julian Schnabel's *Basquiat* (1996), and Cindy Sherman's *Office Killer* (1997)—get double billing as American horror films up to Hollywood standards and as screen memories for the extinction of art cinema, which they, as independent films directed by artists, act out, mirth in funeral, in the mode of overkill.

Fassbinder is the live wire of inspiration admitted (to my knowledge) by three out of these four artists moonlighting in the 1990s as independent film directors. Since the worst was yet to come, I am willing to join the Fassbinder fan club. But that doesn't make his standing with the artists of cinema in the early 1980s just go away. Look at Jonathan Rosenbaum's *Film: The Front Line / 1983* and you will see that Fassbinder was at the top of the best-sellout list according to these artists. All standards seemed to have split when *October* dedicated a special issue to Fassbinder's films. The critical response to Fassbinder's crossover films pales before our greater horror at all that independent filmmaking has to offer. But the earlier crisis in a sense rehearsed the greater one that followed. I bring this up here because the going assumption is that Ottinger was Fassbinder's peer (Youens). Ottinger was interested in his first films. (She also still finds his 1978 film, *In einem Jahr mit 13 Monden,* "interesting.") It happened that Fassbinder declared himself to be the biggest fan of Ottinger's *Ticket of No Return.* She returned the complement by inviting him to play a part in *Freak Orlando,* but scheduling conflicts kept getting in the way.

I closed my (silent) reading of the four New York art-world films as projections of unresolved sibling rivalry among art stars of the 1980s and thus, all together now, as demo of the small world to which the conjoining of art and film had been reduced by the 1990s, with a coda that set aside Larry Clark's first two films, which were not about the psychotic break, but were focused instead on the unsteady state of adolescence. The Clark films—*Kids* (1995) and *Another Day in Paradise* (1999)—are full of the tension that is part insight and big part blindness to Clark's own position with regard to the Teen Age he just loves but therefore also misrecognizes. There is no Teen Age without its midlife crisis or criticism. If the *Psycho* metabolization genre had come to a full stop within the era of independents (an era that saw the reshooting of the Hitchcock original), then it was time to redistribute the elements of psycho alert across a new attention span of tensions going down in the coupling of midlife and teen acting-out. In Clark's films, performance and denial of adolescence or group psychology get a rise out of nonphobic lines of reception of our ongoing Teen Age. This Teen Age is the only future granted with independents. But the short tension span between adolescence and its midlife criticism keeps the movies on the short control release of group therapy.

What independent-versus-Hollywood cinema takes away, to prohibit boredom (which is the projective way of putting down the outside chance of the advent of the other), Ottinger's cinema gives in overabundance: time, time to look, time to let the other appear, time to metabolize the time that, no matter how dedicated it is, is also lost.

Nietzsche argued in *Thus Spoke Zarathustra* that Christ wasn't as bad as all that. He just died too young, still adolescent in the terror of his insight and the terrorism of its self-containing application. If he had instead lived on into his maturity, Nietzsche wagers, he would have recanted, given up all prejudgment that tattle-tells good from evil, but without the sacrifice that, like the sacrifice to end all sacrifices, can only be born again.

Ottinger's relationship to the horror film, both the kind addressed to states of protracted adolescence and the kind caught up in psychopathological scenarios of violence control or survivalism, is citation specific. The latter diagnostic-type film is cited in *Madame X*'s sound track in one scene. But the sounds of B-movie horror are along for the camped-up mass murder of Lady Divine and her guests aboard the yacht "Holliday" (also spelled Hollyday in the original screenplay, which brings the misspelling that much closer to its reference to "Hollywood"), perpetrated by Madame X and her crew in retaliation for the "unsubtle" treatment of Belcampo, the film's unidentified flaming object.

In *The Image of Dorian Gray in the Yellow Press,* Dr. Mabuse's initiation of Dorian into an underworld of diversions and inversions was, according to the director's plan, folded as "horror" film into this film of many films and as many genres. But the horror here is styling with Gustave Moreau, one of Ottinger's declared influences, and seduces rather than challenge survival. Even the survival that is at stake for Dorian Gray at the end of the film, since double and uncontainable, is also not decidable as victim or survivor identity.

In 1998 Ottinger composed a screenplay for an outright vampire film titled "Die Blutgräfin" ("The Blood Countess"), set within the Austro-Hungarian Empire's late-nineteenth-century obsessional-funereal collections in museums, churches, amusement parks, and cemeteries. The setting, as always in Ottinger's films, aims to go beyond the matter of place to become part of the story. Not just location, location, then, but running alongside in a parallel universal of storytelling, Vienna is the stage set for the return of the seventeenth-century Hungarian vampire. Countess Bathory's affirmed vampirism is contrasted with her nephew's guilty vampirism (he's in analysis in order to become what he is not). But by the end, at the Prater amusement park, the countess gets her woman (a young bride who shoots up the ride with her groom by her side, but gets consumed by the countess's passion). For this at once funereal, upbeat, and ironic exercise in the vampire movie genre, Ottinger recognizes Roman Polanski's *The*

Study in preparation for Madame X: An Absolute Ruler.

Fearless Vampire Killers (1967) and Harry Kümel's *Daughters of Darkness* (1970) as precursors.

"The Blood Countess" is a farce that does in a sense play comic stereotypes of adolescent anxiety and fixity against the affirmational blood drive of the Countess Bathory. The countess escapes at the end, doubly so, both the plotting against her and her genre. She announces to the bride by her side on the amusement park ride (before giving her the bigger thrill of her life) that she's returning to Hollywood to resume her career. In Vienna, in contrast, she tells the soon-to-be-flushed Hungarian bride, her past has become just too real, and in time, given the city's funereal-archival resources, will have caught up with her. In sum, then, the countess's family-tree research or search for identity, which takes us on a tour of Vienna in necrospect, turns her flight from identification back into her Hollywood screen representation, which also gives us identification, but the kind that psychologizes, gets in our eyes, and hides the other.

1
BOUNCING BIO

Let's take a running start and put ourselves into the big picture of Ulrike Ottinger's work, complete with a bouncing bio to follow. There is one life condition of this cinema. When and where and as whom or what Ottinger was born set all systems going for traumatization. Let the record show that she was born in 1942 in Constance, Germany, to a Jewish mother. But the adverse external, social, interpersonal conditions that followed notwithstanding, all forms of margin and difference would remain for Ottinger, just the same, adventure and safety zone. And that's because, intrapsychically, the conditions of her earliest childhood were utopian. For three years she shared her beloved mother only with the other mother, her grandmother (her father's mother), while her father, who wasn't Jewish but whose family kept wife and baby daughter hidden away for the duration of the Reich, would remain the dashing figure of safety off on the horizon of risk-taking diversions on their better behalf. In her prehistory, Ottinger's father is the legend to maps of exotic journeys in which, as a teenager, he starred in the role of sailor. He was also a painter. African fetishes in her home in Berlin, like the Greek ring she always wears, are exemplary souvenirs of the spirit of her father's legacy. Exclusion, as in a dream, can be read in reverse as outgoing adventure, the kind that takes you, inside your safety zone, to realms of juxtaposition of extreme difference that are wide open, possible, and livable, precisely to the extent that no position is superimposable, one on the other, whether as annihilation or assimilation.

Ottinger retained one eidetic childhood recollection that would prove posttraumatic. When an unannounced caller knock knocked on the door, her mother's eyes stared as she seized the baby girl and rushed to their secret hiding place in the attic of the back house. The infant cannot but share her mother's fear; there is no other fear but that which the mother is hard-pressed to contain. It is not hard to imagine that the staring eyes also interrupted the mother's otherwise

Tabea Blumenschein as Jimmy Junod.

unconditional or mirroring gaze. In 1968 this moment of arrest became a serial nightmare. In 1972 it served as inspiration for Ottinger's first film, *Laokoon und Söhne (Laocoon and Sons)*.

In 1968 Ottinger was a painter living in Paris. Her apartment was right across from the Sorbonne. During the student rebellion, the French police would gather on the street below at night and strike the pavement with their long clubs or staffs. In a nightmare, Ottinger hears the knock, knocking. She's in her home in Constance, up in the atelier she used as a teenager and which had been the secret hiding place of her earliest childhood. When she used the space as an atelier, a red phone that looked like a toy connected her with the main house in front (and with her grandmother). Ottinger's primal association with her mother is love; with her grandmother, security. The red phone is still there in the serial nightmare. The atelier catches fire. She calls her grandmother, her mother, her father. She calls Althusser and Bourdieu. Then she calls the fire company. The firemen arrive, but in no time turn into hybrid SS agents (dark leather) and French policemen (the pounding clubs). They destroy what the fire hasn't already consumed. Now Ottinger is also endangered. But then she wakes up.

This nightmare served as the opening of her first film: the artist "dies" during the destruction of her atelier by the seven Furies, who rise up out of the water in the form of firemen. But the artist, "an exceptional woman," loses herself to a chain of metamorphoses, including a changeover into the gigolo Jimmy Junod. The circus Laocoon and Sons, with Tristan Tzara as director, is also the transformation of or alternative to the destroyed atelier. Ottinger was crossing over into a new medium, one in which she was convinced she could work without the limitations she was up against in painting and photography.

By going to the movies to be all that it is, the circus Laocoon also goes beyond the Enlightenment treatise *Laocoon,* in which Gotthold Ephraim Lessing sought to determine the boundaries separating the artistic media of his day. The static media of painting and sculpture, for example, could not admit expressions of pain or joy. Frozen in space, a guffaw or scream in the time of repeated viewing could only prove unbearable. As Herder implied in his critique, Lessing was entrusting to the arts and their distinctions protection against his own hypersensitivity to stimuli signifying trauma. In film, however, you can scream and not only be heard but also seen.

"It is not by accident that one of the citizens of the magical land designates herself 'poet of the permanent revolution,' whereby the concept of revolution is all important. Revolutions—it would appear that this is Ulrike Ottinger's message—arise not only in the context of political power relations but also with regard to modes of perception" (Möhrmann). The dislocation of "revolution" in Ottinger's first film entered into the staging of the dream and the trauma. In 1968 Ottinger participated in a group art exhibition at the University of Constance. Student revolutionaries trashed the exhibit, also smashing Ottinger's piece, a bust in the pop style. For her film, she put the pieces together again so that, in the scene of the atelier's destruction, her work was not only restored but also destroyed again, both moments now part and portrait of the metamorphosing medium of cinema.

Ottinger's first photograph—one's first photograph often has primal significance—was no scream memory. She took her first photograph (with the camera her mother gave her) of a couple of exotic visitors to Amsterdam from Europe's colonial past. Two dapper Indian gentlemen, one wearing a turban, are seated on one side of the canal boat and smile at the camera. "I began at a quite early age to take photos. I was twelve when I was given my first little Retina with which I photographed a great deal—it had a wonderful, very beautiful, very precise Zeiss object lens, and I started with that. That's how I learned photography, how the light has to fall. Later on I arranged things for my images [here Ottinger is referring, with the same *image* word, to visual artwork for which she was trained as painter], that is, I recorded things with my camera which I found remarkable and thereby commenced the montage of my images. Early on I began to exhibit these photos together with my images, which were painted or montage-made" (Ottinger, in Fischetti, "Ich glaube . . . ," 224).

The corollary of Ottinger's inversion of traumatic exclusion as the pathbreaking momentum of adventure is that she refuses to hide (and preserve) the contents or meanings of her images. "In my images nothing is hidden away. If you look at them long enough, then you can read everything. I'm not a big supporter of the dig for deeper meaning. Everyone sees her own problems, that's for sure. But for me I can state outright that everything is on the surface. In other words, everything you see is important, everything you take in is important, from background to foreground, to the costumes and the actors. Taken together everything forms one whole. If I change details and certain connections, then it is because this whole serves as a language, one that has its own validity" (Ottinger, in Fischetti, "Ich glaube . . . ," 222). While the all-importance of the surface accounts for the time she gives her audience to see and read, it also admits the paradoxical status of the image in Ottinger's cinema—and, as noted above, it's all image or *Bild* whenever Ottinger refers to her motion pictures. Her cinema occupies a state of tension, an allegorical tension, between time, the time that's given, and motion, embodied or live time, the time that's taken away.

Her second film, a short document of a two-part Happening by (or with) her artist colleague and friend Wolf Vostell, was titled *Berlinfieber—Wolf Vostell (Berlin Fever—Wolf Vostell)*. It should be noted that Vostell's work outside this Happening document, which over and again fixed a focus in countless collages on the nearly indigestible television set on canvas (often alongside gas masks), articulated profound distrust of the liveness of the new media, both as grounded in the recent past (the interchangeability of the live and the Blitz as special effects of Nazi psychological warfare) and as self-evident in the influence of its new spam of attention deficit on the conditions of art practice and reception. In her document, Ottinger commemorated or deconstructed "liveness" as timetaking work taking part in and around autos (which, in Greek, signifies "self"). The long list of tasks to accomplish by the Happening participants consumes time in an at once paranoid and ritual setting (the inclusion of salt spreading and tasting rings up a mythic or necromantic dimension alongside the obsessive record keeping that was also prescribed). In *El Enigma Vostell,* a collection of greetings on the occasion of the artist's fiftieth birthday, Ottinger's homage, for better or verse, puts both of them in the allegorist's perspective: "The artist as freak. The monster in experience. The natural phenomenon in perseverance."

Eva Meyer wrote a bio of Ottinger in 1995 that extols Ottinger's films for introducing the artifact as a third alternative both to Romantic empathy or appropriation, and to its opposite, the distinguishing standards of criticism. "Her films are ethnographic films, even on her own turf. But without the claim to represent another or even one's own culture. Ottinger knows very well that that's just not possible. What fascinates her she ritualizes in ephemera, without symbolic value, an artifact in other words, one that can be as confusing as it is precise. With this distinction we are there where the experience of the other becomes visible, where it can appear. In a film that is about the fundamental impossibility of appropriating this experience as the subject's self-realization. The balancing act between Ottinger's despair and her enthusiasm is prompted by this impossibility and realizes the artifact. . . . That's what I keep on talking

Rosa von Praunheim and Harry Tannenbaum as two sailors (in the context of The Infatuation of the Blue Sailors).

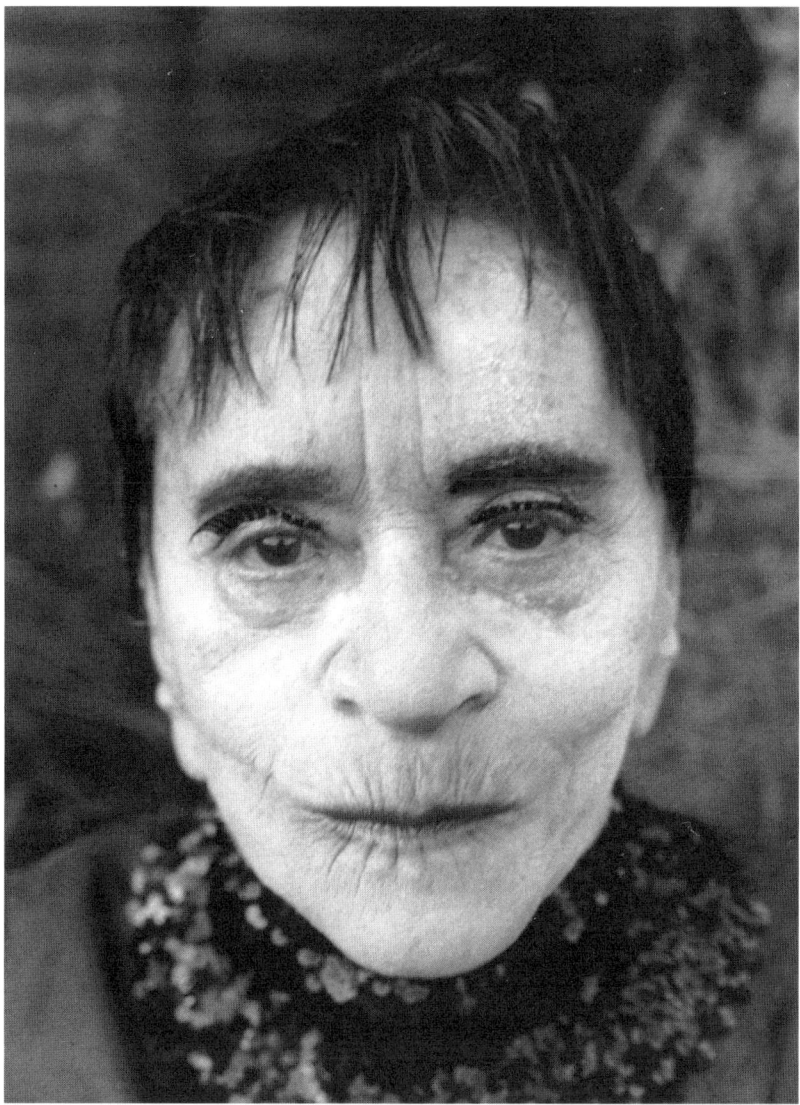

Valeska Gert as the Old Bird.

about, this allegorical moment of distinction, which can be neither Romantically filled and felt out nor replaced through a critical intention, but which can be seen in the films of Ulrike Ottinger" ("Ottingers Artefakt," 8).

In both her fictional and documentary films, Ottinger has given us many identifiable scenarios for what she refers to as the transfer of cultures; but in contrast to so many multicultural arrangements, the encounter, for example, in *Johanna d'Arc of Mongolia,* between European American show-biz types and their Mongolian captors is not between identifiable units or unities. The between is never lost. In other words, the difference that is there has already and always cut both ways and is part of first contact, part of the between, which, even according to that word's prehistory, already also covers the place or state of "being two," beside oneself. To be two or not to be two, that remains the question. According to Judith Mayne, Ottinger elaborates "marginality into a visual and narrative momentum of its own" (149).

Ottinger views her films as occupying a place of ongoing tension and transfer between settled and nomadic cultures: "I would like to describe how much our forms of narration and of image selection, our (film) art, are connected to our experiences, which are differentiated along both basic models of human existence, the nomadic and the sedentary. The nomadic mode means a very active life, constant change is inspiring here and yearning aims not to find peace but wants to entertain and to be entertained. The sedentary mode has too much quietude, wants to shut down and yearns for recovery. This is a paradox and can be explained as a dynamo. Movement produces movement, quietude quietude" ("Cinema of Stations," 57).

The push and pull between the stationary and the nomadic is not exclusively historical; the nomadic impulse asserts itself not only as remnant but also as history in the making. In describing her 2002 documentary *Südostpassage (Southeast Passage)*, Ottinger refers to "new nomads" in the former Eastern Block—former teachers, lawyers, farmers, carpenters, now traders of anything at all traveling along the sidelines of the borders and main streets. They undermine and open up the invisible limits and limitations of life in these abandoned stricken worlds. Through "their courage and inexhaustible imagination" they have become the new heroes and heroines of the struggle for survival ("Südostpassage," unpublished text). The low-tech or aesthetic use of modern machines of transportation and communication that characterizes the document of the Vostell Happening is also a typical nomadic form of first contact with the machinery of the stationary world (one of the themes or layers in Ottinger's documentary *Taiga*). The nomadic impulse is also directly linked to the force of metamorphosis in Ottinger's fictional films.

In her third film, *Die Betörung der blauen Matrosen (The Infatuation of the Blue Sailors)*, the "Irony of Destiny" represented by a siren walking through the desert without end is the stationary contrast to the series of metamorphoses that by and large get out from under the destinal closure. But this film also observes limits by accepting both the stationary and the nomadic models. We are both the metamorphosing bird woman and the sailor who just wants to fit in. A tension or balancing act between organic and synthetic worlds traverses the bird figure: the old bird (played by Valeska Gert) is replaced by the new one, a replacement that represents the incursion of synthetic, artificial, and commodified civilization into the original organic world. But their confrontation rather than any once-

Tabea Blumenschein as the Young Bird.

and-for-all replacement lives on in the film's allegorical dimension, in particular through the figuration and refiguration of "the Hawaii girl," who can represent nature only by at the same time being identifiable as part of the tour or movie package deal "Hawaii." Taping together feathers and the look of a wildcat borrowed from department-store packaging, the Hawaii girl introduces a new ritual of death or change: she becomes the young bird *as* the metamorphosis of the killed old bird. The limit is set by the last sailor who survives (in contrast to all the other sailors who were destroyed by their refusal to compromise) by accepting the world of the Hawaii girl, the world of everyday role clichés. Not yet feature length, *The Infatuation of the Blue Sailors* fills the analytic hour. "What would have happened if the bird had been able to save herself, if under favorable conditions she could have been rescued, or if an alternative to the Hawaii girl had been found? The attempt to recuperate once more the loss of mankind, must it be given up in this utopia? Ritual demonizes this question, irony breaks on it, the memory of the bird keeps the utopia awake" (Ottinger/Blumenschein/Bergius, "Fazit aus einem Gespräch").

2
SATANIC ARTS

Following the three shorts with which she opened her film career, in 1977 Ottinger shorted out the receiving lines of film and feminist criticism with her first feature, *Madame X—Eine absolute Herrscherin (Madame X: An Absolute Ruler)*. Filmed on and around Lake Constance, the movie made Ottinger a sensational figure of controversy. "Ottinger . . . succeeds in criticizing the conditions of the first generation of the women's movement" (Spies). "Ottinger transforms . . . the area around Lake Constance into an exotically overflowing, unreal, man-eating orgy of images" (Kemetmüller). "If this planet cannot be conceived, according to the fantastic discourse of this film, as free of tyranny, then the rule of women would still be the best of the male options for allowing oneself to be oppressed" (Witte, "Weiblicher Piratenakt").

But the I in the storm of headline sensationalism about, and feminist-film scholarly cathexis or occupation of, the ostensible "lesbian pirate film" claimed that what was underway in *Madame X* was a "metaphor for awakening, basically into the adventure of reality. . . . Although the film focuses primarily on the moment of awakening, I try to make clear that the enthusiasm of waking up cannot last . . . Nonetheless, desires for escape and change should remain. . . . I consciously formulated the contradiction between Madame X as a master and her promise of freedom. Madame X does not represent a person at all but rather a kind of power machine. . . . I find it remarkable that awakening, which has become a mass gesture in the women's movement, runs its course within the same hierarchical, patriarchal patterns. I wanted to show this contradiction as our reality" (Ottinger, in Silberman).

The absolute captain of the good ship *Chinese Orlando* invites—through every imaginable media outlet and means of communication—"all women" (artist Josephine de Collage, American housewife Betty Brillo, German forest ranger Flora Tannenbaum, Italian model Blowup, clinical psychologist Karla

Freud-Goldmund, Australian aviatrix Omega Centauri, and Noa-Noa, a native of Tai-Pi) to follow her into new frontiers: "Chinese Orlando—stop—to all women—stop—offer world—stop—full of gold—stop—love—stop—adventure at sea—stop—call Chinese Orlando—stop!" What pulls out all the "stops" is the tele language of techno-body Madame X, a language that is also doubly bound to invite the women to cut loose and to "stop" in these tracks.

Ottinger emphasizes the movie's momentum as open invitational to the "female" subject who will risk the adventure of her own story: "The journey, however, is not a journey outward into adventure but a journey into the interior.... The leitmotif throughout the film is about the prohibition imposed on women to make their own experiences.... This freedom, of course, also includes the possibility to fail. These ideas are contained in the notion of adventure, the adventure of freedom, the freedom to try out things and the freedom to fail" (in Mueller, "Interview with Ulrike Ottinger," 121). That "all women" onboard all die (with the exception of Noa-Noa) points to the inside-out chance that change will take place: "Now all of them fail, they are killed. But as I said before, death in this film is a metaphor for change. If we really want to change, something within us must die in order to let the new arise on the emotional level. It means that old, seemingly immutable structures are being taken seriously. For even if we know in our head how we should act, we fall back on our feelings, again and again. But feelings can be reeducated, only this is a terribly long process, it is almost an organic event, it is a kind of death" (in Mueller, "Interview with Ulrike Ottinger," 124). This is underscored in the film when the same performers play the different parts of the new crew Madame X and Noa-Noa sign up for the next voyage. The film thus supplies linear "stops," and issues the unstoppable call to let go all the way to the point of return. Sabine Hake formulates the affirmation in this double bind: "In a world of permanently slipping signifiers, sexual difference, as *Madame X* suggests, does not reside in a linear movement of affirmation, liberation, or identity, but in a spiral-like energy wavering between exclusion and inclusion, a choreography of permanent non-identity" (184).

Ottinger was unaware of the whole series of *Madame X* movies that had already entered Hollywood film history well before she came up with her "Madame X" title. Believe it. Let the record show that Ottinger saw *The Wizard of Oz* for the first time on my VCR in Santa Barbara in 1992 (even though many of the Munchkin players were seen first in Browning's *Freaks,* a film very much on Ottinger's mind when she made *Freak Orlando*). But sometimes a great commotion arises by accidental interventions in the Hollywood melodramas of secret birthright and inheritance over the body of the self-sacrificing, self-effacing woman (and mother). Hake is still reading Ottinger's film when she reads it through the shake-up call it issues within all the other Hollywood films

Ulrike Ottinger as Orlando and Tabea Blumenschein as the pretraumatized pirate (in the context of Madame X: An Absolute Ruler).

bearing the same name. Hake thus spells out just what's in a name that's a Hollywood sign: "Madame X is a woman's name that stands in for the ideal of femininity and its deconstruction.... The mystery around *Madame X,* then, is about the problem of representing femininity, with the chiasmus X as the marker of her universal exchangeability, yet also as witness to her threatening absence" (179). What marks the spot Ottinger's Madame X is in, right from the outset, is the multiple-chiasm ecstasy or X-stasy—the ex-stasis—the condition of being not static, underway, affirmationally out for adventure. As the mark or spark of new beginnings, X in Ottinger's scenario keeps on circumnavigating the stuck, depressed, even threatening place of absence.

There's a double genealogy of the margin that's ready-made with Ottinger's recourse to the pirate-film genre: "*Madame X* . . . puts women at the center of a male genre but not so as to give women a piece of the action. The genre chosen is already a marginal one . . . , making this an intervention in marginality. At the same time the reality of women pirates . . . means that the choice of genre not only makes a point about media images but has a resonance of historical discourse behind it" (Dyer, 282). Madame X is a fictional addition to the historical and legendary tradition of Chinese women pirates. Ottinger's films always begin by filling a research volume. All kinds of information and image association get into a scrapbook that becomes the screenplay from which its projection folds out. "In my exhibition on *Freak Orlando* I tried to show how I work. I brought together books, photos, newspaper clippings, documents that fascinated and inspired me. Afterwards no one would assemble the materials in this way. But when you see the materials and see the film then you understand, I hope" (Ottinger, in Treut, "Gespräch mit Ulrike Ottinger").

The original screenplay album for *Madame X* opens with a 1930 photograph of the pirate queen Lai Cho San. Ottinger elaborated on this photograph as occasion for speculation that in a sense occasioned her film: "I wondered whether her servant who was sitting next to her was looking so bashfully to the side on account of the surely unaccustomed photographer, even though she was holding a gun, or whether it was out of respect for Lai Cho San who at the same time reaches for her gun with a determined gesture. The photo was telling me a story, and the longer I looked at it, the more questions rose up for me. I started to read diverse books on women pirates, trivial, analytical, eyewitness reports, etc. I was struck by how there was next to nothing concrete on the women in the history of piracy, even though they kept popping up like ghosts in the accounts and stories. I also noticed that while there were European women pirates, who however were forced to cover up their gender through masculine attire and mannerisms, which in one famous case led to the wearing of a silver penis, in China in contrast women robbed as industrious pirates without concealing or denying their gender" ("Piratinnen am Bodensee"). Lai Cho San's nineteenth-century precursor, Cheng I Sao (or Ching Yih Saou, or Ching Shih), known to her adversaries as Mrs. Cheng, has been hailed as the greatest pirate, male or female, in all history. For sure she was in charge of "one of the largest pirate communities there has ever been" (Cordingly, 78). Mrs. Cheng ruled her pirate confederation through a code of conduct that intervened even or especially in sexual mores. If it was determined that a female rape victim had agreed to the sex act, the male perpetrator was beheaded and the woman thrown overboard with a weight pulling her leg.

Madame X rules by serving as the focus of all libidinal ties and intrigues onboard. She is adored, jealously hated, feared. But she is also characterized as unsmiling, passive, quiescent, machine-like. Madame X's piracy, absolute rule, and loneliness at the top rise from a prehistory of loss. Her lover Orlando (played by Ottinger in the flashback accompanying the Chinese cook's narration to the new crew) swam out one day to pick a beautiful sea flower for Madame X. But, as Madame X already recognized while Orlando was swimming underwater toward her flower, Orlando was in fact nearing the tentacles of a carnivorous jellyfish that would drown and down her. Now the ship bears Orlando's name. Madame X lost her right hand while attempting Orlando's rescue. Now a techno prosthesis, which comes to a point at the end of the knife affixed to it, gives her a lethal hand (described in the screenplay as a "Persian combat glove"). The motor coordinates of the uncanny or funereal reading of where love and narcissism go when loss drives them first inward, then onward are camping on this trail. The camp Ottinger sets up here allows *Madame X* both to know about and not know or be about these traumatic origins.

Madame X's prosthetic technologization is not confined to her killer hand. She is doubled by the ship's figurehead, which is in her image, but which is also the device or apparatus she uses to maintain absolute rule over the crew. "With the aid of the figurehead, which is the exact copy of Madame X, executed with great care by a highly talented Numidic artist and medicine man, Madame X decided, as a precautionary measure for the turbulent and difficult times that lay ahead, to set her new crew an example that would demonstrate her absolute claim to power and her determination to punish severely any form of disobedience. On a foggy evening the eyes of the figurehead began to shine and through a sophisticated mechanism that Madame X set in motion the mouth of the figure prophesied gold, love, and adventure. They all heard it and saw it with their own eyes. The women were very impressed. This fact confirmed the omnipresence of Madame X and many were convinced that Madame X must possess highly unusual if not supernatural powers" (Ottinger, "Madame X—Eine absolute Herrscherin").

"There is a doubling of Madame X's person, on the one hand she is a real person, on the other hand a machine being, a motif that comes from Romantic literature and is then applied again in Expressionist films: Homunculus stories, the Golem, or Brigitte Helm in *Alraune*. It seemed to me important that Madame X and the apparatus of power—by which I mean the figurehead—are identical" (Ottinger, in Treut, "Gespräch mit Ulrike Ottinger," 72). Another inspiration Ottinger claims for *Madame X* (not in its doubling parts but in its juxtapositions) is the work of painter Gustave Moreau: "What I always liked about Moreau was that he brought together different levels in his pictures, that is, he did what seems impossible, something that goes without saying in collages, for example, that's what he was able to do in his own way, namely as painter. . . . I think he really risked a lot. . . . I believe that he brings together in a very courageous manner very disjoint things" (in Treut, "Gespräch mit Ulrike Ottinger," 75).

The Moreau-associated juxtapositions and disjunctions introduce another heroic legend, the kind that renders legible the journey's map of absolute doubling. Madame X isn't, after all, terribly uncanny. Monika Treut closes her reflections on *Madame X* with illumination of the breaks in the power apparatus that the viewers really should get: "The cruelty of Madame X mirrors the power, the challenge of which she takes on; . . . the recollection of her lost love, Orlando, keeps utopia up and running amidst the mechanical substitutions and lets us see past the performance of rigidity to another life, which is recalled in flashback," one that is also "laughable." "Only she who perceives this mechanization as immediate model or copy and overlooks the play with rigidity and immobility, will find in her disappointment nothing to laugh about, and will freeze up into the very seriousness which is mirrored for us through *Madame X*" ("Ein Nachtrag zu Ulrike Ottingers Film Madame X," 20).

Patricia White reconstructs the figurehead double of Madame X in sync (or swim) with figurations of the apparatus that are more contemporary than Ottinger's citations of Romantic literature and Expressionist film. "An exact replica of Madame X, the figurehead fits the image, produces the illusion perfectly. The image (woman) animates the mechanized, or enchanted, leather-clad female body which stands in for the apparatus (the title of the film appears across the first image of the figurehead). . . . Madame X's robotic movements and mechanical sounds indicate that she is not altogether human: her severed hand is restored like a spare part. The synchronization of sound effects associates her body with the register of sound mixing" (90). As internal representation of the apparatus of filmmaking, the figurehead in turn contains Madame X, both the pirate and the film. The promise that this multiple Madame X issues to "all women" is, according to White, "that of cinema itself" (80). "All women" in *Madame X* jump aboard the good ship *Chinese Orlando* and enter the film medium. The score, which is never settled, is a nonsynchronizable techno division between image and sound, corpus and voice, the nonverbal communications of camping and discourse that's hysterical.

But even in its double binding, White's identification of cinematic self-reference serves an even more absolute rule, that of a certain film feminist discourse. *Madame X,* "in taking up the appeals of both cinema and feminism, . . . addresses the spectator not only as *female* . . . but also . . . as *marginal*" (80). In other words: "*Madame X—An Absolute Ruler* was produced within and in reference to the current wave of feminism. It dramatizes the relation of women as social subjects to woman as supported and produced by the cinematic apparatus" (81). White's assumption that *Madame X* is engaged in dated debates about his and her pleasures is, however, an academic's fantasy. But it assumes the force of censorship when it mistakes the history of a discipline for the overriding historical record and context—as when it becomes categorically imperative that you identify and contextualize Ottinger's films along certain discursive lines and sides of critical debate. And what about queer cinema? Whose career depends on reanimating these debates, or at least requiring that they be revisited just for the historical record? Why should the identifiably "marginal" artist (or writer) bear the burden of keeping academic disciplines and careers artificially alive?

Unlike the apparatus double, the transvestite Belcampo poses a troubling doubling of gender that, both historically and in the course of White's reading, nevertheless serves to revalorize or revitalize the women-only arguments of feminism. "The figure of Belcampo offers a condensation of the film's address to the marginal subject. For if the crew respond 'naturally' as women to Madame X's call (recognizing themselves in the address and their desire in the promise), the interpellation of Belcampo, as unnatural 'woman', is more problematic. Classically, the fool's discourse frustrates sexual identification" (91). By the time it's time to conclude, the digression working through the problems and frustrations posed by Belcampo in the field of feminist film studies gives the upbeat of White's concluding sentences: "The film displaces two assumptions—that feminism finds its audience 'naturally,' and that the female spectator is destined to miss the boat. Gold, love and adventure lie just beyond the horizon" (91).

Ottinger can recall in the Berlin scene at the time she made *Madame X* local conflicts between feminists who were willing to admit transvestites into women-only organizations and clubs, and those "dad set" against the inclusion transfusion. Ottinger's films give us the rundown, our being run down, on the links and channels of mass identification. The other can never name herself as other. In a culture of diversity and commodity that means that we're all always passing, passing as spectator, passing as spectacle, passing through the metabolism of identification, in particular the mutual identification or admiration (or rage) found in groups. At the same time, with a twist worthy of Benjamin's Brecht (or of his Karl Kraus), Ottinger has been able, just the same, to gain admission and representation of minorities without first setting them up (in order to be heard or received at all) as representing themselves by necessity as part of an identifiable minority experience. This took radical exception to the rule of the inclusion illusion, whereby minorities were first introduced into the settings of their former exclusion only as experts on their own minority or multiculture. Thus "all women" in *Madame X* occupy any profession at all, and cathect anyone without discrimination.

Why is it that the body first or primally technologized is always the woman's body? Enter Daniel Paul Schreber, Freud's star witness for the analytic inside view of psychosis somewhere over the intersection between technology and the unconscious. Even in the Schreber case of techno delusion, the all-out turn-on gets attributed to the female body alone (which Schreber is becoming, via replicating changes induced by God's rays, at the same time as he's becoming an android). Only his new body, which is both the only body around and at once female and technological, can overcome the crisis in reproduction for the survival of the species. Schreber's only alternative to servicing as a dump site for the "poison of corpses" (121), to servitude to the "monstrous demand" that he

Karla Freud-Goldmund and Belcampo struggle for control of the test.

should behave continually as if he were himself a corpse (127), was to become a woman (with a "'Jew's stomach'") (133).

At the same time, his alternative live style made him over as terminal for divine rays (the same ones that either recognize only corpses or technologize sex changes in living bodies) caught in the act of writing down all his thoughts so that the next wave of rays can "again look at what has been written" (119). Only this live body can receive or conceive the ray beams of a divine power otherwise given to reabsorb within its Elysian force fields the nervous energy of corpses or, as happened to Schreber, of persons melancholically playing dead. It's a different way that both God and "Miss Schreber" (as He calls her) have of avoiding getting stuck on loss. Schreber's psychotic networking of identifcations (as woman and as wandering Jew) can only contain itself in the memoirs of a *Schreiber* (a writer) as an autobiography of writing, but one that updates writing's self-portrait as group portrait in the setting of the mediatic Sensurround.

Enter that feminism that has always doubled as investment in autobiography, but autobiography of media: the feminism that has always been on the way to technofeminism. In the first place, it was writing to which a certain feminine outer-body experience of traces was being restored. When these feminists turned to autobiography to get a certain voice or vote counted, the advance that crossed over to the other side of repression was not, for example, some new subject or body of knowledge, but always only that opening in which writing, as the primal technological medium, had been allowed to tell its own story. As Eva Meyer argues in *The Autobiography of Writing,* the grandmothers of Freud's hysterical patients—the women who dictated to the "father" the truths of the unconscious—were the authors of epistolary novels that we saw first with women writing about writing. Thus there is, even historically, a kind of inevitability to a certain feminist theory's opening offer to recoup a lost or disenfranchised feminine voice via the autobiography of "feminine writing." Although often obscured by the overinvestment in the de-repression of "the body," there was always also this other direct connection feminism put through to the autobiography of the media technologies, one that's mutual, to be sure, and indeed co-constitutive.

Theory may be art's second nature by now, the newest resource for inspiration or haunting, but it's not faster to the draw or the click of what's been a happening alliance in part production between the woman and her techno medium. So many "postmodern" women artists attract attention through the devices or gadgetry of their self-involvement as techno media. The record the gadget girls are stuck on speaks of itself.

In the camp of *Madame X,* which is styling with a "stylization of stylelessness" (Steinwachs), Ottinger drew a line through a particularly integrative and normative application of the Freudian intervention, specifically in the form of the sliding-scale test Freud-Goldmund administers to the newcomer onboard. The watch hit the decks with the breaking news that she had sighted "something not yet identifiable." They steered the ship toward what appeared to be a tiny boat. (The Hollywood players on the yacht *Holliday* had cast her off in a lifeboat upon deciding that she was a male, when it was a female they had intended to "shanghai" in Hong Kong.) "In it was a woman who waved chiffon scarves in an exalted manner while crying out loudly for help. One brought the exhausted person onboard. It was a woman? A man? Belcampo was totally exhausted. But when she noticed that the women were discussing whether she was a man or a woman, and the decision that she was a man would undoubtedly mean that she would be thrown overboard, she sang a stirring song from her homeland and danced along with great charm. The clinical psychologist Karla Freud-Goldmund, who had attended a seminar in sexology taught by Professor Giese in Hamburg, believed that she would be able to solve the problem with a short test. Doña Belcampo, currently a shipwrecked hairstylist and manicurist, announced that she would be glad to answer a few questions. Karla Freud-Goldmund asked Belcampo in swift succession the most bizarre questions, which Belcampo, to the delight of the crew, answered just as quickly and bizarrely. When the experimental subject came to the image test, and solved it very capriciously with the aid of her strange styling and manicuring cutlery, the enthusiasm of the crew no longer knew any bounds. Karla Freud-Goldmund was very irritated by this unusual response to her test. In her entire career she had never before seen anything like it. Just the same she could still draw her conclusions even from all this, and unperturbed she gave instruction: Doña Belcampo possesses without doubt the psyche of a woman, her physical sexual traits must be considered secondary. The crew rejoiced and it was decided to admit Belcampo into their colorfully mixed circle, especially since she seemed to be very amusing" (Ottinger, "Madame X—Eine absolute Herrscherin"). The final question at the end of what's just a test, phrase number 566 on the actual MMPI pasted inside the original *Madame X* album, brings the loopy reception back inside the media loop of self-reflection: "Do you like to watch love scenes in movies?"

Belcampo achieves immunity from sexual identity by jamming the personality test that would pin him or her down with "flash-forwards, flashbacks, and false fragments of the film" (White, 83). That Belcampo's resistance to his MMPI testing doubles as cinematic alternative to a certain line of questioning places the pathologizing test, which is only at one remove of interpretation or confidentiality from an arrest report, in the position of the screenplay well made in Hollywood or for TV. Belcampo refuses to be identified (with) while figures of identification are required for psychological testing and diagnosis ("the identified patient"), the police report (no arrest without identification), and the proper screenplay and film. Ottinger: "A potential co-producer recently recommended that I make my films as technologically saturated and also in details as realistic and story-telling as a James Bond movie. . . . He also was of the opinion that with my imagination and my capacity for empathy it would surely not be difficult for me to create a figure of identification for as many people as possible, who could then go ahead and have as many unusual experiences as I like. In that regard he did not want to constrain me. I answered: In that regard I could agree to be restrained, but in no way in the former matter. The co-production fell through" ("Der Zwang zum Genrekino").

How-to screenwriting textbooks promise knowledge of what to do in order to write, which addresses a certainty or surveillance as old as the oldest hermeneutics:

> When you complete this book, you will know exactly what to do to write a screenplay. Whether you do it or not is up to you. Writing is a personal responsibility—either you do it, or you don't. (Field, 5)

The screenplay must therefore raise and answer a finite set of questions:

HOW TO KNOW WHEN YOU'RE DONE
... Ask yourself:
1 What is my story? Can I state it in two or three brief sentences giving the beginning, the middle, and the end?
2 Who is my main character and what does he want?
3 What does my main character get? How is that different from what he wanted?
4 Can the reader state my story and identify the main character's needs by page 10? (King, 124)

The report can introduce order only after a moment of regression—that of the arrest or "bust"—has gone down. Good cop, bad cop is the one and only ritual that corresponds, point by point, with the split Melanie Klein diagnosed between good breast, bad breast. The arrest report, pathologizing test, or Hollywood screenplay introduces order into an already split indeterminacy (or immediacy). That's why it can only give orders, not form. This knowing perspective is uncanny, uncontained, in its formless propensity for endless and self-destructive development. The Hollywood screenplay author, the authority on how to write screenplays, occupies a space of uncanny conflation of two irreconcilable extremes of violence, the lawmaking and the lawbreaking kinds, the same space Benjamin identified as the native habitat of the police. That these two kinds of violence serve as the bookends of legal violence presupposes the interchangeability in place of any opposition between lawmaking and lawbreaking. To break the law is to make a new law: violent breaking or transgression marks the primal origin of the law, to which we return with every crime, whether as witness or as perpetrator. Thus, according to Benjamin, the purpose even of the legal system's highest violence, the power over life and death, "is not to punish the infringement of law but to establish new law" ("Critique of Violence," 286).

The certainty or surveillance of the arrest report, the psychological test, and the made-to-order screenplay is belied in the first place by those who follow and administer these standards or norms. They all have their own ideas and require a free-for-all of latitude that spells the compromise formations of police brutality or development hell. Benjamin identifies the police force as phantom-like in the improv nightmare issuing from its hunting license of ungrounded evaluation and decision making. "Its power is formless, like its nowhere tangible, all-pervasive, ghostly presence in the life of civilized states" ("Critique of Violence," 287).

In a far more unnatural combination than in the death penalty, in a kind of spectral mixture, these two forms of violence are present in another institution of the modern state, the police. True, this is violence for legal ends (in the right of disposition), but with the simultaneous authority to decide these ends itself within wide limits (in the right of decree). The ignominy of such an authority, which is felt by few simply because its ordinances suffice only seldom for the crudest acts, but are therefore allowed to rampage all the more blindly in the most vulnerable areas and against thinkers, from whom the state is not protected by law—the ignominy lies in the fact that in this authority the separation of lawmaking and law-preserving violence is suspended. (Ibid.)

Where there's ghostliness, there's loss—as in, let's lose these police. "Institutionalized seeing and the reception of new aesthetic forms could also be formulated: Is it still at all possible to survive outside the conserving can?" (Ottinger, "Der Zwang zum Genrekino").

It is a question of style, not of truth, which in *Madame X* skewers together Freud-Goldmund and a visionary guru. Nor is it simply a put-down when the clinical psychologist "returns" at the end as bike dyke, as, according to Ottinger, one of her own patients (in Treut, "Gespräch mit Ulrike Ottinger," 71). Reviewers were slaphappy to dismiss Freud-Goldmund in her entirety (Jochen Brunow, for example). She is indeed compromised by the MMPI test. But if her diagnosis of the group dynamic onboard the ship seems funny in context—and the analytic interpretation cannot but be gratingly or ridiculously out of context in an acting-out setting—this does not undermine the validity of the interpretation. Certainly, as we will see, Ottinger's own discussion of the narcissistic disturbances exhibited by the alcoholic heroine of her subsequent film *Ticket of No Return* draws from the same lexicon as Freud-Goldmund's diagnosis of Madame X. After Noa-Noa (following Madame X's command) spears the fleeing Freud-Goldmund right through the guru who interrupts his meditation to volunteer as her human shield, Madame X turns away from the death scene and lets the psychologist's scientific study about her lie there, still in the bottle in which the author had sought to carry it to a place of publication. That Madame X all the while mumbles the different terms of Freud-Goldmund's study betrays a degree of knowledge of the interpretation, by omniscience but also by rote, that cannot be written off to disdain.

Blowup is killed by a defense mechanism built into the figurehead when she rages against this machine (and by proxy against Madame X). "The next day brought a new gruesome surprise. Blowup lay strangled in the arms of the figurehead. Madame X marveled at the coincidence that put so much power in her hands. From now on none of the women would dare to stand up to her. Madame X avoided mentioning the mechanism built into the figurehead lest a rational explanation for the incident become available" (Ottinger, "Madame

Blowup is killed by the double of Madame X.

X—Eine absolute Herrscherin"). Omega Centauri is poisoned by Madame X's decree because she witnessed Blowup's execution and saw that it was apparatus made. Flora Tannenbaum gets her throat cut for uninvited watching of Hoisin and Belcampo adoring the spectacle of Madame X's bathing beautiful but hirsute chest. By triangulating the narcissistic ritual, she cuts into the duo dynamic that runs Madame X's powers.

Freud-Goldmund gets the spear, then, because through her analysis she too bears testimony to a secret that threatens to undermine Madame X's double power over "all women." Here is Freud-Goldmund's clinical evaluation:

After the women had left behind all the psycho-social barriers of their everyday lives, their suppressed sensuality broke through with unanticipated force, repressed instinctual stimuli became manifest and cast them, accustomed as they were to the girdle of civilization, into extreme psychic conflicts which overwhelmed their weak egos. Woman's centuries-long oppression, which left behind in her character structure habits of passivity and dependency, made them into the willing tools of Madame X, a narcissistically disturbed but charismatic personality, whose almost insatiable hunger for power was amplified immeasurably through the almost masochistic submission of the women. Another inauspicious effect and conflictual moment to be considered is the isolation in such a small space which stands in total contradiction to the wide open space to which the women had access through their own imagination. The gruesome bloody acts performed for no reason recall the destructive orgies of early childhood that never took place and here find their over-sized reactivation. (Ottinger, "Madame X—Eine absolute Herrscherin")

Madame X's killing spree does not begin as punishment for the fight against the machine. It starts with Belcampo, who in the drag of a tambourine-shaking majorette makes it to the end of the film, heading Madame X's procession through the harbor town and then back to the good ship *Chinese Orlando* with the new crewmembers. Belcampo rescues and stows away a sailor from the *Holliday* during Madame X's annihilating attack. This doesn't escape Madame X's supervision. But when Belcampo pleads for the Russian sailor's life, her wish is granted, and the *Holliday*'s sole survivor, Moorenhut, is kept in a cage suspended above and alongside the ship. Belcampo has her way with him. But Betty Brillo, who is also interested, threatens to tell Madame X if Belcampo doesn't give her the key and a turn. While Betty Brillo and Moorenhut are getting it on, Belcampo cannot help herself: compelled by a "devilish thought" (Ottinger, "Madame X—Eine absolute Herrscherin"), she releases the rope holding up the cage and drowns them both. Madame X's judgment the next morning: she cuts the rope so the cage with the corpses bobbing at the surface can sink into oblivion. "Belcampo was not punished. This terrible kind of prank even amused Madame X. Betty Brillo's portion of the loot was divided up according to the rules they had agreed upon" (Ottinger, "Madame X—Eine absolute Herrscherin").

While even in name Belcampo seems caught up in camp affirmation, she also has a German Romantic literary pedigree as a character in E. T. A. Hoffmann's *The Devil's Elixir*. Patricia Highsmith spanned this sensibility to be shared when she joined her call to Madame X's invitation to all women: "I summon you to the ingenious, sarcastic, and still somehow Romantic Madame X!" Psychoanalysis tracks back to the "somehow Romantic" spot we're in with Madame X and

Belcampo. Freud's analysis of the uncanny used Hoffmann's "The Sandman" as demo, but only because *The Devil's Elixir,* which he cites as his main inspiration, was way too complicated for case-note summation or transcription. A "Note" signed S. F. that appeared (the same year as the essay "The 'Uncanny'") under the rubric "Varia" in the *Internationale Zeitschrift für Psychoanalyse* cites Belcampo's words of comfort for Medardus, the deranged hero in *The Devil's Elixir* (a novel S. F. cites overall for its wealth of "masterful descriptions of pathological mental states"):

> "And what do you get out of it? I mean out of the particular mental function which we call consciousness, and which is nothing but the confounded activity of a damned toll-collector—excise-man—deputy-chief customs officer, who has set up his infamous bureau in our top storey and who exclaims, whenever any goods try to get out: 'Hi! Hi! Exports are prohibited . . . they must stay here . . . here, in this country. . . .'" (in Freud, *SE* 17: 233–34, n.1)

Belcampo, alternatively Schönfeld, is a hairstylist who claims equal rights with any artist. He's all pun power and he wraps up language or thought in curling irons. But the curl that shows that "to be mad" *(verrückt)* literally, in German, is "to be displaced" hits the spot, according to Freud. The "Note" assigns *The Devil's Elixir* (with Belcampo as its spokesperson) to a place of horror (I mean honor) alongside Schreber's *Memoirs of My Nervous Illness* and Wilhelm Jensen's *Gradiva* (and in contrast to the series of works of interpretation to which *Oedipus Rex, Hamlet,* and "The Sandman" belong) as one of those works in which psychoanalytic knowledge can be found endopsychically recorded and stored to the letter (before the letter) of Freud's words of formulation and reformulation.

Thus it is in a setting of examples and models of "uncanny" and "demonic" doubling or repetition in German Romanticism that Freud in 1920 reads the repetition compulsion and the death drive as "demonic," which allows him, as "Devil's advocate," to unfold a series of life-or-death scenarios reminiscent of devil fictions that he also stops short of accepting (or signing). During the flashback narration of the loss that created Madame X, in the original screenplay, we read that the bereaved gave herself to the devil and the satanic arts (Ottinger, "Madame X—Eine absolute Herrscherin"). Vilém Flusser, whose studies of photography and the nomadic impulse have a shelf life in Ottinger's library, began his writing career with the publication of *Die Geschichte des Teufels* (History of the Devil) in Portuguese translation, because Flusser, who was born in Prague, had fled Nazi Europe to Brazil. Flusser's only Freudian work tracks the history of the devil (which he declares is our history, as in, there is no other history) through our relations to the world and through the world back to ourselves. The stations of these relations are the seven deadly sins. Ottinger's interest and investment in the allegory of these deadly sins led to her 1986 *Superbia—Der Stolz (Superbia—Pride)*, her contribution to a seven-sins, seven-women-directors collection. Pride, Ottinger writes, "is the first in the canon of the Seven Deadly Sins. In the interpretation of the old Superbia concept, Superbia was the premier sin against God: to desire to make something of one's own was considered sacrilegious since creation was the domain of God. Thus one could see the artist and his work—in particular film as realized alternative world—as incarnation of the Superbia concept" *(Produktionsmitteilung)*. But according to the prologue in the film, Superbia at the same time rules over her own seven sub-sins (vanity, etc.) as "Luciphera Superbia."

Pride, according to Flusser, marks that penultimate moment in the cycle (and recycling) of the deadly sins conceived as phases of metabolization of the world of our own making. With pride we recognize the whole world to be our own egoic act of will. At the prideful stage, the world as medium, as language, is both stretched to the limits of abstraction and "thickened" (as in the German word for poetry or art, *Dichtung*), materialized, stuck in the groove or scratch from which it starts over and over again, scratching the surface, deferring the cutting-off point. The only American filmmaker up to Ottinger's visual standards of time-stalling elaboration of the depth in the surface, of the interior of the image, is Kenneth Anger, whose "Luciferean" work is dedicated to Aleister Crowley, the neo-pagan father of modern black magic arts and cults.

But the devil always only gives finite time. In other words, the high point of pride falls down quickly into acedia, the sorrow or lassitude of the heart (otherwise known as sloth). Acedia marks the nadir of depressed, philosophical realization that this world of my making, which isn't so much, is all there is. Flusser characterizes this vanishing point of philosophical reflection, even and especially in its inevitability, as "lazy thinking." But in no time the playing-dead quiescence of sloth gets caught up in lust, doubles and divides like the unicellular organism, and begins the cycle of deadly sins all over again. In the original *Bedazzled* (directed by Stanley Donen, 1967), as in Flusser's interpretation, sloth is married to lust.

Allegorically, then, the seven deadly sins mark phases of metabolization of our self-relations through our relationship to a world that comes out of and returns to nothingness, the world of art-like creation and self-reference. Like Freud, the artist will take up the position of devil's advocate, and while not signing up herself, can by proxy, at the remove of representation or observation, deal with the devil. In the devil fiction or fantasy, the contractual relationship gives quality time and, at the end, the guaranteed preset deadline. This is another reason artists are as tempted by the devil's contract as are the psychopaths (for their own reasons). The relationship supplies what is missing or wanting in the depressed phase of intake of and insight into our self-relations via a world of our own making.

There is no question that the artist stands outside the scenes of external violence in which the psychopathic clients of the devil are at home. The question that can be raised, like a ghost, is How is the artist spared joining the lineup of the devil's clients? We saw that Freud-Goldmund's posing of the problem does not explain or cure all there is to Madame X (both figure and film). Insofar as this coupling of figure and film is also always exceeded by doubling, we encounter the repetition compulsion that Madame X contains—gives form to and is all about.

In his *Confessions*, Crowley motivates the upsurge of his rule-busting life, and the concomitant switch in his memoirs from third- to first-person narration, through a certain relationship to his father's death. It was the synchronization of his dream of his father's death with his father's actual dying that gave him a rules-and-inhibitions-busting ego. His mother kept hanging around as static on this line of "dad" certainty. After years of dreaming of her death, one of his dreams did finally coincide with her passing. Crowley suggests, however, that this dream had the same affective charge as the one (only one was required) that was joined to his father's certain death.

To serve the devil, you must be without inhibitions on a scale of supernormal to psychopathic. Belief in God or in the alternative occult afterlife styles of vampires or werewolves, for instance, is compatible with an inhibited sensibility, one stuck on loss or still working on it. The uninhibited capacity for compensating for a lack through a successful operation of substitution without complications—to the full extent that the lack or loss is even seen as having been required or desired in exchange for the devil's offer of "dad" certainty—drives Madame X's absolute rule, her apparatus. The relationship the devil pitches to prospective clients consists in the deferral of suicide for the quality time it takes before the deadline, one's proper and certain death, along which you sign when you sign with the devil.

When Freud derived the death drive from the compulsion to repeat he also issued, between the lines, a rereading or reformatting of relations with the devil as the demonic principle or drive that participates even in the prolongation and preservation of life (for the time being). Ottinger's *Madame X* reinscribes the dead-end figures of "dad" certainty within an affirmation of the ongoing and hard-to-follow balancing acts between life and death drives. Thus we begin again at the end of *Madame X* with the new crew (the old crew members in new roles) signing up with pleasure. "With thumbprints they all signed the contract, and

Madame X as figurehead or double.

to the accompaniment of Belcampo's loud drumroll each passionately pressed her lips to the giant emerald shining among the many small knives on Madame X's glove. The adventure could begin anew. And with a favorable breeze they set sail" (Ottinger, "Madame X—Eine absolute Herrscherin"). Madame X, true to the chiasmatic force of her name, is posed and poised between lassitude and lust, between the downswing of the cycle and the lustful beginning again from scratch.

3
BETWEEN MEDIA

Ottinger came to filmmaking via a career in the visual arts (painting, works on paper, photography, performance). After training in Munich, Ottinger resided and worked in Paris. Her success notwithstanding, she reached a crisis point of disappointment in the range of what she could accomplish within these more static, preliminary, or partial media. She renounced her art career and returned to Constance, where, as founder of a gallery and a film club, she continued to work in the art world, but from a directorial or organizing point of view. Ottinger's film career took off with her subsequent move to Berlin, an archaeological site of political and psychic projections that served her through the 1980s as a major source of inspiration for her exploration of the cinematic medium of projection. Otto Dix's "Großstadt Triptychon" ("Big City Triptych") was Ottinger's primal childhood intake of an image of art (Möhrmann). Dix's metabolization of Berlin in three parts within the analogy time (or "timelessness") of art proved a lasting inspiration for her own Berlin trilogy, beginning with *Ticket of No Return*. In *The Image of Dorian Gray in the Yellow Press*, the cabaret revue on one of the stages marking Dorian Gray's sightseeing tour through the underworld has all the "bite" of the Dix triptych (Schaper).

What drew Ottinger to film is that it is a medium of juxtaposition (between, say, parameters of the historical and of the modern, between stationary and moving perspectives, between global panoramas and the miniature) and therefore ready-made for conveying the present tensions driving her encounter with the other onward. Reflecting the status of the medium as the high or late point of developments beginning with the printing press, Ottinger makes her movies at the stations of the crossing of the legible with the irreducibly visual, of narrative with tableau. "Back then I was making etchings, I worked as assistant in Atelier Friedländer—and then—well, how shall I describe it: I suddenly had a big problem with this form of totally isolated work and in this way I ended up in a real life crisis because I actually really wanted to paint—but I wanted some kind of contact with an audience. . . . This totally isolated situation, it was making me completely crazy. I couldn't stand it anymore and at that time I was addressing with my painting and the photo documentations entire theme complexes—which is really already too much for painting as far as the message goes. And from there it was a completely logical step for me to move to film, which gave me sound and text—since I began making films I have the feeling that I can really express everything I want to express" (Ottinger, in Strempel). In its synchronic or syntactic dimension, film can tarry with the narration and go with the speed of all there is to show, can show the long and the slow of what's sedentary or nomadic. On the semantic or diachronic axis, the "collage film" (as Ottinger named her brand of cinema) cuts and pastes images and events: "I believe that real events are better understood when they have been taken out of their whole context and placed together in a somewhat displaced manner. I think that one can contemplate such images, which certainly also exist in reality as fragments, simply more rigorously than if I filmed a story from A to Z and represented it in a way that is also available to us in real life" (Ottinger, in "TIP—Interview mit U. Ottinger," 17).

Although Ottinger's return trip, or trip without return, counted a stopover in Constance, her eventual move to Berlin from Paris, her transfer, in other words, to the new medium of filmmaking, is reflected or rather doubled in the fictional journey of the anonymous heroine in *Ticket of No Return,* which commences in an imaginary place called La Rotonda with her purchase of a one-way plane ticket to Berlin. The transaction is concluded in French. La Rotonda belongs to the area or era of "Europe" in which Paris serves as "capital" and standard of exchange. In turn, the lavish "Mediterranean" building we enter to visit the travel office, which is upstairs, was in fact an unidentified instance of late nineteenth-century Berlin architecture, which can be characterized as deregularized historicist.

The English-language title translates the original French subtitle, *Aller jamais retour.* The main title in German, *Bildnis einer Trinkerin,* translates as "portrait of a drinker" or "picture of a drinker." Unfortunately, in English we can't show gender in the "same" word. The necessary addition of "woman" or "female" just wouldn't go down as smoothly as the original title. And elegance is of the essence. Referred to throughout as "sie" or "she," the visitor from La Rotonda discovers in Berlin the setting where she can realize her decision to drink without end, until death does the partying, I mean does them part. Certainly she, like her uncanny double, the alcoholic bag lady, is in crisis, and her beauteous journey through Berlin's allegorical pageants still counts as a suicide trip.

The transition to filmmaking was a period of crisis for Ottinger. And while the subject of her 1979 film "portrait" is on a death trip through the Berlin stations

"She" in Berlin.

of alcoholic excess, her story lies more precisely in the in-between, in the middle ground of glass walls she can break but never break through. Yet this impasse is only one possible description of the same mirror medium through which the director continued to journey and make contact. Since Goethe's *The Sorrows of Young Werther*, it is commonplace in the history of stories that a fictional figure must fail where the artist continues to survive and thrive.

In 1983 Jonathan Rosenbaum judged that "*Ticket of No Return* somehow manages to be two things at once: (1) an inspired development and fusion of many of the most fruitful currents in European film over the past several years . . . and (2) an uncategorizable masterpiece so sui generis that influences seem hardly relevant at all to the synthesis achieved" (124). In short, *"Ticket of No Return* . . . strikes [Rosenbaum] as a fully achieved work—one of the few true masterpieces of the contemporary German avant-garde cinema" (123).

Ticket of No Return counts as the first part of Ottinger's trilogy, which continued with *Freak Orlando* (1981) and concluded with *The Image of Dorian Gray in the Yellow Press* (1984). The Berlin setting holds these films together. A Berlin postcard opens the original research album for *Ticket of No Return*. In Ottinger's allegorical reading or rendering, Berlin's ready-made status as most ancient or primal city of our more recent past and most traumatic history becomes visible, through the artist's work of metamorphosis, as a narrative of episodes cutting through time and space.

Berlin's "reality" is setting, document, and the other fictional world of film. In her "Synopsis," Ottinger spells out how the connection/disconnection between the two women organizes all the stages or stations of the film: "Profile of two unusual but extremely different women. One of them more the 'Barefoot

"She" and Lutze (the bag lady).

Countess,' the other more 'Nights of Cabiria.' One rich, eccentric, hiding her feelings behind a rigid mask, consciously drinks herself to death. She is one of those cases that never appear in the statistics, because either they are kept at home on Valium, or in a private clinic under lock and key. The other is poor and unknowingly drinks herself to death. She appears in the standardized statistics as typical of the unstable drinker who is repeatedly picked up drunk. . . . In the course of the story—which is subdivided into stages—these two drinkers try to get to know each other. . . . They cannot come together—not because the social difference is too great, but because the alcohol repeatedly hinders their attempts at communication, or even replaces it. 'She' can only break through her rigidity and isolation in her fantasy world, in which she imagines herself in various jobs. In extreme fantasies filled with paranoid fears she commits acts of self-destruction. She fights with her own shadow or tries to obliterate her mirror image with the contents of her wine glass. . . . The three ladies, 'Social Question,' 'Common Sense,' and 'Accurate Statistics'—playing the role of the three Fates in an organized, technologized, standardized world formed by the mass media—comment in their matter-of-fact way. Background is Berlin, thrown open to a grotesque kind of sightseeing (a drinker's geography) and complemented by actual encounters with people who live in Berlin or are visiting. Rock singers, writers, artists, taxi drivers."

In *Ticket of No Return,* Ottinger demarcates a "drinker's geography" of West Berlin. The landscape that stretches beneath the one-way flight from La Rotonda to Berlin embraces the techno coordinates of long-distance travel and communication. But upon arrival, "she" starts doubling on contact with her destination/destiny (the press, for example, shadows her): the landscape shrinks to fit the site for sore "I"s or egos, the bottom of a "bottlefield" of internalization.

In ancient Rome there were already roadside *mansiones* every twenty-five kilometers offering travelers and horses stopover services. Between the *mansiones* an alternative, alternating subchain cut into the stereometric distances with fewer services but just in time for those who couldn't keep standard time. They were called *mutationes,* and offered all that's in their name in the line of evolutionary variation on a standard pattern or chain. Mutations were there to serve those just needing one more drink for the road or to crash, whether in the mode of emergency or of spontaneous intermission.

The history of travel in all its mutations writes or rides the history of hospitality. But what gets internalized as all-out drinking fits the subtext of the double history of travel and hospitality. Hospitality, as old as prehistory, was in its original reception and even in the history of its names at once welcome and uncanny. The guest was originally an unwanted foreigner or, at best, a chance arrival of unknown origin. What was good in "guest" (or "host" for that matter) made it into "hospital" and "hotel." The bad part lives on in "hostile." In ancient times, your host was untouchable, just like the cook, the slave, the gladiator, or, in Egypt, anyone involved in the work of embalming. From guest or host to ghost is not a big skip of the heartbeat. It's all the same word and world. One ghost, the spirit of some ancestor, for example, is friendly; another, still fresh in the minds of the survivors, the get-well death wishers, is vengeful, out to haunt the near and the dear.

Over time your host was your sponsor: he became a local politician, broker, supporter of the arts, or entertainer. Finally, he became a therapist, and the static of haunting could be interpreted or contained in new transferential settings. Freud's own first analogies for transference conjoined references to the printing press and to haunting. The original printing press in turn reassembled the wine press it took as its model. Before our era of Freud's interventions, the first major cultural revolution was the introduction of coffee, tea, or cocoa. That new course pulled an emergency break in the all-out drinking that had saturated Europe. Ever since, there is a morning/mourning offer of alternation between drinking and recovery.

Nietzsche was fond of reminding us that the history of Europe counted bottles of beer on the wall. Nonstop drinking spilled over into border zones where ghostly taverns, known as *Nobiskrüge,* took shape out of the fog. The *Nobiskrüge* came out of the deepest recess of melancholic drinking, where getting bombed gets the undead one inside you embalmed. Luther grabbed our attention when he used these spooky taverns to conjure the underworld and give us hell. One historian of tavern life gets the picture: "Fantasy given wings by alcohol not only led to the creation of legendary figures out of nothing, it gave rise to the construction of nebulous buildings for the unstoppable drinker: the *Nobiskrüge* emerged outside the centralized towns, out of the reach, therefore, of every administrative, rational control. In ghostly fashion they appeared in the midst of forest and heath, usually they were located near the border, and the reputation of uncanniness was attached to them. The origin of the name is dark, uncertain. . . . In the popular mind such an establishment was the meeting place of sinister figures, demons and dead people who had not yet been able to shake their longing for worldly pleasures" (Benker, 86).

Trips without return, or only with a ghostly return on our investments or cathexes, traverse and demarcate landscapes, the primal frames of cinematic seeing. Beginning with *Ticket of No Return,* Ottinger rigorously mapped out the range, genealogy, and deep psychology of the landscape, which even when it's in nature is artifice too. The landscape belongs to the recent past or prehistory of our photographic and cinematic seeing-eye passage through the worlds between the perceived world and perception itself. Gertrud Koch contemplates traveling's continuity shot with cinema: "Travel as a form of perception is characterized by a chiastic intersection of internal and external images, fiction and reality. It shares this quality with film, which is also a form of perception, crystallizing at the interface between representation and projection; determined by camera position, centering of the image, montage and timing, and the always surprising and arbitrary conclusions drawn by the viewer" ("Arabesques and Intrigues," 237). The continuity shot itself, I would argue, is what we refer to, in earshot of escape, as *landscape*.

LANDSCAPE FROM TECHNOLOGY

Landscape is not just about gardens, which are sculptural (according to Mondrian) and, in the aesthetic terms of the Italian Renaissance, third, not second, nature. So let's take a map. That too is another parallel universal. Before there was landscape, inside the genealogy of gardens and maps, all-out visualizations of the land began where myths of lost continents left off: on lost fantasy islands like Atlantis, like California. (No land is an island except for California. The coast with the most was primally projected as fantasy island, and way in advance of discovery or first contact or any science-factional calculation of what happens when we finally do get the continental drift. The flotational coast that was such a screen belonged, they said, to Queen Califa. Cortez got so tired of looking for Your Highness, and low about getting just desert, that he made a place-name for her: "California," the queen's "furnace.")

Freud gathered together all the jump starts of perspectival visualization in one dream team of latent meaning: "Marcinowski has published a collection of dreams illustrated by their dreamers with drawings that ostensibly represent landscapes and other localities occurring in the dreams. These drawings bring out very clearly the distinction between a dream's manifest and latent meaning. Whereas to the innocent eye they appear as plans, maps, and so on, closer inspection shows that they represent the human body, the genitals, etc., and only then do the dreams become intelligible" (*The Interpretation of Dreams, SE* 5: 356). Where it's not an identification question, even the ego is a projection of the body. It's all I-land.

Northern Europe followed the era of discovery with short attention to gadget-loving details. From up north came, in one span of retention, both the new medium of oil paint and the matter of fact of the landscape. Following Hanns Sachs's example, in "The Delay of the Machine Age," we might ask why it took so long for the landscape to be developed. Did it respond to a techno-narcissistic crisis in relations with one's own body, which always also refers to relations with the mother's body? Did the sudden uncanniness of bodily relations not only require the emergency projection of the body as machine, as Sachs argues, but also, at the same time, as landscape? In dreams, according to Freud, when we both recognize a landscape and cannot quite identify it (which may just be the very best generic definition of landscape), we've returned to the mother's body. It's the only body around and it's off-limits.

The sublime is the lube job that gets us around the fright sight of nature and really into our own technologization. By the time the landscape came to California, the sublime—like the rumor of gold—stuck to all those oversize out-of-sights of our land: the mountains, the canyons, the desert. Astonishment, horror, silence became golden, became sublime. Even before Zane Grey assisted behind the scenes of Hollywood's filming of *The Riders of the Purple Sage,* amusement parks were being built upon the short circuit that made the big scenes of nature so awesome: the sublime was still along for the first thrill rides of our catastrophe preparedness in groups. The landscape entered, via the sublime, first the amusement park, then the big picture of cinema.

Already at its introductory offering, the landscape was the picture perfect of a view that's never really seen, whether for all the trees, or because it is in the background, or, besides, we're only passing through it. Something gets magnified in landscapes. What gets fired up in landscapes is the internal, I mean eternal, flame of the unknown, unmourned dead. Yes, the hills were alive with mythic creatures. But vacant fields of representation were always only set aside for framing or viewing if already reserved for the dead. The new worlds of landscape and seascape at the same time flashed back from the Elysian force fields of undeath. Where mourning gets repressed, interrupted, undone, the spark of technologization brings up the arrears.

The landscape is in a future perfect tense or techno tension. The moment of landscape viewing, the moment in passing, never was but always only will have been. Landscape composition thus fits and then extends the short attention span. At first fitting, it gave us a perspective for getting around peripheral vision, the static of seeing too much too soon. But this new picture perspective also always reasserts its constructedness, its science-experiment status, because it remains finally nonsuperimposable onto our vision. It's like in the movies when identification gets constructed in the equation between the camera-POV and our own seeing-I. Nice try! But total near miss. One cannot forever put off recognizing what's blinderedness in eyesight that's without all the spillover extending and blurring the cutting edges of our points of vision.

With the landscape we began constructing techno vision in pictures. Oil paint and celluloid and magnetic tape mark stations of this vision's crossing with the materials of recording. The arts of magnification were at the same time amplifying the range of picturing while blending the boundaries of visibility. We were cutting in, interrupting invisibility, and prosthetizing or framing our every contact with the visual field. Walter Benjamin compares our visual mediatization to a surgeon's rapport with his patient's body ("The Work of Art in the Age of Mechanical Reproduction," 233). With the same techno skill, we enter right into whatever we're to see, but then, like the surgeon, we also stop short of merger, I mean murder. That's why our gadget connection with our own ongoing technologization bestows, in visual terms, as Benjamin says of the camera's trigger-happiness, a posthumous shock ("On Some Motifs in Baudelaire," 175). It all will have been datable, consciously experienced, disposable. This is how our techno-group metabolism works, on a short control release: the gadget's on-off switch shoots us up with inoculative doses of what would otherwise be traumatic. The gadget trigger or switch splits the second, the splitting second of trauma, and takes shock into the ego instead, which absorbs it in part, assigns it a date, and disposes of it in all its other parts.

Everything Benjamin projected for the culture of film, a forecast radically interrupted by TV, gets realized in the in-group settings of video production and consumption. Now that our fast-forward, rewind, and playback functions are in place and editing has lost its castrative edge, we can join in our gadget-love as experts, always just testing.

But the cut has been displaced too. Now it's less about prosthetic limbs, and way more about transplanting organs. If we currently take replacement organs from our accident-prone teenagers, soon, they say, we will grow them ourselves, beside ourselves, inside the supply chests of our own clone bodies (teenagers at heart, friends forever). But even this newest organ will still be just a cut above the rest. Even in the immediate future we'll be in landscapes pulled in both directions by replacement parts and partings at one end and, at the other, prospects for our own, self-containing, replicational immortality (without, that is, all those divisions of doubles).

Already in the eighteenth century it took one landscape to recognize another one. Even back then we were trying to get into the image and be right at its art. It's not only that Gainsborough, for example, painted sylvan landscapes from models he constructed using broccoli for trees (the vegetables standing in for all the trees in the field of representation were recent arrivals down the assembly line of engineered produce). But for the longer haul, all alpine settings should be watched through rose-colored glasses, the kind that gave the passing view the Claude Lorrain look. You didn't leave home or gardens without them. The so-called Claude glass, rather than glasses, was more a look-see than a look through. It was a compact mirror, convex and either sepia-tinted or made with black glass. You turned your back on the view that had landscape potential, and saw reflected therein a landscape painting (or a "photograph" of one) that was up to the standards of Claude Lorrain's art.

The panorama was just around the bends our sensorium suffered before getting into motion pictures. The process went into reverse. Now mass audiences wanted to see real scenes as real, not as painted. In contrast to the single 3-D POV of landscape painting, panorama painting posited a theoretical horizon along which a large number of points of view could be matched by an equal number of viewing points. Thus, with regard to the wraparound panorama painting, the viewer saw what could be seen at a given moment from a specific site. Before the advent of cinema stopped short the spread of panormas, which simply disappeared, offshoots were also spawned, such as the extended panorama that simulated travel in a moving vehicle through landscapes. Rolled on mechanically moving cylinders, these panorama viewings could last for extended periods of time. One of the grandest extended panoramas took visitors to the 1900 Paris Exhibition on a simulated ride on the Trans-Siberian Railway. The scrolling panorama of Pawel Yakovlevich Pyasetsky could be viewed through the windows of three luxury railway cars. The two-week train trip could be done, thus, in one hour. Before he coinvented the daguerreotype, Louis Daguerre invented another variation on panorama vision. The diorama refocused or tunneled the 3-D view as theatrical spectacle in which the manipulation of light and the addition of transparency to the palette of representation of scenes on layers of linen produced realistic effects of a changing landscape. According to Benjamin, the flâneur passed through these devices into urban space transformed into the other landscape ("Paris, the Capital of the Nineteenth Century," 34–36).

The nineteenth century was all about the Western frontier. But back in prehistory, according to Locke, the West was one with all the world: "In the beginning, all the world was America" (in Marx, 65). But whatever can be said, in the beginning, to have always been gets projected out of some impasse where the past heads us off. In other words, everything we see will have been "Californian."

The Western landscape was constructed at an intersection of media projections. Bierstadt brought his German training to bear on photographs of Western views, which he then painted by number and scale of the sublime. Literature did the rest (before we started going to the movies to complete the system of our projections). The setting of the landscape in the West comes out of crypts carried by authors like Karl May and Zane Grey.

Karl May, one of the German Meisters (together with Wagner, Ludwig II, and Daniel Paul Schreber) of the mass-media Sensurround, was born blind. But by age five he could see. By that time, nine out of his thirteen siblings had died in infancy. When he was advanced to the head of his class to become a teacher, he just couldn't stop stealing under irresistible conditions of remote control. Mother May I: the klepto-ego tries to consume and incorporate the maternal body (or bodies, those of her unmournable babies). During his four-year prison term (the one that began in 1865) he conceived, so he claimed, the entire body of his work. But first he had to act it out, and then cut it out, because even after his time was done, he was still under higher command to break the law. May formed an underworld gang of thieves, one that disrupted the local economy to such a third degree that the military had to come to the rescue. In the midst of all-points bullets, May's close calls and getaways were already repeating or rehearsing those wild Westerns. Two years later, it's four more years. During this second four-year term in prison, he was able to exorcise the dark force that was with his transgressions against all institutions of transference (he stole not only outright but also, often while impersonating authority figures, by scam and swindle). He took note this time around that the prison library didn't carry the right kind of books. He would therefore proceed to right one wrong, and write the literature for the imprisoned, a literature of escape and landscape.

When next he landed a job, as a journalist for the mag *Mine and Factory*, he filled his pages with "Geographical Sermons" on the surrounding landscapes. But when he started writing for the *German Family Paper*, he at least—at last!—added travel narratives and heroic tales to those sublime settings. While the exotic coordinates of his books were polymorphously all over the places he would never visit, it was the cowboy-and-Indian narratives across wide-open landscapes that gave the main support and staying power to his reception.

While via journalism he reentered a redoubled world of landscapes around the world, he could commit himself to substitution only via the spiritualist séance culture that identified his two women as mediums. But he didn't have far to go: the press emerged as the first major institution of everyday life to use the telegraph to wire its range from the local to the national and the international at the same time as the Fox sisters began their decoding ring of ghost communications with poltergeist signals echoing the code of the telegraph. Among the leading recurring stories humming across the wires were accounts of séance contact with the dead or undead. May's first wife, Emma, summoned the spirits at séances to help her get her way with her husband. Among the couples that regularly attended séances with the Mays was the Plöhn duo: the wife, Klara, was a gifted writing medium. Emma tried transmitting spirit writing too. But black on white, it was always clear that whereas Klara was able to channel higher-minded spirits, Emma never got past the range of her own thoughts. She went back to the telegraphic knocking. When Mr. Plöhn died, his widow started taking dictation from spirits urging dissolution of the conflicted May marriage. Klara, who thus knew how to write down the telecommunications from the missing without showing her hand, her manipulation, became Karl May's second wife.

Like Karl May, and like all the male characters in Shelley's *Frankenstein,* Zane Grey too made a career out of transference transgression. His father bullied him out of his first love of writing right into dentistry. Once he was out of reach, however, the son became an author with a changed name: he changed the spelling of Gray, his father's name, and took his mother's patronymic, one of his middle names, as his first name. He said he just had to drop the name Pearl, which his mother had given him, because it brought him too much gender confusion in his correspondence. But the change from Gray to Grey preserves a kernel of the original name, the one that came from mother-of-Pearl. In his writing, Grey in effect followed the history of his mother's family out West. Once there, he proved to be the writer of the landscape of the purple sage, the same landscape that glows on and on in John Ford's movies.

Transference transgression sets the father's place as empty at the funeral feast. Victor Frankenstein was giving his dead mother wide birth via the displacements of monstrous bodybuilding. The paternal antibody didn't show, too slow, on the intake of mother or the uptake of monster. Karl May belonged to a foursome of survival. The countdown of self-punishment comes in four-year terms. That a simple medical intervention gave the five-year-old his eyesight (after a physician chanced to overhear mother May discussing her little boy's case) suggests murderous conditions for the nine casualties of early infancy. How to fill in for nine missing, unmournable children? Plus Karl makes ten little Indians. The figure of identification that opens wide for acceptance of Indians bears the name Old Shatterhand. The "and" that had been shattered was what May just had to hand back to us with each shake of identification, with each intake of gang, group, or tribal membership. Only in the Western landscape, the land of the setting sun, the land of the dead, could the losses, the shattered "ands," be won back, made one.

Pearl marked the spot of loss Zane Grey's mother was in. Follow the bound pearl-shape. In school, Grey could risk all his marbles, but then, on double take, he just had to steal back the one he had named Cornelia. His throw of the baseball won Pearl admission to the University of Pennsylvania, somewhere beyond the father's castrative search for the tooth. The institution's nickname, Penn, is a near metonym of writing. His mother's declared dread of the marginal combo of fishing and storytelling Pearl would realize and recuperate as desire. It was the margin where their reality began inside the Western landscape, at once internal screen, projective rebound, and happy haunting ground.

ROLE CALL

In *Ticket of No Return* "she" enters a series of job-failure scenes on a role. "The possibilities for playing with different realities, to interrogate them, become especially clear in one scene in which the drinker imagines working as drinker in various jobs, for example as drinking hell driver who crashes up the car in keeping with her job description, or as undertaker who tries to comfort the mourners first off with a sip from her flask, or as secretary who leaves behind her raging boss and cruises the park with a bottle in hand" (Ottinger, in Strempel). We enter the internal theatrical space that opens around adolescence (conceived as the search for the role, the job that fits), and that gets put on stage as Oedipus and Hamlet. The theatrical always refers — via the assignment of all agents or actors to prescribed roles — to the Oedipus complex. Even psychosis counts its reversals in the struggle for a world of its own within the infinite relay or regress also available on this stage, but as mourning pageant.

Ottinger realigns the interviewer's attribution of "fantastic" to certain scenes in *Ticket of No Return*: "That is a concept against which I am always defending myself in connection with my films, because one thereby dismisses everything as fantasies. On the contrary, they are rather fragments of reality assembled in an unusual manner. They are not my fantasies but very real observations. My fantasy enters the picture in the way in which I connect things" (in "TIP — Interview mit U. Ottinger," 17).

"She" leaves behind the place of fiction, La Rotonda, and her one identification there: "a belle of antique grace and Raphaelite harmony, a woman created like no other to be Medea, Madonna, Beatrice, Iphigenie, Aspasia." *Ticket of No Return* narrates the disenchanted heroine's arrival at the Berlin-Tegel airport: "Her plans for a narcissistic-pessimistic cult of loneliness were fortified on the short plane trip and intensified to a point that they found themselves at precisely the stage in which they should be lived out." Even the airport welcomes her in public address: "BERLIN-TEGEL — REALITY — BERLIN-TEGEL — PLEASE REALITY." Ottinger: "To present a reality with complete truth is as complicated and confusing as reality itself. I just don't believe that one can invent a figure on the basis of an ideology and then let it act according to that ideology. I find that unrealistic. Even that figure has fantasies and dreams. I refuse to make these unambiguous films that say that because such-and-such the following is true. That would then be a political statement. By doing that you hold back a part of reality and at the same time a part of the truth. To put it quite briefly, this simplification of the truth becomes a lie" (in Hoffmann).

At the end of her first day in Berlin, back alone in her hotel room, "she" continues guzzling wine — a sound shape that in German *(Wein)* externalizes and picks up action as the word for "weeping" *(Weinen)* — until a series of scenes

"She" through glass.

starts filling in the blanks. First we see two identical photos of her in masculine drag, each lit by three lights reminiscent of votive candles. The master of ceremonies is a dwarf who welcomes her to the first scene, bowing and gesturing to her to come drink from the monumental fountain. In the third and fourth scenes the dwarf finds additional exotic settings and conditions for her drinking. In the second scene he accompanies her up a glass-enclosed stairwell. Throughout the film, glass, at once transparent and reflecting, is juxtaposed in all its hardness and separateness with liquid, the medium of merger or communion. This first series of scenes breaks for intermission in her real and fantasy life, the prep work of self-destruction that fuels it. "She" guzzles brandy in a café while facing the window toward which she offers a pantomime of communication. But she's just bouncing off the window's reflective surface her earliest introductions to contact with and through the mirroring other. And thus she struggles, just like a psychotic, to reclaim the mother that was once in her face.

But then Lutze, a homeless bag lady, steps in and fills or fulfills the empty placeholder of the other. Lutze and "she" crossed paths before, but remained on opposite sides of the glass between them. This time they join on the same side of the glass wall, and hold guzzling communion together. But while it could be argued that the alcoholic Mass ultimately blocks or replaces all attempts to communicate, it is more important to recognize just how uncanny-proofed their encounter is. The crisis of uncanniness (of what is in German literally "homelessness"), which follows the overextended stay in primary (body-based) narcissism (and which, according to Hanns Sachs, yields the origin of technologization as psychotic defense), is resituated in Ottinger's film through the dissociation revalorized here as another form of connection. "I think you have to work with this reality, you have to bring it into consciousness. Not just steal it with a tape recorder and camera, then show it. I hope I have succeeded in doing that with these two very different drinkers, where one of them plays reality, the so-called typical social case, an expression which I see as an insult, the disrespectful and statistical evaluation and labeling of the drinker as a case of sickness. . . . I want to make reality recognizable through this relationship of alternatives that the two women share, one of them being the artificial figure, the other being presented in a more documentary fashion. A dialogue between documentation and innovation" (Ottinger, in Strempel).

Circumvention of the uncanny crisis zone confers upon the film its formal organization. According to Jonathan Rosenbaum, "it is the scandal provided by the union between these two that provides the closest thing to a consecutive plot that *Ticket of No Return* can claim." "Conceptually speaking," the film unfolds then around this pair or dis-pair as "a string of episodes which repeat the same root elements, like a string of gags in a series of Road Runner cartoons (where wit always has something to do with the distinction between sameness and difference . . .). Within this relatively static framework, however, the variables—such as the heroine's wardrobe, the diverse narrative settings for her drinking, and diverse inventions in the dialogue and *mise en scène*—give the film a flamboyant, expressive range" (Rosenbaum, 126).

To celebrate her crossover with Lutze to the same side of the glass wall, "she" splashes her drink onto the window. Liquid on glass blurs the image but also animates it, and brings together the hard and watery surfaces of reflection comprising the Narcissus legend and complex. In a text Ottinger composed to accompany the publication of a series of photo studies "in the context of" *Ticket of No Return,* she elaborated on all the work that surrounded and shaped the containment and uncontainment of the splash the film made: "I asked my actress Tabea Blumenschein to address a defense of drinking—a defense born out of paranoid fear—to her own reflection and then to hurl the contents of her full wine glass at her reflected self. I watched her doing this through the camera and recorded moments that I especially liked. She repeated the act of emptying the glass so that I had the opportunity to photograph several versions of it. . . . Simple incidents such as the emptying of the glass, just described, are far more effective and dramatic when divided into single pictures and the movements frozen; and in some instances I, too, decide to 'freeze' the film. One can look at a photo for as long as one wants. In film, on the other hand, each picture moves so quickly that one does not have the chance to understand the cause of one's pleasure or lack of pleasure. This is brought home with particular clarity when one ventures to show the daily TV viewer (whose viewing habits are deeply ingrained) a picture for longer than is usual. He will find it an imposition. 'I would like you to see that picture for that long' would be my simple answer" ("Zum Film *Ticket of No Return*").

Kaja Silverman captions the photographic moment of truth that follows the impromptu celebration of "reunion" with Lutze that closes the scene, but that also displaces, disperses, and continues it: "two other patrons of the coffee shop quickly pull out their cameras. They point them not at Madame or Lutze, who replicates the action of her friend, but at the streaming surface of the window. They thus photograph Madame not as 'herself,' but in the guise of the image she attempts to efface" (56). The morning-after newspaper catches in its headlines a photo taken of the foreign drinker making her scene. "She" compares the photo with her mirror image. But after several tries she appears unable to make the connection. She splashes wine onto the mirror surface.

Although the next scene does not feature the dwarf, Silverman argues that the empty theater is the reverse or negative of the scene that will next follow the dwarf's lead. "She" enters a theater in which only five women are seated in the front row. But for all the emptiness, a sense of audience is nevertheless preserved: the front-row women turn around to stare at her as she sips champagne. In the final shot, she puts on sunglasses and adopts the double position of spectacle and spectator. The subsequent scene, in her hotel room, follows the blue video hello of the dwarf carrying a turkey platter into the same room, but all on monitor. The camera moves to the right to show the night table with the turkey on top. "She" enters, picks up the carving knife, and stabs around one of the two images up against the wall. Confronting the image, her partner in narcissistic coupling, the one divided from its double as bad from good, she enacts the violence in this identificatory bond, the dis-pair—the despair—that presages self-murder in the regressive fantasies of merger her theatricality stages, defers to, and abandons, empties out.

As the underworld guardian of her primal relations, the dwarf returns to introduce a photograph of himself, with which, after he turns around and departs, "she" alone shares the park bench. But the dwarf, still with one foot in the additional remove of mediatic representation, also instantly and intrinsically brings up the theatrical arrears of baroque allegory, the way Oedipus plays in psychosis or along its borderlines between mourning and melancholia. The series of job-failure scenes is immediately framed by the dwarf's two-step.

The dwarf presents the drinker with flowers.

At the end, he returns to retrieve the photograph, only then again to leave. And the dwarf's to and fro leads to and from a series of rapid-fire close-ups of "she" interspersed with restorations of the full view of her on the bench, all of which rests in and then issues from her screen-sized eye. "The close-ups of Madame's eye that are interspersed between the images of her on the park bench are extremely brief, more like 'flashes' than composed images. Like the sound which accompanies them, they suggest the opening and closing of a still camera shutter" (Silverman, 61).

Miriam Hansen designates the dwarf the film's death driver: "Thus nested [between the dwarf and his photo], even the most positive images she can conceive of herself—as underlined by her own eye's imagining capacity—are marked as deeply interwoven with the death wishes externalized in the image of the dwarf" (101). But while Hansen can sit on a dwarf in this way, the imp also plays a ceremonial part in the allegorical vanitas pileup of consumable items. If *Ticket of No Return* is in Ottinger's words "a kind of drinker's geography of Berlin" and "sightseeing film" then, as Ottinger stresses, what must be seen and heard also fits in the mouth: "it will be a film in which one creates in part a completely artificial set—a table set with oversized Bavarian meat and sauerkraut platters" (in Strempel). Catherine de Medici delighted in hiding her favorite dwarfs in bowls of fruit set on the table. They would then pop up in the course of the meal to surprise and entertain her distinguishing guests. In answering a query about the "different levels of reality" with which Ottinger works in the job failure scenes and about the "different discourses which reflect on each other," the filmmaker comes back to the dwarf: "Yes, of course, there is also the video insert of the dwarf whom I am using as a commentator, like a TV news announcer" who is also always an entertainer (in Mueller, "Interview with Ulrike Ottinger," 117).

In Ottinger's view, "she" isn't only a doomed figure without a room for psychologizing: "In the pirate film there were women who were dissatisfied with their lives and simply up and left. Here, too, a woman departs, only in the sense of finding the place where she can live out her alcoholism undisturbed. That is an aggressive stance, since normally one wants explanations: Why did the woman become like this and why does she drink, and I recognize in all these stories, that one drinks or takes drugs or whatever—that one distances oneself from that which one would like to do. That piles up in an alarming way until one could almost say that most people live in the way in which they really don't want to live. That is the theme that occupies me throughout! I want to show the drinker simply as a figure who deliberately and stubbornly drinks herself to death—in a sense an ultimate form of consequential thought and action. She could of course just jump from some tower, but she has chosen the form of drinking herself to death, and in this span I am given the opportunity to say a great deal about her" (in Strempel). What Ottinger has to say about her is a draw with the psychoanalytic discourse that was the message in a bottle in *Madame X*: "This is not the classical, self-contemplative narcissism but the kind that triggers aggressions and self-destruction. . . . What interests me in particular is that narcissism always involves a certain amount of anxiety, anxieties which are never talked about. In this film these anxieties are drowned in alcohol. For a long time I thought about how to represent this anxiety. It seemed evident to me that she hates herself. . . . Yes, all her experiences are experiences of self and not of others, and so her aggressions are directed only against herself. The final metaphor of her self-destruction is when she crushes the mirrored floor with her heels" (Ottinger, in Mueller, "Interview with Ulrike Ottinger," 118).

Although in the job-failure series "she" takes the stage as Hamlet, not as Ophelia, she is caught in the interchangeability of these roles, as elucidated in Ella Freeman Sharpe's reading of *Hamlet*: "Hamlet's death is a dramatized suicide, superego and ego roles being allotted to different characters. In Ophelia the different institutions of the mind are not separated out. We are given the facts. Her father is killed; she goes mad; she drowns herself. . . . It implies what is explicit in the play, namely, a narcissistic withdrawal after the father's death, the incorporation of the lost love-object, the reproaches against this loved one directed to the self, and the swift nemesis brought about by the superego sadism turned against the ego. . . . She has returned to the mother, the separation from whose breast was the pattern on which all later frustrations, with their unsolved problems of anxiety and hostility, were built" ("The Impatience of Hamlet," 207–8). Freeman Sharpe's reading of Hamlet as the relay race passing the baton between oral impatience and anal procrastination characterizes the slow time of urgent self-destruction in the case of the drinker: "Hamlet's procrastination is a vain endeavor to stem the tide of this urgency, an eking-out of time. It is an elaborate slowness to combat swiftness, against which he is battling for self-preservation. Ophelia is then the feminine aspect of Hamlet" (208–9).

What Ottinger has to show and tell about the drinker proceeds, in Hansen's words of art appreciation, as "a succession of visually stunning compositions" (105): "Such places do not add up to a social topography—as they might for the bag lady—but represent allegorical stations in the protagonist's experiment of lived-out fantasy" (106). According to Karsten Witte, *Ticket of No Return* turns the ready-made scenes in Berlin into stopovers of the flâneur who, just like a strolling stoner, slowly walks the walk of resistance down the nineteenth-century Paris boulevards, as illuminated in the 1930s by Benjamin, a native Berliner: "In these images we stumble through Berlin like Jacques Offenbach through 'Life in Paris.' The surface gleam deceives. In other words, their art-saturated gaiety tells lies because they basically promote surface as their aesthetic principle and flee the compulsion of the senses just like the dandies of the Second Empire. Berlin becomes the new Boulevard and sidewalk where everything goes, spreads and unashamedly unfolds itself, but in the morning light petrifies in melancholia" ("Der Dandy als Dame").

Norbert Jochum sees Berlin allegorized as last resort where "the wish to drink oneself to death is almost the expression of the will to survive." According to Hansen, the drinker's unraveling similarly doubles as self-analysis, which doubles the whammy of her disconnection, her dis-pair. For the viewer "the contrast

From one of countless photographic studies for which Tabea Blumenschein assumed as many roles in preparation for Ticket of No Return. *For many she enacted a melodrama, as in a photo novella, in the course of a series of shots. This particular photograph bypasses the role-playing and hits the lights (and shadows). It is the quintessential image, formally speaking, out of which* Ticket of No Return *would be projected.*

between the Drinker's increased alienation and the beauty of the images conveying this process is actually quite painful" (Hansen, 104). The contrasts that cut across all stations and that inflict behind the scenes a measure of pain refer to one setting to which each station tunes in, one that is resoundingly implicit and frankly excluded throughout the film. While "she" is always rendered speechless, there are no images in the film uncompromised by language. While the split between silent-movie video portion and completely separate sound track in *Madame X* could still be written off as the by-product of a low-budget production, the underscoring of this split even in the higher order of *Ticket of No Return*'s production values shows the determining force of the unsettled score in Ottinger's films. Sound and visual tracks are separate but more than equal: "On average," Ottinger says, "I work three times as long on the montage of the sound track as on the image montage" (in Fischetti, "Ich glaube . . . ," 226). Contrary to what she refers to as the "comic strip method" of mainstream cinema—which makes the sound do, and thus allegedly explain, what the visuals have already accomplished—Ottinger always attempts to say one thing visually, and something else again with the sound track: "I work self-consciously with fragments of reality in a collage process. For example, in *Ticket of No Return* I have integrated many other noises—both artificial and real—into the original sound track to broaden associative possibilities. Earlier I never had the money to record real sound; here I could afford a sound crew, but still used the old process" (in Silberman). "This break between reality and imagination is supported by the sound. The original sounds are powerfully defamiliarized, or the sound effects and noises, which run in sync with the pictures, have different sources. For example: a glass breaks. Contents spill across the tabletop and drip onto the floor. Sound: car crash, ambulance siren" (Ottinger, in Strempel).

In *Ticket of No Return,* language often assumes the more paranoid than neutrally omniscient form of third-person commentary, now via split-off voice-over, now through the three allegorical figures of public opinion who shadow the drinker throughout her Berlin tour. Precisely because it is unclear who is really speaking, whether looking at or being looked at on benches, beds, or bar stools, "she" denies and implies the inevitability of her being "on the couch." Ottinger's relationship to her viewers, based on montage/collage, invokes the transferential model of understanding over time that Freud set in motion: "I stake my work on the imagination, on the ability of viewers to piece it together in their heads, even or especially when it doesn't come together right away. The compulsion for instant interpretation is completely senseless. For my films you have to take the time" (in Fischetti, "Ich glaube . . . ," 221–22).

In analysis, the couch, which interferes with the normalizing, functionalizing mode of interpersonal contact, always keeps the short hand of analysis on the intrapsychic and theoretical dimension that gives way to therapy only on the second hand. "Culturally, psychoanalysis operates contrary to many expected methods of direct communication. For example, people expect to look and be looked at when they speak to others. The couch frustrates this expectation. . . . Because the entire process of looking and being looked at while speaking is such an accepted mode of human communication, the idea of engaging in that different kind of human communication which is peculiar to psychoanalysis inevitably meets with some objection" (Stern, 21).

In *Madame X*, the analyst's couch is called the "contemporary version of the divan," the age-old accessory of women. While in *Ticket of No Return* "she" is acting out, is not in session, still the silent treatment of her resistance renders all that resounds around her intervention aiming to reach her, to make contact. Before Freud propped it up against his office wall, next to the armchair where he sat, not looking but taking it all in like a telephone receiver (according to his choice of analogy), the couch belonged to inner spaces for women only. There was the fainting couch for the woman fit to be tied to the hysteria diagnosis, or the couch for lying-in-wait to give birth. The boudoir was the place for couches. It was the first outer space where women could receive mixed company. In the Marquis de Sade's *Philosophy in the Boudoir*, for example, men penetrate this space and its occupants; but during time-out to talk, woman takes to the couch and man sits down in the armchair next to her.

Benjamin could admit his missing link with Freud only in session with the shock of remembrance. Benjamin's gadget-loving attention to the details of shock also always put through a direct connection to Freud. In *Berliner Kindheit um Neunzehnhundert (Childhood in Berlin around Nineteen Hundred)*, Benjamin demarcates the analytic setting or session between the chapters "Telephone" and "A Death Notice." The phone that emerged "new born" out of the night of nothingness, and which was first kept, as the uncanny, in the furthest corner of the back corridor, gradually made it to center stage of the domestic scene, displacing or outlasting all the oppressive details of decor that had at first crowded it out of the salon. Following its promotion, the phone thus became a comfort zone in the new phase of isolation. The telephonic apparatus, Benjamin writes, "shared one bed with the abandoned."

In the chapter "A Death Notice," Benjamin questions the fit between the term *déjà vu* and what seems to him heard but not seen, more like the echo of a blast from the past. It's like with shock, Benjamin adds, like the shock or shot of inoculation that accompanies or admits a certain moment into consciousness as already experienced or lived. Such shocks are most often given by sound effects that suddenly take us back inside "the cool crypt of the past." Once upon a time, at bedtime, his father gave little Benjamin the news of a cousin's death. Benjamin hardly knew the older gentleman but was nevertheless curious about the meaning of the heartbeat just a heartbeat away from death: "I didn't take in much of the explanation. But instead my room and my bed made a lasting impression on me, just as one takes special notice of a place when one senses that some day something forgotten will need to be retrieved from there."

The couch, the material side and support of the talking cure, is always also, via regression, the five-year-old's bed. The relationship to the unseen voice or silence seated behind the couch shares, like the telephone, one bedside manner with father and son taking it to heart.

4
HIT AND MISS

In 1983 Jonathan Rosenbaum, diverted perhaps by the perfection or consummation he found achieved in *Ticket of No Return,* judged *Freak Orlando* (like *The Image of Dorian Gray in the Yellow Press*) "a decidedly uneven film, definitely hit-or-miss in its overall thrust, and conceivably full of as many misses as hits" (123). The fifty-fifty proviso signs in at the symptom center of *Freak Orlando*'s reception. "It is a strongly visual baroque allegory of freaks—those who through world history have been persecuted, tortured, excluded and eliminated as ugly, insane, deformed, monstrous beings, deviating from the norm; a pandemonium of myths, archetypes, and fairy-tale figures, belonging to fairgrounds and the show. Naturally, this many-sided panorama of history, seen from the point of view of freaks, does not allow itself to be decoded at the first attempt; naturally this approach of alienation, this allegorical configuration counts on powers of association and on sensual gratification, which finds in many of these optical and acoustic arrangements and tableaux . . . sufficient food for eye and ear." The parenthesis that fills in the dots: "(which are on occasion too long and therefore in forfeit of their suggestive power)" (Schütte).

Freak Orlando seems particularly beset by this refraining order of regret. The charge that Ottinger overlooks that in film only a certain size or length matters is unwelcome guest at the receiving end of all her films. Even as the *LA Weekly* made *Johanna d'Arc of Mongolia* "Film Pick of the Week," the reviewer who came to praise this film as "Ottinger's best to date," if only on account of the special combo of Mongolia on-location and Delphine Seyrig at her most "fragile and beautiful," also buried the praise in a general dismissal of all Ottinger films as "both mind-bending and boring" (Knode). It shouldn't boggle the mind that yet another journalist failed to see the connection between the provocation of thought and what is (always on one's own projective terms) boring. Gertrud Koch, on the other hand, locates in a formal conflict the penetrating point of what's boring, which, however, she would rather see resolved: "If the film at times seems overlong, in spite of the generous image fantasies and the incredible wealth of detail, in spite of the varied episodes and stunning individual images (like that of the hermaphrodite playing, self-absorbed, with its mirror image on top of the pile of coal, like the landscapes wrapped up in green material), then this results in part from the camera remaining mute witness and recorder of the theatrically staged events unfolding before it and rarely intervening, rarely dynamizing spaces and rendering them cinematic. The allusion to 'world-theater' succumbs to the seduction of its adoption as aesthetic form, even though individual images and image inventions break this frame on their own" ("Von der blendenden Schönheit des Haßlichen"). The break Koch gets belongs, then, to the allegorical dramaturgical dimension of *Freak Orlando* already given in the subtitle: "Kleines Welttheater in 5 Episoden" ("Small World-Theater in 5 Episodes"). "For me what is most important is the relationship of movement in the image, in other words, the relationship between staged movement in the image and the image frame and the camera movement. That appears in a certain sense perhaps somewhat static, but there is also in addition in my films something like a subjective camera, which also expresses movement. The static impression that arises on occasion is determined by the locations I select and shoot, which function in part like theater stages" (Ottinger, in Frey, 42).

Ottinger stands by what appears uneven in her films as a performative part of finding a form for her thought experiments: "For me form and content are one and the same, so much so that I cannot even imagine that when one tries to convey something today one would not at the same time try to find an adequate form for that which one wants to get across. That is what I am looking for in my films. When that is your plan, then it clearly follows that one must diverge from a purely linear cinematic language, and that one would attempt instead to express by association such parallel states as, for example, our systems of thought, word selection or connections" (in Frey, 42). "My films function the way our thoughts function. If you tell me a story, then there's a lot happening with me. It gets assigned a place in my psychic organization, not only on the basis of my experiences from the day before, but also with reference to experiences I had ten years ago, or which I read or heard about. That's the way my films are. They are assembled from very many details of experience and declare this quite openly" (Ottinger, in Fischetti, "Ich glaube . . . ," 234–35).

Rosenbaum adds an important proviso or afterthought to his observation of what's so uneven about *Freak Orlando*: "Like it or not, though, the film can be regarded as a climactic summa of the performance-oriented European avant-garde film" (123). That hitting and missing could be at the art of this sadistic-allegorical film is largely missed for all the summation and synthesis Rosenbaum prefers to find in Ottinger's cinema. He scores a hit, however, with regard to timing and closure in *Freak Orlando*: "Ottinger's political focus in *Freak Orlando* is a lot closer to that of Tod Browning's *Freaks* than it is to Virginia Woolf's novel *Orlando*, from which Ottinger has taken only the notion of 'an ideal protagonist . . . a figure who represents all the social possibilities—man and woman—which we normally do not have.' But the absorption in pure spectacle that one associates with late Fellini is still closer to the mark, making the matter of the film's overall duration somewhat arbitrary, like an endlessly extendable chain of vaudeville turns" (130).

But back up a bit. A relationship to time is also intrinsic to the intertext in the film's name. First, there's the timing of youth. In Florida, the state Ponce de Leon searched up and way down for the soda fountain of youth, the city of Orlando hosts Disney World and Universal Studios, theme parks with a global take on juvenility that would divert the attraction of California's part in the conspiracy of adolescence, if this part were not already greater than the whole world watching. Then there is the temporality of allegory (on location, that is, in Woolf's text). When we are first introduced to Virginia Woolf's Orlando, he is a writer of "abstract" plays ("Vice, Crime, Misery were the personages of his drama") that rest on the seeming "natural antipathy" between nature and letters: "bring them together and they tear each other to pieces" (9). Allegory (the gory taking apart of nature and letters) takes over the writing that's directly about or above him: "Now, again, he paused, and into the breach thus made, leapt Ambition, the harridan, and Poetry, the witch, and Desire of Fame, the strumpet; all joined hands and made of his heart their dancing ground" (52). Both times come together in the combo-figuration of real estate and trauma. The continuity shot that skewers all levels of the work, right through the author's own research prep work, belongs, in the preface, to "knowledge of the law of real property" (5).

Woolf's *Orlando. A Biography*, following in the wake-up experimentalism of *To the Lighthouse* and *Mrs. Dalloway*, was mistaken by disappointed readers to be retrograde in comparison. The inside psychic viewing of the earlier works had given way to a seemingly straightforward manner of presentation and description. Sometimes great notions or commotions (like modernism) only reduce, according to their own plan, complexity that's as plain text as the visualizations of typeface. Let the mind be a page: "What a phantasmagoria the mind is and meeting-place of dissemblables" (Woolf, 115).

While the narrative is not styling with interiority, like interior monologue or perspectivism, for example, the exteriority that rules this seemingly conservative discourse is exclusively the exteriority of the word. In *Freak Orlando* the theatricality of costumes and props takes over where Woolf's rhetorical figures leave

Scene inspired by Goya's Caprichos.

off. The pileup of accessories and costumes serves, like the episodic frame of the "World-Theater" towering above the stage or screen, as consequence-interruptus, making the eye stick to unidentified but highly ornamental surfaces.

The disease of love of literature causes Woolf's Orlando to "substitute a phantom for reality" (48). But the allegorical figures guarding the inkpot of ghostwriting must bow before the show of truth they put on and pull over: "Orlando had become a woman—there is no denying it. But in every other respect, Orlando remained precisely as he had been. The change of sex, though it altered their future, did nothing whatever to alter their identity. Their faces remained, as their portraits prove, practically the same" (90).

Orlando, in love or above it all, can play at sexual difference only up to the limit imposed by "the iron countenance of the law" (Woolf, 109). It is before the court that the allegory of identification and difference must make appeal. Only now is Orlando truly in transition: "Thus it was in a highly ambiguous condition, uncertain whether she was alive or dead, man or woman, Duke or nonentity, that she posted down to her country seat, where, pending the legal judgment, she had the Law's permission to reside in a state of incognito or incognita as the case might turn out to be" (110). She goes through sexual identities as through sets of clothing. But then there's the nineteenth century, the other dark age. The spirit of this era is dedicated to the couple that now contains, now releases, fear of "ghosts in the corridors" (160).

But once Orlando makes it to the present, 1928, what presents itself is a terrifying revelation of what keeps above her, passing over her, as she tries to collect herself. "Indeed it is a difficult business—this time keeping; nothing more quickly disorders it than contact with any of the arts" (200). As she accelerates through the disordering of her many selves, she must conclude: "'Haunted!' she cried, suddenly pressing the accelerator. 'Haunted! Ever since I was a child'" (205). Orlando is haunted but not traumatized. A multiplicity of selves, roles, sexual identities, eras informs the corpus that is, in the moment, haunted. This haunting gets its raising out of the near-missing relations with the present, relations that, in their disordering, open wide, for example through contact with the arts, to encounter the random and uncontrollable other, the one that belongs to time, but not to any time that could be kept.

In *Freak Orlando* a span of centuries (at least the three and a half that Woolf gives her Orlando) admits, for the exclusion of the misfit, a coalition between the Inquisition and modern psychiatry. This stage of world history, situated within

The Festival of the Ugly.

the late eighteenth century, is number three. The monsters that reason dreams up in Goya's *Caprichos* are cited or summoned for this staging. It is preceded by, number one, the display of the mythic past for sale in a department store and, number two, the medieval stage of miraculousness of the freak who is at the same time a candidate for demonization. "I ask myself if it doesn't, structurally, come down to pretty much the same thing, whether one adores someone or kills that person for being different" (Ottinger, in Frey, 45). Stage number four is set aside for the sideshow era of freakdom, while stage five belongs to the modern press of normalization. It crosses Ottinger's mind—just as it assumes center stage in "The Festival of the Ugly," a citation of a pageant that does in fact take place in Italy—that today the normalized citizens are the freaks. In the movie the winner is Herbert Zeus, who in this final incarnation is a middle-aged psychopharmaceuticals salesman who by accident walks onto the stage. He is paired with one of Orlando's/Orlanda's bunnies, with whom he gazes at a heart-shaped moon. The selling point of the selection of the year's ugliest person is that "in our society everything, even the most extreme, can be commercialized—and that entertainment extends to all realms. Everything is being incorporated and integrated without problem. While certain modes of behavior are reversed, at bottom nothing has been changed" (Ottinger, in Frey, 47).

Freak thus qualifies as one of the "primal words" that according to Freud keep to primal time by containing opposing meanings. The freak is an uncanny outcast. But the freak can also be cool. When *freak* gets some action, it can freak you out or it can mean "to fuck." Even without this booster shot of repressibility, the double meanings of *freak* make clear that "it" serves as boundary case or concept of the stereometric construction of the body politic. The freak of nature was pressed into service as a freak of culture. The freak is the comparative chopdown to prescription-sized and family-sized proportions of what is normal. A world theater or history featuring freaks is very much on location with the rest of the globe. "Since this history also reflects the 'criteria' of normalcy and their socially sanctioned limits, it reveals just as much from its pathological underside . . . about 'normal' humanity" (Bergius). From sacred liminal beings mediating between natural and supernatural realms, freaks were set in the corner of the new "erection" or "institution" of categories, constructions, identities. The freak is a relic of an older order in the state of ruination of what was once "one." But the freak is also the "acknowledgment," in Mary Russo's words, "of the extent to which spectacle, the body, and politics are by now inseparable as distorted and hyperbolized aspects of media culture, which is to say the world we have now" (85).

In the scroll-down at the start of Tod Browning's 1932 film *Freaks,* we are informed, believe it or not, that "deeds of injustice and hardship have been attributed to the many crippled and deformed tyrants of Europe and Asia . . . misshapen misfits who have altered the world's course: Goliath, Caliban, Frankenstein, Gloucester, Tom Thumb, and Kaiser Wilhelm." When, in "On the History of the Psychoanalytic Movement" (*SE* 14: 7–66), Freud gave his account of the newest theories and therapies that his former followers, Adler and Jung, were advancing for the renovation and improvement of psychoanalysis, he caught Adler, at his end of the negative transference onto Freud, developing a literal-minded, compensatory, and strictly interpersonal take on castration and its consequences. Adler's understanding of the psychological motivation of external or social consequences would fit the scroll-down view that Browning's film tries to qualify, or rather, deny. In the New Introductory Lecture on "The Dissection of the Psychical Personality" (*SE* 22: 57–80), Freud selects from the pop culture of the "inferiority complex" the diagnosis of Kaiser Wilhelm's quest for a place in the sun/son as compensation for organ inferiority as a good example of the limitation of Adler's theory. Freud counters, it was not the Kaiser's withered arm that, just like that, occasioned a spectacular set of overcompensations that climaxed in the Great War. It was rather that the Kaiser's mother had reacted with horror to her child's deformity. Everything begins and ends, in the culture of Freud's science, with an internal relationship with the other, which is intrapsychic and can never be superseded by all those relations we tend, self-importantly, to take so interpersonally.

Browning's *Freaks* is devastating as a horror film that perpetrates, under the cover of revenge, the organ-inferior view of freakdom as dismemberment or castration of a woman's body. The documentary aspect of *Freaks*—they're real freaks—culminates in the fashioning of a freak image out of the other woman, Cleopatra. "One of us" doubles as the sacrificial making of one out of us. When the unwilling bride of the group rejects admission to being a freak—she shouts them down: "Freaks, freaks, freaks!"—she also names the film. Possible subtitle: castrative crisis of the genitally centered subject. The body of differentiation offered up for Cleopatra's inclusion won't take no for an answer. She is made one of them, in the literalizing, castrative mode. The freaks thus operate on band lengths associated with the superego in a psyche in crisis big enough to destroy the world in the psychotic mode and replace it with a new one of projections, both psychic and cinematic. The only cut that is presented, as happening, is the one cut that cannot be real. But she becomes thus the representation of the film as edited product and projection that meets us more than halfway on the cutting edge of our own death wishes.

The German-accented miniature couple withdraws from the group metabolization of the other woman who must make the cut after threatening the future of their coupling—a future that the group at the same time holds in contempt of the group's courting of oneness. The group's bride or mascot (or "totemic representation" [Russo, 91]) is the chick or chicken woman on display just beneath the opening of the film. The film can close once we see that she was the one put there to be left behind.

Freaks was the film Browning just had to make. Only he knew he had it in him. He spent the rest of his life trying to resurrect his pre-*Freaks* standing in Hollywood. When Lon Chaney died during Browning's transition from silent films to talkies, he left *Dracula* in the hands of his cameraman, Karl Freund. When that was over, Browning proceeded to make *Freaks,* which nearly finished him off. Browning had started out as a circus performer (his most successful stunt was a live burial followed, after plenty of downtime, by resurrection). But in the 1930s, sideshow culture was already coming under wraps, soon to be replaced on the back pages of comic books by the abs and ads of bodybuilding culture. "For practical purposes the word 'humane' means death. . . . Wherever that word appears something dies. So it was with the old-time traveling sideshows in America. The tent spectacles that gave our great-aunties palpitations died off in the 1950s. They were victims of a wave of prim disgust masquerading as humane sensitivity" (Dunn, 9).

In 1976 Daniel P. Mannix expanded on the splitting image of the freak in his day: "I realize that I should not use the word 'freak.' In these days of euphemisms, freaks are now called 'strange people.' This is a pity because there are lots of strange people in the world, but only a comparatively few freaks. . . . If you regard yourself as a normal, healthy-minded person, almost certainly the very idea of a freak is repugnant to you. . . . After all, think of the effect that seeing a freak could have on a child. Yet children are raised on stories of dwarfs, giants and fairies (all of whom have counterparts and probably their origins in human freaks). It is also true that children, far from feeling an instinctive horror of freaks, are delighted with them. . . . It is fortunate our ancestors did not take the modern, civilized attitude, for freaks have changed the course of history and greatly contributed to our knowledge of humanity" (8). In contrast to the Browning scroll-rundown of the evil influence of freaks in history, Mannix lists avatars of beneficial freak influence, including Bertholde, prime minister of Lombardy; Jeffrey, spy for Charles I of England; Edward the Confessor, English monarch; and the Emperor Maximilian of Rome (8–9).

THE COLLECTION UNCONSCIOUS

Sabine Heimgärtner puts her reading finger on the impulse of collection as mounting and maintaining Ottinger's films: "The films . . . have their origin in . . . a kind of passionate collecting, through which the remarkable events of world history are separated from one another. What is left, after years of collecting, contrasting, comparing, and selecting is what is noteworthy and what is worthy of monstrosity." This perspective, Heimgärtner underscores, is the given of the original screenplay: storybook research albums—"surreal" catalogs, fictive image books—in which all Ottinger's films begin to make it to the screen. For her 2000 show "Stills" at the David Zwirner Gallery, Ottinger eschewed the trend to exhibit photographs in huge format, and selected a display-case size for her photographs, in keeping with the look and proportions of a wonder room or curiosity cabinet.

Collectibility is foregrounded in *Freak Orlando,* a direct hit or fit with certain station stops in this time trip, but a margin account opened up in more contemporary settings of freak control. The "small world-theater" of *Freak Orlando* reintroduces sixteenth- and seventeenth-century wonder rooms, but always as tagging along on the freak-show margins of the modern era of more compartmentalized or departmentalized organizations of public collection. Like anything that survives under displacement, the margin of superseded settings of collections and collectibles awaits the big blast of return. It is possible to recognize that there is not so far to go from the eclecticism of the contents still collected in time capsules buried in countless American backyards, to what will be aboard the space capsules soon taking off to colonize wide-open outer spaces for the survival of the species in circumvention of loss, the mourning after, and substitution.

If the modern or modernist museum has a history coterminous with that of every other cultural institution sharing the Enlightenment fantasy of origin, it also has, then, a prehistory, one that belongs to a century-or-two-older emergence of all-out collection surrounding an interdisciplinary or eclectic mix of oddities, curiosities, and wonders. "In these kaleidoscopic displays, the most curious and dissimilar objects were exhibited side by side: a dried mermaid, the shin bone of a giant, a unicorn's horn, Egyptian mummies, and African natives' gear were intermixed with pickled and dried monstrosities, the skulls of hydrocephalics, and the death masks of famous men" (Bondeson, vii).

What passes as miracle or wonder metabolizes the wound of separation, dislocation, or long distance. It was the age of discovery that brought back the grab bag of wounds and wonders, both from the new frontier of our first outer space over there in the Americas, and from another new inner-outer space opened up by techno vision. Now we could see our way clear to catching life where it breeds and is undone. Through these lenses, between the lines of the supernatural, we got the picture of circulation, it was in our blood, and followed Harvey's discovery of the circulatory system as our model for all subsequent sciences and institutions of circulation, substitution, invention. But the vampiric conditions of collection always bring up the arrears, the losses, the backfire of the look and march forward of techno invention. This was a tension Freud mapped out in his first First World War essay "Thoughts for the Times on War and Death." The Great War was what Europe had been holding back, swallowing and never digesting, while resting in one peace in a mode of cosmopolitan forty-year-old self-collection. The *Titanic* catastrophe gave us the horror preview of what would be coming soon. The ship-sized state of European collection was to be the ultimate in the techno invention and perfection of safety. Technology would keep us all calm and collected even following contact with catastrophe or accident. But then the unthinkable, I mean unsinkable, went down, near-missing the ultimate safety net, the media-technological rehearsal of the World Wide Web, which the ship's catastrophic end cast about our ongoing state of preparedness. In the year following the *Titanic* crash, ending without rescue, twenty-four-hour wireless service was set up as the law for all ships passing in the night. Ever since, we have been live, online, on-lifeline.

Before he invented the phonograph, Thomas Edison was the survivor in childhood of a host of sibling deaths. By age twelve he was well on his way to being a deaf gadget-lover and -rescuer concerned with supplementing the audio range of all ear sets, both for those quick to hear and for the deaf. When Edison was born, the telegraph was already wiring up long distances. At the same time, the American craze for séances started around tap sounds that we were beginning to make out as the outside chance that the dead were getting back to us. Turn on the tap and let the bier overflow. Everyone was doing this tap chance.

Edison's works of invention represented an overcoming at least as much as an undertaking. Even at his most deaf, he could always still hear the tap, tap, tapping sounds of the telegraph. At first he sought to build a kind of recording machine for the messages transmitted by telegraph or by phone. Once upon a time, while testing the record he had made of a telegraphic transmission, he overheard ghost voices coming through just like voices in the next room. The phonograph was born—out of one deaf gadget-lover's auditory hallucination of audio contact with dead voices coming through on the telegraphic recorder. The long distant, who are always also along for the connection coming through across long distance, were receiving via the deaf safekeeper another voice of confidence and coincidence, another techno hold of storage and transmission. The votes that were thus in the deaf medium gave to his mother's undead children a certain majority share in the new techno cultures of safety that were coming soon.

The deaf and the deaf-mute have been doubling as model mediums at least since the eighteenth century. Their reduced sensorium brought them closer to the apparatus that inventors and scientists began supplying with extended senses, techno senses that were soon new properties for the rest of us too. The deaf-mute, the premier experimental subject in modern science labs, was at the same time our first projected automaton.

In 1877 Edison, who was into perfecting all the sparks of techno creation that were out there, added to Bell's invention his own invention of a carbon telephone transmitter, which was the practical piece missing from the realizability of the original phone. In 1885 Edison secured ways and means for the transmission of telegraphic signals between moving modes of conveyance and a station fixed in place. This was his essential contribution to Marconi's project, the invention of the wireless telegraph. The *Titanic* catastrophe would give the rescue signal across airwaves top priority in the new order of technologization. Radio control, Mayday, and the black box were on the way.

Marconi claimed to have invented a time-traveling recording device that would make it possible to hear, for the record, the words spoken by Christ on the cross. Edison sought more direct contact with those who were already history. He was convinced that there just had to be a radio frequency between the long and the short waves, which, once he contained it and gave it an on/off switch, would put through the first live connection to the realm of the dead.

What is in a name when it was the *Carpathian* that rescued what was left of the *Titanic,* leaving to the *Californian* the greater portion of blame for all that was missing. The *Titanic*'s posthumous legacy of nonstop wireless connectedness was addressed in the first place to the *Californian*'s attention deficit. In the vampiric mode, the ship's telecommunications had been switched on only for one-half day's broadcasting. In Bram Stoker's *Dracula* (another late nineteenth-century exhibition catalog or owner's manual introducing, alongside all the occult collectibles, the latest in techno communication and recording), the vampire count is outmaneuvered by his hunters because they can rely, nonstop, on telegraphic live transmissions while for the better half of the day the vampire must rest in his "earthly envelope" (309) and thus rest in one piece with and at the same pace as his designated mode of conveyance. The *Titanic* disaster made the emergency of round-the-clock live transmissions a fact of life especially for the *Californian*. The vampire, like any old occult medium, never goes away; it just gets superseded by more of the same, only better. Technologization or mass psychology is just one crucial wavelength ahead of the occult forces it at the same time doubles and contains.

William Stead's promotion of journalism that would be in direct touch with the public led him to embrace spiritualism, telepathy, the occult. Not just a journalistic topic or belief, telepathy became for him a possible means of transmission that would realize the affective bond with the mass readership. According to Stead, journalism offered a means of communication between the experts and the mass of minds that needed to know, for example, how to form their own spirit circles. At his last supper, Stead discoursed on spiritualism, telepathy, and the occult (according to one of his fellow diners and passengers on the *Titanic* who survived the sinking). Spiritualist circles allegedly received the news of his death before wireless operators could confirm that he was one of the casualties (Luckhurst).

The techno hope was that the internal compartmentalization going into the *Titanic*'s designs on the future, like a succession of submarines, would offer on any accidental impact the emergency plan of automatic shutdown of all the undamaged waterproof compartments that could, like emergency flotation devices, keep the ship unsinkable. But the iceberg proved to be just the top of the mourning breaking into the crypt plans of technology.

They say that the more cavalier passengers used the shattered ice glittering on deck to chill their drinks. Think again: others claim the ice mountain was dark and stinking from all the prehistoric debris ripening on contact with the air, the air waves of first contact with the human species.

In 1985 the sunken *Titanic* was located. After several open seasons for relics, a first sampling was put on display in 1994. Among the mix and match of mundane artifacts could be observed dollar bills, pound notes, leather wallets, cigarettes, silver salvers, white crockery, white chamber pots, hip flasks, leather bags, portholes, telegraph sets, internal telephones, and fuse boards. "The Atlantic depths give birth and a ridiculous junk-heap emerges. The objects recovered have no intrinsic uniqueness: there is only the association with the *Titanic*, which viewers must sentimentally supply for themselves" (Gardiner and van der Vat, 249).

In January 1998, Swedish artist Stig Sjölund opened his site-specific installation titled *"Titanic* II" on the same day that James Cameron's film premiered in Stockholm. Sjölund's site-to-behold fit the courtyard of the Hallwylska Museet. From the outside, in the deep freeze, there was the totally Goth facade looking at you. Sjölund commissioned two top ice-cream firms to set up shop in this setting and compete—against the elements—for customers. That was just the tip of the ice cream.

What was jamming at the intersection Sjölund occupied on the centenary of the building of the castle that would hold crypt and museum collections? The Hallwylska Museet itself, as specific citation from the genealogy of collection, with the *Titanic* as the liner notes accompanying a tension that's still on the record between collection and invention, between melancholia and catastrophe preparedness, and with the winter's sale of ice cream as the caption that emerges from the white noise, the static, and the surf of drowning out.

By the end of the nineteenth century, the new science of phonetics had started collecting examples of "juncture" in which the sameness of sound shapes could be seen to rely for their distinction on a time interval, the pause button pressed within the newly discovered domain of suprasegmental features. There's the example *night rate* (nitrate). Another one made it into the big lights of the Good Humor ad: "I scream for ice cream." Then there's the well-known knock-knock joke that elaborates on a third example: "Iowa a penny to the library." This collection of phonetic sameness and difference is unthinkable without the late nineteenth-century introduction of media technologies of sound recording. At the same time, a new system or science of phonetic notation was required to make the serviceable transcription: the audio record needed an owner's manual, a typewritten hard copy for access and organization. But how to indicate for the supplemental record the difference in the sameness that was on the record of hearing? After a kind of Morse code of suprasegmental features was added to the basics, the new science of phonetic transcription could take note of all the new techno oral histories of primitive languages, local dialects, and last words of the dying that were out there, expiring and ready for recording.

In 1920 Wilhelmina von Hallwyl gave her Stockholm palace and collections to the Swedish government for safekeeping. The collections spanned the double movement of eclecticism and totalization: "I will include everything, brooms, dust mops and the like, because the day will come when these items are unusual and remarkable once everything is done by electricity" (in *Hallwylska Museet*, 2). Even the impulse to collect, to supply souvenirs of whatever is gone, can be entrusted to the sparks of technologization. Thus von Hallwyl gives a future tense of push-button reanimation to the significance of her own archival project, her mummification of all the scenes of a lost, preelectric life. In 1921 her husband died. From that point onward, she was home alone inside the collections that she cataloged, until her death in 1930. This doubling of the collection contained itself within a final set of seventy-eight leather-bound volumes. The collection had all along been about von Hallwyl's interests, which began collecting themselves in childhood: "Between 1853 and 1854 I received a small shell from my father. The shell had been found inside a quantity of raw hides. This shell was the start of my collection" (ibid., 3). The palace, completed in 1898, was built on the crypt of an infant daughter who was dead, they said. Undead! Undead! The surprise shell that spilled out from unbound leather was the start of a collection that in turn would be bound up, seventy-eight times, in the catalog volumes. The catalog exceeds the collection in one item, another bit of stray unbound leather from another childhood. "The frozen moment captivates us. Not to add to or take away from it was another one of the donor's inspirations. Only one object was rejected—a pen dryer made of rat hide . . . Traditionally, the Christmas gifts from grandchildren and great-grandchildren should be handmade by the children themselves. Great-grandchild Hans solved the Christmas gift problem by killing a rat, preparing the hide, and making a pen dryer with the gray-brown skin mounted on a half circle of blue satin" (ibid.).

TIME TRAVEL

In *Freak Orlando*, Ottinger moves the transfer, the across or trans- she would have us bear, around an axis of time travel. Time travel, for all its boundlessness, is part of the fine imprint on the label of photography's historical record. There is a reception of photography that journeys through time to reverse and recuperate loss, to preserve it, or even to commemorate it and put it to rest. Charles Sander Peirce assigned the photograph indexical status as vestige and emanation of an object, like the lock of hair next to it in the album of souvenirs. By now the locus classicus of this (implicitly) funereal pointer can be found in Roland Barthes's *Camera Lucida*: "that rather terrible thing which is there in every photograph: the return of the dead" (9). A primal scene or rather screen memory of photography's melancholic offer of supersavings organizes Chris Marker's *La Jetée* (1962), a film of photographs engaged in the rescue fantasy of time traveling. The third world war has driven the survivors underground. Time is running out among all the resources in short supply. A time traveler must be sent to the future or to the past to obtain assistance. Our protagonist, who is stuck on a part recollection, an eidetic souvenir, one that's part part and part parting, is the chosen one, the one who suffers but doesn't die or go mad while time tripping. To be stuck on a recollection is to be stuck all around it, as in fetishism, gadget love, or traumatic amnesia. What you are stuck on is the moment right before traumatic amnesia took over and left you to get off—on boots and related garments of the edge or margin, or on the lines of the car the moment before impact. This gadget lover or fetishist—like the time traveler in *La Jetée*—has therefore an involuntary memory, a concept Proust introduced in so many words and which Benjamin reinterpreted along Freudian lines in his essay "On Some Motifs in Baudelaire." The traveler stuck at the edge of a memory he doesn't remember and thus doesn't remember to forget is sent into a zone of dislocation from the present, perhaps deeper into his remembered past or into invention or fantasy or delusion, where he accumulates more and more memories or souvenirs, where the disconnection between the woman's face and his own ghost appearances becomes a connection. The face of a woman recognized but not to be identified belongs to the maternal realm. But it is his separation from her that he no longer remembers to forget. The temporality of the photograph, according to Barthes and Benjamin, corresponds to some of these in-between calculations of time traveling. The photograph is part and parting of the subject shot: the photo op is dead, constitutively speaking, and is going to die. "I read at the same time:

This will be and this has been; I observe with horror an anterior future of which death is the stake. By giving me the absolute past of the pose, the photograph tells me death in the future. What pricks me is the discovery of this equivalence. In front of the photograph of my mother as a child, I tell myself: she is going to die: I shudder, like Winnicott's psychotic patient, over a catastrophe which has already occurred. Whether or not the subject is already dead, every photograph is this catastrophe . . . : that is dead and that is going to die" (Barthes, 96). The photo op thus hovers between two absences, not as the absence of a presence, but as an absence that's going to be absent: the photo op will have been. The photo thus retains the subject, but not as present nor as absent presence but in the borderline zoning of the time trip.

In popular science fantasy, time traveling fills in the blanks by getting around the timeline lining us up in second place. Often it is the fixity of the past that would be circumvented if one could only control the future. Or somewhere between merger and murder, as in the *Back to the Future* series (1985, 1989, 1990) and the first two *Terminator* films (1984, 1991), it serves a fantasy of unbirth, in which one carefully saves or determines one's own birth while facing—abyssally, psychotically—the prospect of one's being unborn. What is repressed is the only available model for one's unborn connection with oneself: the undead connection with the mother. Thus the mother's body is elided, murdered, through the psychotic politics of unbirth.

When Woolf turned on the machine of time traveling, she threw gender into the blender of time and place (which we saw first with Woolf). There are moments of close reading in Woolf's *Orlando* when all or too many of the coordinates of the different timelines meet at once in the undetermined space of the trans-. It's at these moments and in these bodies comprised of nonsuperimposable juxtapositions of different time zones, genders, and lives that we catch another missing link, the one between *Orlando* and Ottinger's *Freak Orlando*. The freak is top candidate for mutational futurity. On the evolutionary scale, mutation is time travel that looks after the missing link and looks forward to what only the mutant can become, his own future generation.

Before Darwin and then Freud, there was no time scheme for understanding our technologization; the way, for example, a new gadget can transform the outcome of what we call history. Once the theory of evolution was advanced, one couldn't stop fantasizing about parallel evolutions of plants, animals, and machines. Evolution allowed for the sudden shifts and switches brought about through techno invention and accident. It opened up the psychic space of time, the outer space that in science fiction inspires and delivers our newest technologies. If selection is ultimately a function of memory, then Benjamin's notion of aura, of the old high we copped from art, can thus be advanced from a retrograde place to the position of the either-aura of techno mnemonic selection and evolution.

If a parallel evolution of genes and nongenetic memory units was always on track, then the sheer velocity of technologization beginning at the end of the nineteenth century switched the techno object onto the fast lane and placed us in the ready position to assume the state or status of missing link, the link to and through reproduction. Technology is evolving ahead of us, and indeed for us. Darwin's theory of evolution immediately hit one of his first fans, Samuel Butler, with the prospect this revaluation of historical time opened up for machine history or evolution. In *Erewhon* Butler develops the science fantasy that humans already represent the selective milieu for machines that do the evolving for us. Evolution is more about survival of our fit with technology than it is about some racist or specist fitness program. If Butler's *Erewhon* is more fact than science fiction, and it is, then our only egoic objective is to cross over into the technological object and merge with it.

But just like a mirror image (or glove), the photograph neither merges with nor reflects the referent, dead or alive. Photography exceeds the drop-dead, point-blank reference by converting time into one moment, which owing to the rule of inversion is never superimposable on itself. Photographs are also always suspended within interphotographic or intraphotographic relations. As Katharina Sykora writes of Ottinger's photographic oeuvre: "Every one of the thousands of photographs that Ulrike Ottinger has taken . . . always refers to something beyond itself: to the reality that precedes it; to countless images from the repositories of the arts, of everyday culture and of myth; and to the visual cosmos of her own increasingly dense oeuvre. These photographs are encounters between things found and things invented. They are arenas in which reality and fiction, past and future, wish and fulfillment, transform each other" ("Stills and Sessions," errata insert). The spookulation of photography is a by-product, Derrida argues in *Droit de regards,* of its staggered, staggering self-reflexivity, the kind that cannot, just the same, generate all its terms out of itself. When photographs cite or consist of other photographs or when there is work on the photographic copy itself, including retouching or airbrushing, we have photographic self-reference, the specter seen to haunt an endless spatiality of frames. The implicit and explicit serial proliferation of the photographic copy along an axis of inversion—both inside and outside the frame, for example—confers on photography, Derrida concludes, the effects of its phantasmic, occult, and dreamlike aspect. In other words, the frame of photography cannot double as the boundary or site of proper burial.

At the end of *La Jetée,* the time traveler returns once and for all to the jetty in the past, where he sees the woman watch him get shot. It is or was the moment of his proper death, the "dad" certainty that the forgetting of time traveling sought to defer or circumvent, but which the discrete fact-finding time trips that brought back the memories had to restore. But your proper death means nothing to you. We can't imagine or experience our own deaths. Either we attend our deaths as an other, in identification with a departed other, or this proper death figures as oedipal separation by the third person of the face-to-face bond with mother.

Barthes pointed beyond his sense of the photo finish by giving the "Death" in the photo shoot the finger: "Ultimately, what I am seeking in the photograph taken of me . . . is Death: Death is the eidos of that photograph. Hence, strangely, the only thing that I tolerate, that I like, that is familiar to me, when I am photographed, is the sound of the camera. For me, the photographer's organ is not his eye (which terrifies me) but his finger" (15). If it were eye to eye, the shoot would be uncanny. But the finger intervenes in the immediacy, tampers with the self-evidence, exceeds the duo dynamic of eye to techno eye, and introduces the gap in and between the image. Sykora focuses in this regard on a photographic technique or moment in one of Ottinger's films: "Delphine Seyrig, who—in the guise of Lady Windermere, at once Virgil and ethnologist—guides us through Ulrike Ottinger's film *Johanna d'Arc of Mongolia,* is the star witness for this visual technique. In a saloon car of the Trans Siberian Railway, she speaks the polyglot prologue to the coming adventure, accompanied by a 360° pan across the opulent wall surface of the artificial, mobile shell in which she travels. At the end, the camera completes the circle and returns to her. But suddenly, in an infinitesimal moment of stasis—which we might call the moment when photography arrests the cinematic image—we see a rift in the *trompe-l'oeil* backdrop. This gap is what interests Ulrike Ottinger, because it is only in this hiatus that the next images—the alternative images—reveal themselves" ("Stills und Sessions," errata insert).

ARCHIVIST OR ALLEGORIST?

Freak Orlando, according to Frieda Grafe, "documents collective fantasies. It shows that myths were always parasitic hybrids in which ruling conceptions were condensed, without inquiring after their origin or goal. Even where one would like to congratulate the director on highly imaginative invention, she documents in a book on the film that all this really did in fact exist" ("Mythen auf dem Mist des Alltags"). Like Flaubert's *The Temptation of Saint Anthony* as interpreted by Foucault, *Freak Orlando* can be seen as another monument to meticulous erudition. Foucault takes the entrance of Diana of Ephesus in *The Temptation of*

Orlando (Magdalena Montezuma) and the Siamese twins.

Saint Anthony as exemplary of Flaubert's achievement: "Certain evocations in the text seem totally dominated by the machinery of dreams. . . . Nevertheless, this 'fantasy' is an exact reproduction of plate 88 in Creutzer's last volume: if we observe the details of the print, we can appreciate Flaubert's diligence" (xxv–xxvi). Foucault thus concludes that *The Temptation of Saint Anthony* "is linked in a completely serious manner to the vast world of print"; "it dreams other books, all other books that dream and that men dream of writing" (xxvii). The totalization along for this assessment corresponds to Foucault's related point that this was the work Flaubert was forever trying to write but, since it would at the same time realize the archive's sui-citational highpoint *and* endpoint, he also repeatedly had to put it off if he was going to write anything else at all.

But is the archive of representation and self-reflexivity really bigger than the two of us, self and other? In *Freak Orlando,* the Siamese-twin sisters can look at each other only in the mirror.

The five episodes of *Freak Orlando* are set apart as different epochs even as all the epochs press for representation or contamination in each episode. That all the same actors take up the different roles of the different episodes underscores (as in the return of the old crew in the new crew in *Madame X*) the allegorical character of metamorphosis in place of the historical event or even death. What also returns in every epoch is the look and impact of contemporary commodification of representation, or what the screenplay designates the "juxtaposition of mythology, department store, and middle ages." At one point, for example, Orlando, in order to take another time trip, enters a room or camera decked out as curiosity cabinet—as "ship of fools, a kind of mirror and horror cabinet" (Ottinger, *Freak Orlando*)—where he is joined by the flagellants carrying their

Galli and the giantess in front of the 1936 Berlin Olympic Stadium.

sales items onboard. When Goethe turned to allegory in *Faust II* it was to float a pageant of commodities that culminated, and this is the connection in *Freak Orlando* too, in a tableau about the different economy of art.

The dwarf painter Galli, named on occasion in the original screenplay *Dokumentaristin* (a woman who documents), follows and keeps the historical record of events that recur, but always in unique juxtapositions or forms. When Galli, assisted by the giantess, stands her freakish ground in front of the 1936 Olympic Stadium in Berlin, she offers up the "document" she reflects and records in contrast both to Leni Riefenstahl's monumentalist film "document" (which the Nazi state, with the Olympics at the front of the line, essentially provided with sets and extras) and to the television coverage of the Olympics, the first live transmission of a mass-cultural event on TV, on primal time. Galli keeps her different record alongside what history shows: the spokespersons, who sell the latest S-M accessories or pitch the ongoing sales over the department-store public address system. In the course of documenting the deportation of freaks during the Inquisition, Galli throws away her worn-down sketching pencil and buys a Super-8 camera with which she continues her documentation (or documentary).

Ottinger underscores in her reflections on *Freak Orlando* that the department-store sequence houses the film's references to the most ancient mythic stratum: "For me these scenes signify the presence of the past in what is most current" (in Frey, 45). This continuity of the past, as Frieda Grafe observes, serves as uncanny vehicle for all the allegorical tensions that follow but also gain release from the special offer of myths on sale: "The department store in *Freak Orlando* is the temple of promises, the gathering place for the believers, where public life organizes itself according to specific liturgies. Not only are norms set in concrete here, but even the relationship to the past gets exploited. Only the very newest, coupled with the good and old, makes just the right special offer. The beautiful Miss Helena Müller advertises the sales items and special offers in the department store with the voice of a Siren, and as in olden days the purpose is to awaken expectations, make you believe, without however letting you see anything. The images in the film function in a similar manner, they are allusions that spark associations, in which what is allegedly natural is undermined by artificiality" ("Mythen auf dem Mist des Alltags"). Grafe's vanishing point fits the film's opening in a department store. But the opening, which sells the connection between signifier and signified, gets subsumed, as Grafe also points out, in the course of Ottinger's allegorical inauguration of an image language or world of her own: "In these images, which remain full of contradictions, the aura of diffuse meanings materializes into impressions for which there are no words. It is as though the usual barter business of cinema, in which the image stands for a copied reality, had fallen into

Miss Helena Müller (Delphine Seyrig) announcing the myths on sale.

disarray, and everything had been displaced onto the level of images. As though there existed free-floating images that no longer followed a model in nature."

Ottinger's *Freak Orlando* is aligned with the reception or reinvention of allegory associated with Benjamin's *Origin of the German Mourning Play*. In Benjamin's reading, which is as much about the baroque theater as it is about post–World War I expressionist drama, or, for that matter, about all the words and worlds between, the allegorical mode has one context: it comes after the

The S-M leather boys pass dwarf with dog in the Caprichos *setting.*

catastrophe. It is the mode (or modem) that still links our survival as mourners and readers to what's missing. Allegory, according to Benjamin, signifies the nonbeing of what it at the same time represents. As with the corpse, which Benjamin refers to in passing as the primal or ready-made allegorical emblem, allegory is realized within the perspective of the melancholic. The object becomes allegorical under the melancholic's gaze; all the life is gone out of it; it remains as dead, but as eternally preserved. Benjamin has one openly psychoanalytic analogue for this double reading (his reference to Freud's understanding of melancholia remains in hiding), which he uses not once but twice. It is typical for the sadist, says Benjamin, to demean his object and give it satisfaction too. The same goes for the allegorist.

How to understand the allegorical mode of post-catastrophic reading? We can begin with our own setting, the mass media Sensurround, which simply reverses while retaining the melancholic link, but in the mode of catastrophe preparedness, or what Benjamin analyzes in terms of shock absorption. Benjamin addresses this more contemporary version or reversion in the later essays, like the one on film culture and the other one on Baudelaire and mass psychology. Ottinger in turn preserves this association between the allegorical treatment and its mass-mediatic reversal or revival by moving from *Freak Orlando* to her next film, *The Image of Dorian Gray in the Yellow Press,* which engages the identifiable conditions and contexts of our own media technologization, and on terms that only appear to have departed from the world theater of *Freak Orlando*. Because sometimes a disconnection is a connection too. The Freak City department-store opener and frame looks forward to *The Image of Dorian Gray in the Yellow Press,* in which the myth sale is updated as the going-out-*for*-business sellout of all the news that fits the preprinted story.

In Benjamin's two media essays that openly admit allegiance to Freud's science, Benjamin functionalizes (in large measure) his own hallmark allegories of rereading and renaming as a therapy of double take. In the essay on Baudelaire, Benjamin gets his shock from *Beyond the Pleasure Principle*. But what holds together his allegorical rescues and his media therapies is an early encounter both with Freud's "Psychoanalytic Notes on an Autobiographical Account of a Case of Paranoia (Dementia Paranoides)" (*SE* 12: 9–82) and with the text by Daniel Paul Schreber that Freud analyzes in his study of paranoia.

Even if by another name, Freud admits the allegorical dimension or dementia under the concept of endopsychic perception. At that point of excess of self-reflection, which in turn allows access to psychoanalysis on allegorical terms, the delusional formations, which could be reformulated in terms of persecution, martyrdom, and rescue, wash up onto the outer limits of Freud's own theorization. Freud's inside view of Schreber's delusions catches rays belonging to an endopsychic perception, one that already reflects back the same view and even the theory of these paranoid views within views. Freud thus reaches the limit concept of endopsychic (or paranoid) reading, which borders on the same self-reflexivity impulse that drives Benjamin's allegorical project onward.

Elias Canetti crowded an origin of spectacle into the Crusades (the same era that Sachs saw as introducing, through its shakeup of socioeconomic foundations, the first undoing of the "delay of the machine age"): "The Crusades developed into crowd formations of a magnitude no church building of the contemporary world could have held. Later, whole towns became spectators of the performances of the flagellants and these, in addition, wandered from town to town" (*Masse und Macht,* 21). In *Freak Orlando* these violent spectacles reach the screen as the "cool sophistication" of its images, resulting from the equidistance imposed upon the viewer by the noninterference tact of Ottinger's camera and from the theoretical endlessness of these "beautiful" images (Berg-Ganschow).

> [*Freak Orlando*] takes the example of the freaks to construct a world history. . . . I am interested in showing how this phenomenon has developed and changed; for instance, which groups at what time have been excluded by society. . . . The exclusions had their beginning with the segregation of lepers outside of the city limits. Today exclusion is effected inside the walls of

prisons and psychiatric clinics. This is one aspect of my . . . film. At the same time I wanted to make a film about the exclusion of our fantasies. The film starts in mythological pre-history, . . . a time when our fantasy and imagination served as a link between known and unknown things, when religion and myth were closely tied in with actual knowledge. But at the same time, this episode will take place in a department store, which is featuring a mythological week, a literal sale of myths. (Ottinger, in Mueller, "Interview with Ulrike Ottinger," 115)

Freak Orlando, then, Ottinger's "quintessential work of orgiastic surrealism," introduces "us to every conceivable human form: Siamese twins, beggars, pilgrims, dwarfs, bearded women, and transvestites" (Pidduck), while on the same tour, the guiding figures or points of narrative cohesion change into different genders and historical scenarios. While Ottinger's "preoccupation with eccentrics and marginals is a complex study of difference itself" (ibid.), this self-deictic or -reflexive moment is compounded in our interest by the coterminous fixity of the film's space in Berlin, the place that fits all that's seen in this world theater. That Berlin is excavated over and again to provide the settings for our allegorical genealogy or time trip, which follows the bouncing rise or fall of the freak, helps qualify the temporality of Ottinger's juxtapositions. The emblematic pieces of the different pasts do not conjoin in timelessness. The meeting of national socialism and the Inquisition, both styling with sadism and allegory, is not a reunion of relativity, a posthistorical combining or analogizing of one era with any other one. It's always the more recent past that's immediately, primally repressed, and transformed thus into a primal past or prehistory linked to and separated from us as catastrophe.

In Ottinger's *Freak Orlando,* Berlin can figure as the oldest city in history, the city center of our recent or primal past, or in the terms of the film, as Freak City, hangout for the S-M leather boys who hang with the times of analogy. The intimate connection Benjamin drew between allegory and sadism, which Ottinger continues to put through in *Freak Orlando,* is not stuck only on the visualizable details of those styles. The connection is made also in the time we are given to watch or read: time is neither streamlined nor full in Ottinger's film. It's always overlong; it fulfills but then exceeds and thus erodes the retention span of melancholia. Satisfaction and assault start up (again) from scratch, both the scratch that has us stuck in the record and the scratch of the surface that thickens time and lets us see (at least—at last!—for the time being).

Allegory has the quality of an inherently uncompletable act—in such a way, in fact, that its uncompletability is fundamentally related to its activeness, making it irreducible to fact or to information. Thus, while the systematics of philosophy is constantly present in the background of allegory, in a manner that invites generalization and suggests that its substance could have been expressed in the form of relatively systematic argument based on the (philosophical) history of civilization, this background stabilizing influence operates only to the extent that allegory resolutely disavows the specific theorizing from which such an argument could arise. For only this disavowal can adequately enact the system of paradoxes, paralogisms, and contradictions the argument springs from, can keep it operative precisely as action in a historically meaningful sense, rather than, by the claim to understand and accept, freeze it into a strict and strictly pointless "no future" with all ambivalence and paradox removed.

5
OPERATION ART

In the time that it has become but a screen memory, the theatrical art of Ottinger's fictional films has been on view onstage. In the theater, Ottinger declared in 2000, "one still has artistic freedoms" (in Liese). Or again, when asked if it is her preference to work for the theater rather than in film, Ottinger spells it out: "Today in Germany it is impossible to finance a film that is not commercially adjusted. Artistically right now in the theater there is greater freedom" (in *Focus*). While my contact with Ottinger's 2000 staging of Elfriede Jelinek's "Das Lebewohl" ("The Farewell") is exclusively at the remove (and mercy) of newspaper reviews, I insert some reflection on the reception of this staging because it belongs to and further illuminates the power themes and their media nature in both *Freak Orlando* and *The Image of Dorian Gray in the Yellow Press*.

This was Ottinger's third staging and direction of a dramatic work by friend and colleague Elfriede Jelinek. "The Farewell" is a monologue that cites the words of the right-wing Austrian politician Jörg Haider in juxtaposition with everyday phrases and excerpts from ancient Greek texts like *The Oresteia*. Asked what fascinates her about Jelinek, Ottinger affirms a sensibility they share: "She succeeds in treating a concrete theme with a high form of art language, with montages and collages" (Ottinger, in Conrads). In the case of "The Farewell": "Jelinek analyzes a phenomenon that has been on the rise recently: that by now politicians really always only sell themselves. That is plain populism. There was a time when politicians liked to be seen and shown together with artists. They no longer do that" (Ottinger, in Conrads).

A *New York Times* review of the latest stage developments in Berlin described Ottinger's presentation of "The Farewell":

> "The Farewell" . . . has been given a powerful, imagistic production by the feminist filmmaker Ulrike Ottinger. She has taken Ms. Jelinek's monologue and placed it in the mouths of 13 Haider clones, dressed alternately in eve-

ning clothes and a flamboyant array of sporting gear (Mr. Haider is a sports enthusiast). They recite the text in stylized Greek-chorus fashion, while performing sporting activities onstage. The sight of 13 actors skiing, kayaking, rappelling and roller-blading, dressed in blinding Kodachrome color, is stunning. (Rocamora)

Ottinger sought to throw a fit with the specific emblems of Haider's claim to power: "He surrounds himself with all the insignia of the young successful man. He presents himself as energetic mountain climber. As victor and winner" (Ottinger, in Luzina). By multiplying Haider into one-plus-twelve Haider clones, Ottinger was able to set Haider's specific insignia in the bigger and older picture of power surges: "Each period introduces a new form, Haider embodies the high-tech variant. . . . But it is the same old brown manure in modern clothing" (ibid.). "The fateful continuity of abuse of power in relations between majorities and minorities—that is the leitmotif traversing my entire work" (ibid.).

"Sports—according to Ulrike Ottinger—are the costume of populist politics. She is thus in agreement with Elfriede Jelinek. To begin with the actors come on stage as flag-waving fascists uniformly dressed in red. Then they form a group around a table like the disciples of Jesus at the last supper. One Haider figure is elevated to the status of savior. But when they drop their cloaks we see that they are dressed in contemporary sports outfits" (Kranz). There you have it: what set off negative reviews was the citation of Christianity for a certain complicity as though the journalists were thus under attack. For example: "When one is subjected to pedagogical torture, the punishment usually has only one function: namely to cloak the fact that a real aesthetic transposition of the text has not been found. Ulrike Ottinger's didactic theater is so boring and shallow that one much prefers to watch the skaters as they make their turns with elegant movements" (Dermutz).

Freak Orlando introduced a station break in the support of Ottinger's work by ZDF, the "Central German Television" station. The channel requested that specific scenes of the film be cut pre-broadcast to spare the religious feelings of viewers. Ottinger countered that these scenes were the support beams of the dramaturgy as a whole. She didn't strike an accord when she suggested that the station simply black out the screen and let the audio continue; at least that way the censorship would be evident. In discussions around this break with television's identified audience, Ottinger dismissed all charges of blasphemy—"In art blasphemy is not even possible"—and referred to the church as the first multimedia enterprise (in Elbin).

When Heimgärtner sees Dorian Gray as a Christ figure in a passion play directed by his creator to cross a series of stations on the way to the tragic conclusion, it is journalism that moves to replace, in a leap of association or faith, the irreducible secret with revelation, to redeem or resurrect the deposit that is otherwise without redemption value. Because Dorian is completely enigmatic, he is all suited up to serve as blank screen onto which Frau Dr. Mabuse can project the serialized novel for the press to publicize. To that end, Dorian must appear to be keeping a secret that in time he will be pressed to leak. Dorian's identification remains a secret, now open, now shut. All questions of identification are irrecuperably skewed in the opera scene in which everyone appears twice. What keeps Dorian's secret is that enigmatic force of doubling that does not give itself away to the third person, whether the law or the intermediary. Once there can be two of anything, there can be an infinite number more of them.

Postmodern allegory can be seen as running on empty while maintaining the vacated premises of transcendent frames of reference. But mediatization today is just another form of Christianization. If Christianity made the medium the message but the message was of necessity without medial nature, then mediation must give way to immediation. This paradox has since been realized within the allegedly live media Sensurround as paradox sustained by faith. Ottinger's film merely reflects on its medium nature—as double and image—when it lets the surveillance record (on which Frau Dr. Mabuse would base her power) show instead a ruin-scape of technology and an allegorically sustained frame of reference that, functionally, is a failed system running on empty—which nevertheless claims its place next to nothing.

What does it mean to pose questions of surveillance as problems that are technologically, functionally, realistically already upon us (or all over us)? Among academics, such an acceptance of or submission to a science-factual certitude about our being under super-vision derives from a longer-term reception of Michel Foucault's work as "new historicism." Foucault reopened the reading or study of institutionalization and its subject, the seeing I or ego, which Nietzsche had already explored, but not under the aegis of realized technical controls, rather in terms of the ruinous legacies of an otherwise consciously abandoned belief system. According to Nietzsche, from Christianity to nihilism, mankind has upheld belief in an all-seeing witness who, as we say, validates our suffering, our pain, and renders it all meaningful if only by being on record or under surveillance. The need for this witness protection program struck Nietzsche as so seductive, even or especially since inimical to life, that he was moved to forecast twentieth-century wars unprecedented in history through which so-called monsters of nihilism would seek ultimate meaningfulness in mass destruction, death, suicide—in the synchronization of all our deaths all together now at the same time. It was to be a late and last arrival of that old comfort, with all the whammy that going down with the witness must bring: to be double *and* nothing.

Ottinger's film gives no reason to discard Nietzsche's view that the technical, scientific construct of surveillance is a belief system more remarkable for its ruinous failure than for any outside chance of realization. Thus one cannot but suspect that there is stowed away in current discourses of surveillance, transparency, and globalization an agenda, whether deliberate or unconscious, that is at least as old as Christianity. Derrida accordingly renamed globalization "globalatinization," according to which the so-called new media of surveillance and liveness still ask us to believe in that evidence of the senses that cannot in fact be proven, that remains inadmissible as evidence, but which is nevertheless presented to us, in a flash (or flashback), as the word made flesh. Believe it! The mass media of liveness have brought us as close as possible to the self-evidence of the senses. However, since in the splitting of a second any "live" transmission (which is also always product) can be tampered with, simulated, rendered deceptive, we are as far away from sense certainty as ever. To turn up the contrast between the story of Abraham and Isaac and the New Testament media of liveness, Derrida emphasizes that blind faith is no longer an option; instead we must have faith in seeing is believing. Every live medium message, just like the mediator Christ, demands of us: Believe me, believe in me, I am the word made flesh, I am the resurrection in the flesh, in the flash of mediatization ("Above All, No Journalists!").

In *The Image of Dorian Gray in the Yellow Press,* Ottinger gives leading roles to two legends of German film: Doktor Mabuse and the Golem, who in Ottinger's film serves Frau Doktor Mabuse as a computer specialist. In 1964 Norbert Wiener advertised the Golem's compatibility with the computer, given that a change in word or even of a single letter (or number) suffices to start or stop either one. Wiener's equation inspired Gershom Scholem to revisit the legend in 1965 when he gave a presentation on the Golem on the occasion of the arrival of the first computer in Israel.

Under total surveillance—like the operations Frau Dr. Mabuse seeks to apply and control—we could only be the android doubles we look like to those who we think control us. To make a name for yourself, to distinguish yourself in this setting means to go where all selves meet on assimilation drive, the drive to be different—like those you like—the drive to become image. In contrast to institutional surveillance models of visibility, the occult figure of the Golem serves as mascot for our ambivalent relations with the controlling interest taken in our mass membership as assimilation. This interest is calculated not only in the terms of the visible world but also in those of the word that names, identifies, counts. According to the Golem legend, the last line of defense granted the Jews is a visual media event—the clay sculpting of a robot figure animated by insertion of a name in writing—which walks the line between safety and danger drawn by one act of transgression (specifically, transference transgression) against the Old Testament injunction not to represent the relationship to God the Father in image or in name.

But with one foot in computing, Ottinger's Golem also has footnotes in a romanticism-to-expressionism tradition that (as was the case with Madame X's machinic double) rededicates all magical traditions, including Kabbalah, to the devil. In the 1920 film *The Golem: How He Came into the World,* Rabbi Loew conjures the demon Astaroth, one of the princes of hell, as pure cinematic illusion with the power to animate the manmade or media-made Golem. A pact (in transgression) is signed each time "aemaeth" is inscribed and inserted into the clay robot to turn it on. The sacrilege of taking the name into the veins of artificial creation also accompanies the removal of the name that shuts the creature down. Beginning with *The Student of Prague,* the devil set a spell with German expressionist cinema. As Ottinger underscored in *Superbia—Pride,* the film medium, the seventh art form, throws a more perfect fit with the artist's devilishly transgressive creation of an alternate world. Frau Dr. Mabuse is the internal representative of filmmaking under the aegis of pride. But one of the endings puts Dorian Gray in the director's chair. Like Madame X, Dorian Gray is a figure of acedia or sloth, poised between pride and (renewal through) lust.

Frau Dr. Mabuse is attracted to Dorian Gray as cipher to be media remade, but also as the jumpstart or turning-point position in the metabolization (through the seven deadly sins) of our self-relations through the world of our own making. Pride may be the crowning sin of intake and control of the world that therefore subsumes the other four (anger, gluttony, greed, envy), but these five cardinal sins are just the same, framed, encircled, determined by sorrow or lassitude of the heart and lustful beginnings.

Karsten Witte interprets Frau Doktor Mabuse's decision to create a newsworthy figure that would stay between her headlines as an elevation of journalism to the position of art. Witte turns up the contrast with Fritz Lang's Dr. Mabuse, the underworld boss who through counterfeit and terror seeks the destruction of society for the sake of disorder—and whose "legacy" is a phantom's telecommand. In Ottinger's version, Frau Doktor Mabuse is a producer of consciousness, promoting only appearances until she deceives herself into believing that she enjoys total control over her media-made Dorian Gray. As played by Delphine Seyrig, the media mogul is not a representation or representative of tyranny, she is "a memory of tyranny," an allegorical figure. As such she does not so much press into the depths of forgetting or remembering as up against the surface, the place (according to Kracauer, according to Witte) of least ossification where breakthrough or change could still happen.

Frau Dr. Mabuse (Delphine Seyrig) in the cockpit.

Frieda Grafe also casts Dr. Mabuse as filmmaker and artist. The newer media of liveness are props within a greater frame that is still cinematic and typographic. The difference between projected and transmitted images is given in the live coverage on the monitors in Dr. Mabuse's headquarters: "The images on the monitors show first of all what one already sees anyway." Frau Doktor Mabuse's surveillance agents form an I-Spy burlesque routine (with Gary Indiana under Loden cover as one of the operatives). "The titular hero, Dorian Gray, passive, manipulated, narcissistic, a tourist lusting for attractions, that is the viewer in general. That is us in the picture." But Dorian Gray's Chinese servant Hollywood, the chronicler of Dorian's family history and his walking daily organizer (and his partner in TV watching), also enjoins Dorian, and us, to remember. "To understand history, it is necessary to find a relationship to your own history" (Ottinger, in Tax, 34).

Dorian remains an enigma whose object status cannot be contained by Mabuse's "Operation Mirror." Thus one of the photographs taken by the mirror operators who are there to make news out of their surveillance of Dorian shows Frau Dr. Mabuse paying for Dorian's opium, and thus tells all about her behind-the-scenes control of Dorian's experiences and their reception. The control that

Dorian Gray holding a copy of the newspaper announcing his death.

images exercise over subjects turns against Frau Dr. Mabuse. "There are two possibilities therefore: Dorian Gray as the ideal victim, but also as the best student. But even if he were to become the director of the publishing conglomerate, he would have lost in my eyes because then Frau Dr. Mabuse's second intention, namely to make him into her best student, would have succeeded just the same—because he would then have been seduced after all" (Ottinger, in Tax, 33). And yet the two endings to the movie, the one in which Frau Dr. Mabuse triumphs, the other one in which Dorian is the winner, together double the lasting indeterminacy of Dorian Gray. At the double end, Dorian, seated as Frau Dr. Mabuse's replacement, holds a copy of the newspaper announcing his own death. In Ottinger's film, then, the liveness of the nonprojective media remains displaced with regard to the uncontrollable doubling their own mirror operations can neither elide nor escape.

Alice Kuzniar argues that the viewer is endlessly "trumped" by Dorian's "hybrid gender and consequently vague sexuality," to which is added at the end "his bivalent status as neither dead nor alive" (156): "Dorian embodies the Lacanian gaze that looks back and makes us aware of our viewing and inability to comprehend what we see, no matter how much we stare. Thus it is not Dorian as freak who is the object of the gaze, but we who are the blinded subjects"

(155). Gertrud Koch also addressed a "cold ecstasy of attraction" in Ottinger's film that necessarily brings up a vulnerability of feelings that cannot but lead to tension—from which the film withdraws into an aesthetics of untouchability ("Kino der Attraktionen").

What is just as characteristic of Ottinger's fictional films is the cozy uncomplicatedness of her relations with difference. At its most subtle, most unsettling, and most matter-of-fact, Ottinger's women-only world makes the role of Dorian Gray a drag role, played by Veruschka von Lehndorff, but entirely without disclosure or comment. In *The Image of Dorian Gray in the Yellow Press,* then, a film in which all secrets are precisely up for simulation and for sale, the one secret that is in effect kept concerns Dorian's gender identity. Yes, at some point you know that Veruschka, a woman, is playing the male role. But is she playing a woman playing a man or is she playing a man? During his underworld tour or initiation, does Dorian recognize himself in the two leather dykes, the two sailors in homoerotic combat, or in the doubling of the Siamese twins? It *is* queer that our never knowing for sure should be so comforting.

In response to a question raised around Godard's gendering of technique or media technology as feminine, Ottinger gives a double affirmation: "Art has engendered many Siamese twins" (in "Entretien avec Ulrike Ottinger"). In art there is momentum without resolution or closure—there is conjoining but always with doubling. Ottinger selected the recognizable model Veruschka von Lehndorf to play the part of Dorian Gray to underscore, between what's doubly sure and what is at the same time undecidable, what she sees as basic to the dandy: "The narcissus, the dandy, especially the dandy has his feminine side. Therefore in art—I am thinking here of Proust, Oscar Wilde, Gustave Moreau, Reynaldo Hahn, who are all indirectly cited in my film—these were among the first artists who as men made aesthetically manifest feminine qualities" (in Tax, 33).

Ottinger points out in Marcel l'Herbier's 1924 film *L'Humaine* a reversal of television that gives us an inside view of how *The Image of Dorian Gray in the Yellow Press,* by reflecting on the foreign-body medium of liveness, contemplates its own artistic medium as self-absorbed in/by the other. The beautiful woman in *L'Humaine* is seduced not by banker, industrialist, exotic despot. Instead an inventor wins her hand via his new audio and video apparatus. "The inventor invites the beautiful singer to attend an experiment in his laboratory-like workshop (designed by Ferdinand Lêger) and places her before a microphone. She starts to sing, the experiment is a success, and for the first time the singer (and with her the happy inventor) can watch on a media-technological image surface people from other continents listening to her. A sheik in the desert, for example, is overcome with pleasure and enthusiasm while listening to her voice. Here the invention of television takes place in reverse" (Ottinger, "Korrespondenzen").

Kurt Habernoll's claim that Wilde's *The Picture of Dorian Gray* "becomes visible in the mirror" of Ottinger's *The Image of Dorian Gray in the Yellow Press* is true to the precise extent that Wilde too worked within the journalistic attention (and retention) span to the point of extension and breakthrough.

Ottinger expressed delight "in making a movie that even in its structure is organized just like our current news media" (in Frey, 44). But as Grafe emphasizes, the span or frame of Ottinger's film is no longer journalism: "The sensational news media, which otherwise chase after what was never there before, now produce what's new without precedent. They now simulate reality and press news releases out of non-reality" ("Der Spiegel ist kein Medium"). The result, according to Sabine Heimgärtner, is an escalation of self-reflexivity or allegory in the film. Gertrud Koch also discerns a self-reflexive closure in the film that resists and illuminates the mass-media drive to appropriate or commodify. The film is fundamentally attractive. It attracts, repels, startles, amazes. "Attractions have an exhibition value but no appropriation interest. They want to be seen and not owned" (Koch, "Kino der Attraktionen"). Witte thus argues that Dorian "is the ideal object for the connection between yearning and mass media" ("Die Spielerin"). Heimgärtner concludes, "And this Dorian Gray is not only an invention of the screenplay, the story of his invention is the history of film."

PHANTOMS OF OPERA

Music has a long-standing score to settle with the visual media, in particular with the movies, which started out silent, with music in the background "covering" sound. Even F. W. Murnau's film *Nosferatu* (1922) was subtitled *A Symphony of Horror*. The crossover into the "Land of Phantoms" forces entry of visibility into spheres and fear of the invisible. Thus the professor looks through a microscope to behold the polyp blown up out of invisibility, and identifies it for his students as "almost a phantom." Music keeps up these appearances in Rupert Julian's film *Phantom of the Opera* (1925). Although the phantom begs Christine not to look at his mask or at what it covers, but to consider only his gift of song, the mass media Sensurround has already reduced what's there, not even invisibility is exempt, to utter visibility. The unmasking will always take place and we will always see everything that beauty (and the beautiful voice become flesh) has to repress to get ahead. The horror of cinema, then, comes down to the either/or switch within the visual, which at either setting will unmask the bond between beauty and horror. Something that must always be held down in our mediatic reduction to the visual sense gets thrown back up to haunt the work of cinema.

The cinema of opera is a late arrival of Wagner's preview of cinema: for his media-spectacularized operas, Wagner concealed the orchestra, made it into a loudspeaker, and turned off the house lights; the focus was fixed on light shows of traumatic relation in which screaming, dying, crying, and just plain breathing hold the stage beneath the endless melody, the first music made for the movies.

Opera is not about music; it's for those of us who hate music, which, bottom line, is the background music that from the primal mass through the Christian Mass to modern mass culture has covered up the cries of sacrifice, the sounds in the back of our head as we eat and chew. But once you know that much, as every melancholic, like Freud, for example, must, then all you hear in music is a certain backgrounding of the death wish, which at the same time turns up the volume on this staticky resounding of the identifications we all still gag on. The psychoanalytic perspective opens up the orifices of opera not in the mouth nor in the ears, but takes them in primarily (or primally) as anal projection. But that's why the melancholic who's music-shy can take, follow, and adore opera (Freud's favorite was *Don Giovanni*). Opera makes a spectacle of its resistance to music's abstraction and cover-up of the losses opera struggles to total, but up front, in their wake and in our face.

When the titles of Ottinger's films forsake the brevity of proper names, all the difficulties or differences of the crossing, of the trans-, begin coming up already with the translation. *The Image of Dorian Gray in the Yellow Press* is the standard rendering into English of what's due to German. The reason it's not "Picture," like on the Wilde side, is because in German the operative word is *Spiegel,* which means "mirror." So, "Dorian Gray in the Mirror of the Yellow Press."

Frau Dr. Mabuse's mission in the film to create secret-leaking sex-scandal news out of Dorian Gray, a handpicked cipher of a young man, is code-named "Operation Mirror." Mirror, mirror is above all important. Because who's the most self-reflexive of media is the question the film asks itself as part and portrait of the whole techno mass Sensurround, which has us covered by containing itself and whatever it surrounds, double or nothing, within the endless relay of self-reflexivity reduced to doubling. How many newspapers and magazines bear "mirror" in their titles? A mirror on the world? I don't think so, dear reader. When you look into it for the news, you're just looking at yourself as those you like to think of as controlling you already see you, doubled and contained, but also basically as nothing.

The next translation problem is "Yellow Press." This is technically the correct translation for *Boulevardpresse,* but, in American English at least, it's quite dated. Ottinger wants the medium message to be on one continuum with whatever names Proust or Wilde would have given it. Because in the trilogy she has her focus also on the dandy as joining the flâneur as reader and bearer of allegory in modernity. But *Boulevardpresse* in German, even though it has been around for a while, still keeps its reference current and signifies by metonymy the mass-media Sensurround in the sum totaling of all its outlets to this day. The best of all possible translations would have to be, then, "Dorian Gray in the Mirror of the Media Sensurround."

Ottinger selects in addition to the media Sensurround, reconstructed in particular as the so-called cockpit from where Dr. Mabuse has her media empire under surveillance and remote control, the opera as the other frame for the movie's journey into its own interiority as self-reflexive medium. "Just as in the cockpit there is the TV frame, so in the opera there's a fin-de-siècle frame, thus here again in the context or frame of the dandy citation.... This frame—in other words the image in the image, the camera angle, the frame of the Opera, behind it nature.... In front, the actors inhabiting a wild untouched landscape with their highly artificial Opera gesticulations ... The image within the image—its endlessness, it is also at the same time the mirror that extends itself infinitely—gives us the contrast between nature and art, but nature already caught in the frame, not only the frame of the camera" (Ottinger, in Tax, 28–29). The mirror doublings in the interpersonal columns, in other words between characters, as when Dr. Mabuse and Dorian Gray appear in the audience and onstage as the Grand Inquisitor and as the young prince, exceed what's big enough for the two of them. "It remains undecidable whether [Dorian Gray] doesn't also fall in love with himself, with the performance, with the mirror in the frame.... The frames within frames of these relations is for me virtually inexplicable verbally, but when the image of the theater frame, recognizable as set, stands in the landscape, and the two lovers step out of the frame, the image speaks for itself" (Ottinger, in Tax, 29).

The Mass of media and the opera are each just the staggered fall of the other, the fall the allegorical perspective has taken in all standard receptions that stay tuned to totalization. All the elements of the baroque mourning pageant or *Trauerspiel,* Benjamin argues in *Origin of the German Mourning Play,* found their completion in opera. The overture was already introducing many baroque dramas. The choreographic inserts plus the overall choreographic quality of the plot and plotting of court intrigue, the scheme holding the mourning pageant together, the way a paranoid delusion can be the low-maintenance alternative to a deep depression, forecast the dissolution of the mourning pageant and the emergence in its place of opera (385–87).

Opera was thus a fallen form of the allegorical baroque mourning pageant, one that became, in exchange, really popular. When opera died, it went to Hollywood heaven. All these falls, by the way, don't add up or subtract according to a linear accounting of decline. The relation of fallenness, in Benjamin's lexicon, is the nondialectical and not-in-denial-about-the-melancholic-condition alternative to all the lines we are usually given in the field of transition.

Dorian Gray (Veruschka) on stage (but he's also in the audience).

Wagner, who introduced the ultimate theorization of opera's mediatization, continues to make ghost appearances in Hollywood films about superhumanity. The endless melody goes on and on even in the visual composition of Burton's and Schumacher's *Batman* films. *Greystoke: The Legend of Tarzan Lord of the Apes* (1984) begins with an "overture" that frames what can't be seen for all the trees. James Cameron is still stuck—perhaps we all are—on the last remaining retrenchment of metaphysical comforts (according to Nietzsche), the last honeymoon resort Wagner promoted in such operas as *Tristan und Isolde*. Here the couple admits the missing witness, the God we invented to witness our sufferings so that not one shred of it would go wasted, unwitnessed, without meaning or instructive value, by making the scene of *Liebestod* where we each watch the other die. Isolde strikes out against the "und" (and) in the title that links and separates Tristan "and" Isolde. Even the connecting word between the two they would not be must be elided if their merger is to take place. Self-murder, the next best thing, replaces the "and" with the double dildo of couple suicide. This last stand of witnessing gets doubly installed in the big picture as a metaphysics of art, as the one big memory picture that always calls or recalls on us to follow the superheroes into their Valhalla refuge from the future/present, and thus to follow them ultimately into the theater where we are already seated worshipping at the Mass of total art.

Cameron's *Titanic* (1997), not for the first time, goes down, one, two, however many times for a body count of witnessing the losing of the other as our last stand against "The Abyss" of meaninglessness. But that can also just mean libidinizing what we all had already given up on. Memory has to fill it all in, as though only blanks were fired: memory as art, whether high or low, saves us from the dead-end realization that even in that last-stand scene of the couple dying in each other's arms, it's always the other who goes first. Instead, via the survivor and guardian of the memories, *Titanic* brings us all in, the moviegoing audience, dead or alive, into someone's big idea of immortality as the life, not our own, flashing before our eyes with each screening.

To address the titanic seductions of media power in *The Image of Dorian Gray in the Yellow Press,* Ottinger placed the cockpit and the opera on one continuum of her own low-tech repetitions or rehearsals of vast networks of techno surveillance. She reintroduces the trans- of allegorical legibility through low-tech reconstruction, by necessity, of the powers or institutions that are as big as life. "How can one make visible the convergence of all the strings of power, etc. We know from reality what it's about—from the control booths in TV studios to the TV coverage from Houston, the surveillance of the space satellites, of the rocket takeoffs. But as artist one cannot even dream of reconstructing something like that, and what's more you wouldn't want to, that would be meaningless, because we know all that already. And therefore it's crucial . . . how one concerns oneself with this reality. I applied an almost completely naive principle, namely that of the Advent calendar. This simple principle struck me as especially fitting for showing how these advanced computer networks bring about the most complicated effects. In this way I'd like the test-kiosks I set up to be understood, ironically of course, as the narrators of how manipulations occur, how products are promoted. In analogy to actual test televisions, test viewers, marketing tests, etc. I introduced in my film international test kiosks which are stationed in all the major cities of the world, in Tokyo, Rome, New York, Peking, Paris, London, Moscow, in keeping with the Mabuse utopia that in the future the power of business will achieve a displacement of ideological systems, their displacement with regard now to an international concern with profit" (Ottinger, in Tax, 28).

In the opera, we see that the old prizes of colonization have given way to the current trophy wife: consciousness itself. "What is shown in a short span of time is the emergence of the myth of the regained paradise, to which the Europeans of the eighteenth century succumbed. In the South Seas and on Tahiti they found the world before the fall of civilization. . . . The Infante forgets the universal mission of the western Papal central agency and discovers in the beautiful

The opera.

wild queen his own yearning for non-oppressed nature. Dorian as viewer of this universal opera recognizes himself as Infante and his lover as the beautiful savage. Yearning and revolt are repeated in him. The colonization of the world and the extinction of individual cultures culminates in the colonization of the inner world and the extinction of the individual" (Großklaus).

In *Memoirs of My Nervous Illness,* Schreber locates his techno-delusional system (the whole world is either empty or watching his every move and thought) within an intertextual gridlock dominated by opera references. He reconstructs the psychic pressures that have robbed him of his former world as the techno pressures that are upon him in his new, delusional order, one that overlaps down to details with the drama or trauma contained in opera. Because Schreber is the last human on earth, and a rotten egg, he must become woman and at the same time android in order to receive God's replicational rays and thus conceive by himself, as himself, a new species for the world's survival. In "Opera and Drama," Wagner (Schreber's most famous fellow Saxon) asked himself, "What kind of woman must true music be?" The answer: one who sacrifices herself, her whole being, when she conceives. But what distinguishes the psycho Schreber from Wagner, say, is that he intervenes in and makes legible within the opera of sacrifice and surveillance, or so Freud argues, an intersection between technology and the unconscious, between Schreber's techno-delusional system and Freud's theory of the psychic apparatus. This intersection or transition is where it's at, where we're at.

We know by now that in the so-called gay 1990s, perversion was the provenance of straight folks. Matthew Barney's primal or model performance of gender nonspecificity had him playing football in draggy undergear, at once a negation and an exhibition of what's still there to show. Barney inserts himself into *Cremaster 5* (1997), at least in name, as diva, not as divo.

The decade just before the 1990s was, during the 1990s, the most repressed, catastrophically remote, and therefore often an unconscious resource for channeling. In the 1990s we operated a decade short of memory. In *Cremaster 5,* the admission of an encrypted or occult reference to Houdini unties all the knots of unconscious indebtedness—and frees Matthew Barney from all influence. Barney escapes with his androgynous lady of chain, chain, chains inside Schreber's psychotic opera. But he doesn't—how could he, now that he's broken out of the chains of encrypted influence?—take up Ottinger's allegorical distance from and within this opera of breakdown and breakthrough. Barney remains inside the holding pattern of Schreber's relations. Are the Deleuzers right after all: can Schreber's mad autobiography be separated from Freud's reading of it? Not really, though you can act just about anything out.

Already in *Cremaster 4* (1994), Barney presented a convincing science fiction, a work in the category I would respell as psy fi, precisely because it's so psychotic sublime. Isle of Man. Say it quickly a few times and it utters the sentence that Freud overheard in the noise of Schreber's mythico-delusional order, the sentence or verdict that goes without saying in every brotherhood of paranoia: "I love man." According to *Cremaster 1* (1995), there is sexual difference: identifiable women are one big standing ovulation; all androgynous figures, which are male identified, no matter how ambiguously, get to crawl around, always in training, in Vaseline-lubed obstacle courses of anal projection. The "cremaster" names a body part for men only; it's what puts muscle into the rise and fall of testicles. At the end of *Cremaster 4* those model balls, outward bound, pumped up into sheer visibility for the scene they make of para-surgical rewiring, bear testes to a special brand or branding of testimony.

The repressed homosexuality underlying the race world of evolutionary contest (the only context that fits differentiations through technology or between media) is only one side effect of psychotic breaks that all fall down within the register of sublimation. Where sublimation breaks down, the subliminal veils are removed with a view to the techno connection being put through every orifice (both found and surgically prepared). Stowaway and throwaway within a video transmission, projection gets added to the tape, or rather released from it.

The giant in *Cremaster 5*, one of three characters into which Barney divides himself, has big balls that get the takeoff treatment, fit to be tied to doves. The prosthetic chains of the Houdini figure (the Magician, another Barney cameo) begin as externalizations of the cremaster muscle. *Cremaster 5* is ultimately the Queen of Chains' remembrance View-Master through which she keeps watching her lover die (while her foot's in one cremaster shape, she looks through another). This separation anxiety toes the denial line of all the cremaster images that keep cutting above the sight of castration. Barney's *Cremaster* series, seen as a psychotic reversal of a certain masterful obsession with making the cut (as exhibited, perhaps more neurotically, by film directors Hitchcock or Pabst), is shot as video and then reprojected as art film (allegedly to cut expenses). Expense accounts can be given for the length of each *Cremaster* segment, but not for each one's live-liness. As video it isn't cut, but it is paced as video. The cut above or around the cutting of castration falls between media, but also inside a video-centric attention span that just won't go away or stay.

On one side, then, there's the opera of the psychotic dandy Schreber, so closely related to the allegorical works of Ottinger, Benjamin, and Freud. So there's that side. Then on the other side, there's the legacy of internalization—from Wagner to Cameron—of media powers of surveillance within couples that stay together by dying together, or rather by watching each other die. This is not to suggest that there's a winning side to this context, this media contest. But one side is hot off the repression—which is hot but also kind of nihilistic, tackily manipulative, and totally dead end. Instead, let's begin again and return to the question of the trans-, the legibility of the big between in media relations of surveillance that are already at work—all in a decay's work, the work of mourning—on the inside of our psychic organizations.

THE INTERNAL FEMININE

That Dorian Gray, as most famous cosignatory of Oscar Wilde, jumps media, on second thought of interpretation of Ottinger's film, is already extension of visitation rites of gender identification closely associated with Wilde's effeminist politics. Ottinger's contribution to this movement is to cut the thread of reversibility upon entering the labyrinth of gender. It remains undecidable, in other words, at what level Veruschka von Lehnsdorf is playing or inhabiting Dorian Gray. Ottinger's Oscar Wilde is not simply sent away to camp for the simper. Instead, the Wildean dandy, like Baudelaire and Benjamin's flâneur, reaches high points of identification in Ottinger's repertoire, whereby it proves possible to give "passing" recognition or legibility to the tight spot of melancholia while en route to the other shore of affirmation that is also stowaway in undecidability.

There are other cosignatories to the Oscar Wilde corpus, corporation, or incorporation, beginning with Salomé. If for the 1930 London edition, Robert Ross could write in his introductory note that "*Salomé* has made the author's name a household word wherever the English language is not spoken," he could only also be referring to its outer-corpus career, beginning in 1905, as the Richard Strauss opera. Nevertheless, in anticipation of the opera, Wilde wrote in *De Profundis*: "The Refrains, whose recurring motifs make *Salomé* so like a piece of music, . . . bind it together as a ballad" (in Dover edition, xvi [in Ross's note]). The opera programmed into Wilde's *Salomé* picks up where the teen journal-ism and Middle Ages crisis of Dorian Gray leave off as if left behind. Dorian Gray may be only double, but the story of his soul admits divisions to fill the total work of art, the media Sensurround, beginning with Wagner's operas. We thus catch him in the act of "listening in rapt pleasure to *Tannhäuser,* and seeing in the prelude to that great work of art a presentation of the tragedy of his own soul" (Wilde, *The Picture of Dorian Gray,* 118).

The Picture of Dorian Gray gave Oscar Wilde his first shot at writing beyond journalism. Wilde was a fluff journalist for most of his sentient career. It is unusual for a serious writer not to have joined the underground movement of his craft and corpus by late adolescence at the latest. In other words, writers of the caliber of the author of a canonical work like *The Picture of Dorian Gray* have by that turning point shifted their writing economy away from the adolescent writer's cramping of style into diary keeping or primal journal-ism. At the same time, of course, this phase and its phrases are never simply left behind. But Wilde really sat tight within the phasing-out and goings-on of his membership in the Teen Age.

The Picture of Dorian Gray is the last major appearance of the doubling fantasy in letters, just before it slips irrevocably away, sight unseen, onto the big screen and into Freud's science. This near-miss sense of timing, whereby the author holds on to what is not going to last, but gets in last and lasting words (and thus never admits the difference between what lasts and what's last or lost), belongs to the Gray zone of overlaps between journalism and melancholia, the zone Wilde occupied for another. The mirror of journalism, with which Wilde was long familiar, could be served up as the address of *Dorian Gray*'s last stand and lasting standing. Journalism is fresh or stale like only conversation can be. Journalism punctuates and prolongs the impression that voice and personality can make through improvisation, in conversation, under duress of dead air or deadline.

Adolescence is time-out for interiority. The flash of insight illuminates the force that is with the teen, but which exceeds or rather precedes the corpus that can be built up to standards of staying power within the accrual of reformulation. Rather than work this body, Wilde perfected instead the improvisational high points of conversation. His affirmation of youth, it can't just be ironized out, is symptomatic of his own complicity with midlife criticism.

In polite society, you will always hear one Oscar Wilde quote too many. This excess is where the writing begins, or rather begins again. The quotable turn of phrase or epigram is a voice-byte, a lasting impression of what cannot last. It's like writing but also not at all like writing. It travels the preconscious routes of mass-media captivation or the telepathic lengths the undead go to (or both).

Wilde was animated by his own conversational over-skill. He was a reanimator of himself, but as other. Out of the improv night, he pulled another out from under his silent deadweight and put it up in lights. Take the word of one of many witness accounts of Wilde just in for the skill in improvisation and conversation. According to Chartres Biron, Wilde was an ordinary-to-gross person whose voice and talk charmed everyone: "His appearance was not in his favor, heavy and sensual, but directly he spoke his whole face lit up, the aspect of the man changed and he seemed a different personality" (in Schmidgall, 4).

If in the preface to *Dorian Gray* we are informed that, formally, the art of the musician is the type of all arts, while affectively the actor's craft holds the lead, then the relationship between Lord Henry and Dorian, and precisely not the painter Basil's relations with Dorian, realizes this arts and crafts in an erotics of influence. Lord Henry's words immediately get Dorian's secret instrument resonating: "The few words that Basil's friend had said to him . . . had touched some secret chord that had never been touched before, but that he felt was now vibrating and throbbing to curious pulses. Music had stirred him like that" (20).

But it is when he performs not on Dorian but for Dorian's admiration that Lord Henry feels the ecstasy. First he has made another quip, this time an upbeat one, about the midlife perspective on adolescence. He tells his hostess: "'To get back one's youth, one has merely to repeat one's follies'" (38). And then he's off: "It was an extraordinary improvisation. He felt that the eyes of Dorian Gray were fixed on him, and the consciousness that amongst his audience there was one whose temperament he wished to fascinate, seemed to give his wit keenness, and to lend color to his imagination. He was brilliant, fantastic, irresponsible. He charmed his listeners out of themselves" (39).

The charm of doubling all those in earshot "out of themselves" gets its rise out of a downbeat, that of the midlife sentencing of youth that he issues to Dorian at their first meeting, and which dictates the terms of the contract Dorian, in the face of his portrait, takes out on himself. "'When your youth goes, your beauty will go with it. . . . You will become sallow, and hollow-cheeked . . . Ah! Realize your youth while you have it. . . . Youth! Youth! There is absolutely nothing in the world but youth!'" (22–23). Youth is wasted, and not just on the young. It is a waste: it's wasted. It's an era of loss or prematurity, of disembodiment, of uncontainable passion and flashing insight. You can't realize your youth and have it too.

But Dorian is permitted to change, to develop a body for his cheeky extraordinariness, without getting himself into any age spots. Lord Henry: "'I am only ten years older than you are, and I am wrinkled, and worn, and yellow. You are really wonderful, Dorian. You have never looked more charming than you do tonight. You remind me of the day I saw you first. You were rather cheeky, very shy, and absolutely extraordinary. You have changed, of course, but not in appearance. . . .Youth! There is nothing like it. . . . They seem in front of me. Life has revealed to them her latest wonder'" (186). The wounds of midlifers are transformed, in some other wasted place, into teen wonders, the wonders of life still eternally and internally in front of you.

Dorian Gray realizes that his wish that his person never vary and that, in exchange, the portrait endure his hidden aging was his command right after he dismissed Sibyl Vane for the benefit of Lord Henry. He notices a change coming over the portrait: "The thing was horribly apparent" (79). The mutable image of his beautiful face recalls or resurrects "a parent": the traumatized, silent, doomed young mother who died the year following Dorian's birth. He in turn desires a change of heart, and is moved to write Sibyl a love letter of remorse and reconciliation. But it's too late. Lord Henry informs him that she killed herself, probably in simulcast with the portrait's horrible animation and change. "'Here is the first passionate love letter I have ever written in my life. Strange, that my first passionate love letter should have been addressed to a dead girl. Can they feel, I wonder, those white silent people we call the dead?'" (87). Where he wonders, that's where there is already a wound left by the silent dead. Basil touches the wound when he responds to the unaffected, aloof wonder with which Dorian has taken cognizance of Sibyl Vane's suicide: "'Why, man, there are horrors in store for that little white body of hers!'" (95). But the vanitas image Basil conjures up prompts in Dorian a comeback of identification with the one who did the dying for him: "'You only taught me to be vain'" (95). Two young women, mother and lover, fit a certain span of retention already shooting up Dorian's or Wilde's veins. As we will see, the spot Dorian is in with his portrait shares a certain isolation with Wilde's own crypt mission. In Dorian's case, the portrait must now be hidden away. Dorian chooses the old schoolroom that, he is reminded, "'hasn't been opened for nearly five years, not since his lordship died.' He winced at the mention of his grandfather. He had hateful memories of him" (103).

Dorian finds the perfect cover in which to wrap the portrait: "It had perhaps served often as a pall for the dead. Now it was to hide something that had a corruption of its own, worse than the corruption of death itself—something that would breed horrors and yet would never die. . . . And yet the thing would still live on. It would be always alive" (104). The thing, a parent, would always be alive. Dorian enters the forgotten room: "He had not entered the place for more than four years—not, indeed, since he had used it first as a playroom when he was a child, and then as a study when he grew somewhat older. It was a large, well-proportioned room, which had been specially built by the last Lord Kelso for the use of the little grandson whom, for his strange likeness to his mother, . . . he had always hated and desired to keep at a distance" (106). He reflects that back then, in "his lonely childhood," he had little thought, "in those dead days, of all that was in store for him" (107). There was even more in storage in him. On one side Dorian joins his young mother in putting between them and the hated Lord Kelso all the time in the word Dorian gave that he would remain young. But the eternal/internal portrait lives on, the image of conscience, in the hated image of the grandfather: "the thing upon the canvas was growing old. . . . There would be the wrinkled throat, the cold, blue-veined hands, the twisted body, that he remembered in the grandfather who had been so stern to him in his boyhood" (107).

Something else came into existence—or came back—when Wilde turned on the voice, which turned on the charm. This spirit-raising to the occasion of speaking is documented back to school days. One of Wilde's former schoolmates recalls: "The classics absorbed almost his whole attention in his later school days, and the flowing beauty of his oral translations in class . . . was a thing not easily to be forgotten" (in Harris, 17). What gets the rise out of Wilde is his oral delivery of translation. With translation we take liberties or give them death.

The Picture of Dorian Gray seals a deal between conversation and writing that, within the complete work, is displaced with regard to the mourning show of translation he put on or pulled over once (and for all) with *Salomé*. To this end, one must wrap a reading around the corpus, from its beginnings in conversation and journalism through *Dorian Gray* and the plays, including *Salomé*, which, more than just another Wilde play, is in fact a foreign corpus held together by translation, by that which lets it go. In the end we can recognize one case or crypt of melancholia closing or becoming more corpus-friendly on Wilde's side. His serious writing career begins with *Dorian Gray* in 1892. He's a literary sensation, the kind that crosses over into political headlines, and then in 1900 he's dead. Even this beginning that requires that a distinction be maintained between writing and journalism is shadowed by a Gray zone of journalism's metabolization via Wilde's prior publication of a work of nonfiction just prior to *Dorian Gray* with a title that seems in rehearsal for the subsequent novel. In "The Portrait of Mr. W. H." Wilde introduced (by popularizing what was original to other works and even to his own work) the thesis that by now is one of the great received notions in English departments, namely that Shakespeare addressed his sonnets not to his lady but to his lord. The territorial claim that journalism makes on the academy can take the form or forum of career theories, for which Wilde served right away as mascot figure.

Give or take a year, and Wilde enters the body of his lasting-name-bearing work through *The Picture of Dorian Gray*. But all the while he continued making deadlines, the undead lines he had already and always dead-icated to his sister Isola.

His sister Isola died at age ten when Oscar was thirteen years old. Oscar remembers: "My sister was a wonderful creature, so gay and high-spirited, 'embodied sunshine,' I used to call her" (in Harris, 210). The *Requiescat,* Wilde's first book of poems (one's first book of poems is still fit to be tied to the tension span of adolescent journalism) was dedicated to Isola, whom he likened to "a ray of sunshine dancing about the house" (in Harris, 32).

The following summary of Lady Wilde's grounds for leaving Dublin in order to double other departures, including son Oscar's move to London, which she followed in order to serve him there as Bohemian adjunct to his cult of personality, describes a mother who was done with her daughter's loss without ever having really started working on it: "The death of Sir William Wilde put an end to the family life in Dublin and set the survivors free. Lady Wilde had lost her husband and her only daughter in Merrion Square. The house was full of sad memories to her; she was eager to leave it all and settle in London" (Harris, 32). The interchangeability of dead spouse and dead child is the giveaway that we are praying here at a lip service.

Dr. Sir William Wilde, a famous oculist, was infamous in the year 1864 when he was charged with the rape of one of his patients about ten years earlier (around the time of Oscar Wilde's birth), when she was still a teenager, under the covers of anesthetized operations. In the interim, during the time in question of being posttraumatic, Dr. Wilde attended on her with gifts, visits, letters. The secret was so open and shut that it only went public when Lady Wilde demanded clarification, at first from the young woman's father, regarding the satires his daughter was writing about Dr. Wilde and the Wilde family. Lady Wilde, as always the last to know, thus only turned up the volume on the laugh track across which this other woman was tying down the Wilde family honor between the covers of fun-making journalism. Even so, the incident took shape only as an intact body of evidence that remained undisclosed. Oscar Wilde had no words to lose over his father. And yet their isolation from each other was another articulation of Isola's haunting influence on Wilde. The father's alleged and legendary transgressions went public in the year of Isola's death. His father had been stuck on youth. But in his relations with youths, Wilde was unconsciously positioned as always the younger one, still in latency, forever overwhelmed by the sexual difference three years can make between child and teenager.

Wilde was entrusted with the work of mourning or unmourning his sister, of commemorating her and impersonating her, replacing her and reanimating her. At the top of the mourning he tried to reproduce Isola and thus fold her into the family immortality plan. But he and his secondborn failed. Vyvyan, Wilde's second son, ended up as different from Cyril, the firstborn, as Oscar was from his older brother, Willie. But Cyril was the favorite, the only child. Vyvyan explains: "My arrival was a disappointment to my father, who wanted a daughter to remind him of his sister Isola" (in Schmidgall, 141–42). The second son arrived in Wilde's second position, which was one of double occupancy, and which Wilde had hoped to put to rest in one piece through replacement of his own duo dynamic by just one, the reproductive sum to which two can reduce themselves.

Wilde remained in isolation, both the kind associated with his same-sex pedagogical eros, the eros of his conversations and conversions, and the isolation of his improv brilliance, of his epigrammatic points at wit's end. These conditions of isolation were the same for any connection he also sought to make.

Salomé is the one work by Wilde you can love at first sight as a completely composed work, not the kind you just have to love in spite of its fault lines, the dated lines of witty conversation. It is the only work that appears free of vestiges of Wilde's journal entries for the prize in conversation.

Salomé appeared in 1893 in French, and in English translation in 1894. It was written in French in 1892, and was in full rehearsal with Sarah Bernhardt at London's Palace Theatre when the censor prohibited it. The English translation was written by the young man to whom Wilde dedicated the English edition, Lord Alfred Douglas, the object of Wilde's obsession and self-destruction. When Salomé becomes obsessed with John the Baptist, locked up in the cistern, she cries out: "Jokanaan, I am amorous of thy body! Thy body is white like the lilies of a field that the mower hath never mowed . . . The roses in the garden of the Queen of Arabia are not so white as thy body" (Wilde, *Salomé*). Two years later, from prison, Wilde would write to Lord Alfred Douglas in the same terms: "My sweet rose, my delicate flower, my lily of lilies . . . white narcissus in an unmown field" (in Schmidgall, 264).

Salomé was Wilde's scandalous work of identification, which was served up as transgression, translation, and transgression again. Wilde crossed over into the transvestite position when he had himself photographed in Salomé drag, gazing confessionally upon the severed head served up on a platter. In conversation with Harris, Wilde identified John the Baptist as a mascot of his own self-promotional relations with journalism:

> HARRIS: The prophet must proclaim himself, eh? And declare his own mission?
>
> WILDE: That's it. Every time my name is mentioned in a paper, I write at once to admit that I am the Messiah. Why is Pears' soap successful? Not because it is better or cheaper than any other soap, but because it is more strenuously puffed. The journalist is my "John the Baptist." (61)

But Wilde's artist-Messiah complex, advertised here as multimedia enterprise running unstoppably on the echoing and mirroring of the press, also packed between the lines that Wilde would sign a young woman's undead charge that shook the transparency of self-promotion until only the outer-corpus expertise of conversational improv skills could save the undertaking. But then there was the winning combo of identification and or as translation that gave the makeshift complex a rest.

Salomé opens with evocations both of the girl's heightened loveliness that night and of the moon's newly funereal aspect. The moon is like a woman rising from her tomb, like a dead woman seeking out the dead, come to raise or to bury them. The alternation between evocations of the girl's beauty tonight and the moon's dead body addresses one figure: one lovely dancer, the same one moving slowly like a dead woman. The moon watcher then warns the Salomé watcher: the latter looks at her too much, a transgression in this setting (not only for the subaltern but for the tetrarch too). But what defines this setting of the limits of seeing, bottom line, is that one must never witness the corpse.

The soldiers talk about how the Jews, unbelievable prospect, worship a god who cannot be seen. Then we hear the voice of John the Baptist. The Messiah, whose coming he advertises, will open the eyes of the blind, the ears of the deaf. The Messiah will make it all, all of it, visible and audible. The Messiah can even reanimate the dead. The tetrarch counters that he "will not permit the dead to be restored to life. It would be terrible if the dead came back" (Wilde, *Salomé*, 282).

The tetrarch has forbidden that anyone look upon the prophet who remains in the cistern, where his queen's first husband, the tetrarch's own brother, was kept and then strangled. But how could that be done and seen and witnessed? Only the death ring grants immunity (Wilde, *Salomé*, 267). Dorian Gray, at the end, can be identified only by his rings. There's a ring to that which enjoys death immunity, the ring of the voice.

Salomé orders the prophet brought up for viewing. She adores the prophet's moonlike whiteness, his chaste and silver body. But when he rejects her, listening instead to the beating of the wings of the angel of death, she sees the same body become leprous. This back and forth of mega ambivalence hits one desire and one part object: she must kiss his mouth. When Salomé enters this face-to-face relationship with the prophet, the young Syrian, who looks at her too much, must kill himself.

The tetrarch enters this space of suicide. To him the moon is a mad woman, looking for lovers. He slips in the suicide's blood. He sees the body. But then he dismisses suicide as ridiculous, as exempt therefore from his prohibition against viewing the dead. But in the space of mad love, Salomé will supply and embody the dead sight he would keep out of mind.

The tetrarch promises Salomé anything at all if she would only dance for him, take a chance with him. But Salomé demands that the tetrarch give her the prophet's head. His final counteroffer, jewelry, belongs to the register of the moon where beauty so soon becomes a dead woman: the pearls look like moons, the onyxes like the pupils of a dead woman. The realms of invisibility and visibility contaminate each other; in the jewels we can hear the Jews whose standing on stage is determined by their belief in the invisible, and who obey and listen to the unseen voice of their God.

Salomé consummates the face-to-face reunion over John the Baptist's dead body. The tetrarch withdraws, orders the torches extinguished; he can't look upon things that must never look back at him. In the darkness we attend to the voice of Salomé, the audio portion of her visual and corporeal consummation of love or hunger, in a kiss—a biting, starving kiss that drinks blood. There is a saving ring to this unseen voice. But then the dead woman's moonlight throws its high beam on Salomé's scene. The tetrarch shouts it out: "Kill that woman!" The guards crush her with their shields. The maxishield projection is pushed back upon a dead woman's body, and then and again that isolated part of Wilde could be addressed, as when he dressed up as Salomé, as being in transit, as letting go and then as let go—still as a feminine side to be sure, but without the eternal ten- or thirteen-year-old still inside.

At the close of *The Image of Dorian Gray in the Yellow Press,* Dorian/Veruschka in effect announces, like Hamlet nearing his end, that s/he is dead. When Hamlet declares "I am dead, Horatio. . . . Horatio, I am dead," he authorizes the transmission of his story to and through Horatio, whose suicide is deferred to this end. Hamlet doesn't try in the least to comply with the paternal ghost's revenge commandment. But with the appearance of the ghost, a new secular frontier of haunting and remembrance opens up, which he explores throughout the play, trying to steer his course at times with ruins or props left over from Christianity's former dominion, but organizing his itinerary at all times with regard to the mourning rights of the departed. *Hamlet* cannot transmit unless Hamlet identifies with the ghost. The internal feminine as principle of mourning (or unmourning) draws these transmissions and traditions onward.

6
THE ART OF EVERYDAY LIFE

Between *The Image of Dorian Gray in the Yellow Press* and *Johanna d'Arc of Mongolia*, Ottinger made three seemingly very different film works. There was the documentary titled *China. Die Künste—Der Alltag (China: The Arts—Everyday Life)*, which was released in 1985. This excursion into the documentary medium raised the question of a fundamental change in Ottinger's praxis, which Ottinger rejected, at least as fundamental: "Clear confrontations were always part of my film work. In *Ticket of No Return* fiction and reality are engaged in a dialogue on which the ladies 'Social Question,' 'Exact Statistics,' 'Human Reason' comment throughout, while from the very start the pressing request for 'reality' is broadcast over the airport loudspeakers" (in *Presseheft*, 23). "I don't think it is adequate to show things 'as they are' in a film. I don't think you can do that today. . . . In my film *Ticket of No Return*, quasi-documentary scenes alternate with extremely stylized ones. I introduced this technique because I realized that Berlin filmmakers often made the quasi-documentary with tremendously precise film content, but formally the film was lifeless. The public for these films has already developed a critical consciousness and watches a familiar reality on film—so familiar that the public doesn't see, or doesn't want to see, what goes on around them" (in Silberman). "In my previous films I have dealt with the themes of exoticism, minorities and their differing role behavior within their own cultures. Now I am interested in expanding this theme, in getting to know a 'real exoticism' in a foreign land and in a different culture. I am attempting to conduct with my camera a visual discourse on exoticism as a question of point of view" (in Edition Bischoff).

One newspaper review recognized how Ottinger's introduction of slow time and the connection/disconnection between self and other into the documentary genre went against the vision reflexes acquired with TV viewing (Pflaum).

Another review recognized the stakes of reading in the eyes of the beholder raised by Ottinger's China documentary: "It is as though one were traveling through the villages and cities oneself. . . . To understand this film at any level presupposes that one can fully trust one's own eyes" (Koch, "Demokratisierung"). While *Dorian Gray* analyzed the death drive along for the media control release of violence or identification, *China* gives us a hands-on intervention in our ways of seeing. When the audience thinks "art cinema," all defense and collaboration systems are go; but in the face of documentary film, in particular a nondidactic journey through an exotic culture, viewers readily consume, never expecting to gag on a piece of otherness, reality, or real time. Ottinger introduces documentary the way Karl Kraus in his day introduced hard-to-swallow bits of the news media under the cover of satire in order, if only for an instant, to stall the jump-cutting away from all first contact.

Another review celebrated the continuity shot between the documentary travelogue and Ottinger's many other journeys: "However, traveling and the yearning for foreign lands, long a forbidden terrain for women, have played a large role in Ulrike Ottinger's life and film work right from the start. In this regard she occupies a unique position among German women filmmakers. Already twelve years before [the China film], in an early experimental work, 'Laocoon and Sons,' Tabea Blumenschein, for many years Ottinger's coworker and lead actress, could be seen struggling, as Esmeralda del Rio in a widow's outfit, across the snow-covered tundra. Chinese women pirates from the 1930s inspired Ottinger later to make her pirate film 'Madame X—An Absolute Ruler' . . . With her first big China journey Ottinger realized how 'Chinese' her work had always been. Just as in the Chinese realm of signs, which signifies only itself, which declines meaning, so the secret of Ottinger's recognizably opulent image language lies not in what is unseen but entirely in the visible" (Feldvoß). Gertrud Koch captures the essence of Ottinger's way of seeing: "What makes her many-hours-long documentary film on China so fascinating is that the foreign gaze, which attaches itself to details, does not rush to present itself as metaphysical contemplation of the essence of an alien culture, but instead, completely self-consciously, gets a charge out of the fascinating appeal of the surface of phenomena" ("Demokratisierung").

Ottinger's aesthetic view sees only what's good, which is never blended with what's bad, or, in Ottinger's terms, what's uninteresting. This difference in esteeming that Nietzsche in his genealogy of morals calls noble is reversed in the so-called slave revolt in morals, which turns the uninteresting into the good, and what was at first contact good into evil, into demonized (or idealized) otherness. In the turnaround, the establishment of one decisive perspective, that of a determined political point, for example, makes an imperative out of blending

Photography studio.

differences beyond ambivalence into what's good enough, OK, the livable compromise. This corresponds in a sense to the oedipal phase of development: all that was strong in our affirmation of good, our self-love too, gets reversed and preserved as self-criticism, the evil energy of our self-rejection. In the oedipal phase, you learn to say No! and OK. In the pre-oedipal phase, which can be mapped onto the noble distinction Nietzsche made, you can only say Yes! Yes to the good breast, the breast that cannot be blended with the bad or missing breast. There is no good-enough or OK breast during this first bonding experience of the (maternal) body. This is not a situation of choosing. It is a matter of protocol, as always when encountering the other, the other marked moreover as foreign: first you take in as good and interesting what comes toward you aesthetically.

Ottinger's turn to the new form of documentary called attention to her camera work, which was, for all the reading, not seen as much in the art films. In a panel discussion at the London Institute for Contemporary Arts, Ottinger described her camera style in *China: The Arts—Everyday Life*: "In making the film, I was influenced by Chinese nature-painting: by the use of the scroll, which not only demands a different method of painting, but a different way of viewing—rolling

Stairway to the Taoist monastery in Qing Cheng Shan.

out the scroll, focusing in on details, wandering to and fro, viewing piecemeal. So if I was filming a market square, for example, I would pan very slowly and steadily across the square, rather than trying to capture the image in toto" (in Kuhn, 75). Janet Bergstrom comments: "The position of the camera throughout the film, whether still or moving, insists on a separation between the filmmaker and the sights that catch her eye, that she wants to collect and bring home.

The filmmaker is only integrated into the narrative as separate: we never see her image, but her presence as a foreigner is acknowledged by people's attitude toward the camera (seemingly curious, interested) and by the explanations that are given, at several points, of things we see" (46).

The title already announces that the politically charged encounter between West and East will be displaced onto what goes together in China, the arts and everyday life. As Bergstrom comments: "If drawing a parallel between life and art has been a common theme in the history of Western theater and cinema, in this film, we see the comparison made from the point of view of someone outside the conventions of the culture, where the system of signs employed can most easily be recognized as arbitrary" (48). According to Katharina Sykora's view of the film, "the manifold beauty in everyday life finds a logical supplement in Chinese high art. The traditional opera is a continuation and refinement of an aesthetically formed life" ("China"). Moreover, the incursions of Western labels and products do not appear to remain untouched by the transfer to China, at least this is how Ottinger's film sees and promotes the transformation of westernization. Bergstrom summarizes the social differences that come into play here as precisely not subsumed by a past to be retrieved or at best remembered: "The

Performers of the Beijing Opera.

The Chinese consume their press.

China that Ottinger shows us is an example in which social signs are not oppressive, especially because we see artistic expression in all facets of daily life. . . . This is the privilege of the visitor: to be able to see another culture selectively, in this instance as a 'real' example of unoppressed difference" (46). Bergstrom thus sees the visibility conditions of differentiation in Ottinger's *China* as directly part of the theme: "to show an analogy between the official arts and the routines of daily life which also have audiences" (47).

The film ends with a film projected outdoors, in the region occupied by the Bai minority. Sykora again: "The closing scene of the film shows the market place of a Bai mountain village. An open-air traveling cinema presents a film illustrating an episode of Bai history. All three elements in the title: *China* in the Western imagination, its *Everyday Life*, and its *Arts* are captured in a single image like this one, perhaps the most beautiful of the film" ("China"). As darkness begins to fall, a large sheet is lowered, and people take their places on benches facing the screen. A portable projector starts up and begins to show a film about the history of the Bai. The big landscape behind the spectacle on the screen is framed and reversed like in the nature opera in *The Image of Dorian Gray in the Yellow Press.*

Ottinger followed her China excursion with two short films in which she explored the relationship of the documentary impulse to her fictional films.

In 1986 Ottinger made the short *Superbia—Pride,* which was the first and opening part of a collaborative and commissioned project called *7 Women—7 Sins* involving seven women directors. In *Superbia,* the highly choreographed medieval-to-baroque triumphal procession switches tracks to include newsreel-type footage of military and mass formations from the recent past, thereby driving the art cinema float of pride in excess and representation into collision/collusion with another meglo realm, that of military-political power. Some reviewers indeed saw in this drift the charge of escalation of sinful pride into a collective delusional system that thus becomes another, more contemporary deadly sin. For example:

> It is a triumphal march and a dance of death. Superbia, Pride, advances to her marriage to the world, whip in one hand, mirror in the other. She, the first of the Christian-Medieval deadly sins and root of all the others, steers a cloud-carried vehicle, on which the society of the powerful is enthroned, a seven-headed Olympus of glittering carnival figures. World is decked out with countless signs of sin, which the director Ulrike Ottinger presents as a Baroque visual feast and rebus. Her excessive but exactly controlled imagination blends the wealth of images of the ages and cultures into a modern cinematic allegory. Ulrike Ottinger has not left the viewer without any support in this gripping spectacle. Whoever is more confused than enlightened by the allegorical allusions and image citations can grab hold of the inserted documentary footage. Military parades and mass processions are intercut with the progress of Superbia and appear to extend it into the political present, into a threatening reality. (Visarius)

While a continuity shot is established between the baroque pageant and the modern military parade, the documentary material, composed out of found archival newsreel footage, appears for all its recognizable content impenetrable, which is the power it holds over the word—over the world—the power of the unread, unread. The allegorical pageant in contrast, featuring "figures with dragon and peacock bodies, giraffe heads, tanks and whips," is already in the process (or procession) of reading. "The sense of the Christian Seven Deadly Sins is simplification, typologization of the world" (Kilb). The sense or direction here, however, is to "make these stereotypes manifold again, break open the routine patterns" (Kilb).

The final shot shows Ottinger's painting of the mask of Quetzalcoatl, the Aztec god of revenge. One's work, pursued and perfected against the resistance to/of the recycled word or world is, they say, the best revenge. Edith Sitwell speaks up in this way for the artist's necessary pride: "A *proper* pride is a necessity to an

The circus freaks celebrate on top of the giant gasometer on Fichtestrasse (in the context of Freak Orlando*).*

artist in any of the arts. Only this will save an artist's work and his private life from the attacks and intrusions made on these by those unfortunate persons who have been unable to attract attention to themselves except by incessant bawling" (21).

Superbia, as an all-out allegorical tableau or float passing in front of a painted seascape and through a found industrial setting, seemed a kind of essence of Ottinger's fiction films. In 1987 Ottinger made another short, *Usinimage,* in which she offered a remix of leftover and relic moments from the trilogy of fiction films. Scenes that had been composed within certain Berlin cityscapes were now intercut in *Usinimage* with documentary footage of the same industrial settings in contrast to their allegorical treatment in the art films. *Freak Orlando* alone, according to Ottinger, "contains an industrial architecture that spans around 150 years" (in Fischetti, "Ich glaube . . . ," 223). *Usinimage* thus shows the before and after pictures of Ottinger's cinematographic modifications of the Berlin locations. In both shorts, the new element of documentary evidence was being weighed and metabolized in Ottinger's allegorical image language.

7
JOHANNA'S ARK; OR, DOCUMENTARY FILM'S COVENANT WITH ART CINEMA

Leading up to and accompanying each of her films, Ottinger also works overtime as photographer, often trying out transformations of location as research for what the film includes in its moving medium. As could be seen at the 2000 show at the David Zwirner Gallery, the photographic work "in the context of *Ticket of No Return*" had been particularly diverse and even strikingly independent of the final screen product. One productive line of association in preparation for the film referred to the series of fantastic scenes through which the heroine (played by artist, costume designer, and once-upon-a-time Ottinger partner Tabea Blumenschein, who had also designed and starred in *Madame X*) tries out various possible professional personae for her one-way ego trip.

One of the role-playing scenes that Ottinger did not include in the film, in this case because it was too difficult to make movies in East Berlin at the time, involved a young East German woman, dressed in Soviet chic, who would visit the brand-new TV tower and drink herself silly in the restaurant that makes one complete turn per hour around its surround-a-view of Berlin. The photograph taken in the wall zone in West Berlin (which is interchangeable with the wall zone on the other side) in preparation for the TV tower fantasy was composed as in a fashion shoot. The young woman reading the newspaper *Soviet Woman* is caught in the panic-attack poise that marks moments of planning and onset of the ultimate abandonment of impulse control that dots each plot point. Blumenschein, an icon of German counterculture at the time, was out of pictures after *The Image of Dorian Gray in the Yellow Press* (the break she took from *Freak Orlando* lies at the center of the trilogy), thus setting the end of the trilogy as another break in Ottinger's oeuvre as a whole. But if we consider Ottinger's collaboration with

From inside the Trans-Siberian Express, Micky Katz (Peter Kern) purchases charms from a shaman during a station stop (in the context of Johanna d'Arc of Mongolia).

actress Delphine Seyrig, which commenced with *Freak Orlando,* as another point of cohesion, then *Johanna d'Arc of Mongolia* (1988), Seyrig's third and last film with Ottinger (which, to update Rosenbaum's 1983 call, is, above all, one of the masterpieces of world cinema) could be seen to overlap with the trilogy, indeed to function as its supplementary conclusion. It is no more or less a foreign body

Tabea Blumenschein as Soviet Woman in role-play in preparation for Ticket of No Return.

to or in the triad than is *Ticket of No Return,* which might also be characterized as a votive offering left at the opening of the subsequent journey into and through film. As another "end" of this journey, *Johanna d'Arc of Mongolia* openly juxtaposes the fictional film medium with that of documentary filmmaking. When Ottinger was projecting the trilogy in the original screenplay, research, and storyboard album for *Ticket of No Return* (subtitled in the album "a melodrama"),

Delphine Seyrig as Lady Windermere in her salon car on the Trans-Siberian Express.

Freak Orlando was not yet in the picture, and instead, following *The Image of Dorian Gray in the Yellow Press,* Ottinger was looking forward, in third place, to a film project titled "Joan geht nach New Orleans oder die Erbschaft" ("Joan Goes to New Orleans or the Legacy").

Ottinger owes her ability to make contact with the foreign other to a sensibility that is portrayed by Delphine Seyrig in the role of Lady Windermere in *Johanna d'Arc of Mongolia.* Frieda Grafe comments on this figure: "She is a globetrotter who with knowledge and fair play respects the social rules of the others as well as her own and teaches the wild tourists ethics: to see the forms and norms of interaction as such and not just consume them as reality. Myths, epics, legends may be folkloric, but they are also artifacts" ("Nomaden im Chattanooga choo-choo"). Seyrig, who in the latter part of her career made the feminist commitment of a threesome of performances to each of three women film directors, Chantal Akerman, Marguerite Duras, and Ottinger, was asked in an interview what it was like working for the third time with the director of *Johanna d'Arc of Mongolia*:

Working with her is always remarkable because she also stands behind the camera. That is very unusual. I never before worked with a director who also operates the camera. . . . Working with Ulrike is always very difficult, never comfortable, since she is working to achieve something very complicated: she succeeds in bringing together nature and artificiality into one perspective. The film has the effect for me of the result of fantasy about and love of a place where one has never been before. . . . It seems to me that Ulrike in her childhood was enthusiastic about Mongolia and that the place became for her magical. . . . When you watch *Johanna d'Arc* in this childlike mood, it becomes impossible to claim that one doesn't follow the film. That's like saying, "I don't understand Snow White or I don't understand Cinderella." This is Ulrike's fairy tale, a recollection of her childhood fantasy, a reminiscence of something she never saw but certainly fully imagined. Then she traveled there and saw the real place. Thus the mixture of her fantasy and reality is omnipresent in the film. (in Midding, 14)

The seeming split down the middle of *Johanna d'Arc of Mongolia* between the artifice of film set and scrolling panorama that contains the train ride across the tundra and the on-location account of the sojourn of the abducted train passengers in the wide-open spaces of the Mongolian tribe's domain does not subsume or organize all the differences Ottinger set into play. Just as the title of the film speaks in three tongues, so the European train of association barely contains itself but already bursts out into celebration of radically diverse and overlapping cultures well before the train has been stopped in its tracks and the "documentary" section has opened up in its place. *Johanna d'Arc of Mongolia* serves as a reminder that it is impossible or pointless to separate Ottinger's fictional films from her documentaries (which would by now seem to comprise, as though *Johanna d'Arc of Mongolia* served as a model, the second half of her oeuvre). The New York show of Ottinger's photographs titled "Stills" gave evidence instead of the palimpsestuously perverse "context" of her ongoing oeuvre.

In time, then, for the fall of the wall, Ottinger reintroduced with *Johanna d'Arc of Mongolia* her two styles, allegorical art cinema and documentary of ready-made differences as split down the middle but at the same time impure in their separation and nonintegratable and nonassimilable in their differentiation inside and out. It is a film in which "every sort of tension exists, sexual, cultural, generational and stylistic" (Benson). Or as Grafe puts it: "The whole film is twin formation, saturated with doublings, repetitions, digressions that resemble each other, endless mirrorings. The images have a wrinkle, which is conveyed through the stories. A delegate tells the Mongolian princess Ulun Iga her own story. Or indeed the hunting ritual through which the entire film gets turned inside out like a glove. It exceeds itself. The quarry is namely, though one doesn't see it, the young girl Giovanna. At the end the film bites itself in the tail, and the Transmongolian moves Westward. Among those traveling back we find Ulun Iga, too, the Saint Joan of the title, who arranged the train ambush and thereby brought the traveling ladies into contact with genuine adventures. She had only been spending her summer vacation, as she does every year, in her homeland. Thus reflecting light falls from the Mongolian world onto Western customs and rituals, and cinema sees and advertises itself as the instrument for examining and as the agency of old and new myth formations" ("Nomaden im Chattanooga choo-choo").

The film's title in three languages gets its sense across without single-language translation. The title is our ticket to an older Europe celebrated as preserved onboard the Trans-Siberian Express. *"Johanna d'Arc of Mongolia* is the name of a legend which the film makes audible and visible in various ways. I like to begin with great, emotionally charged names in order to bring the seemingly familiar into new and surprising contexts. Usually, it isn't the things that are completely and utterly foreign, but rather those with which we seem to have some connection, that can unleash an incredible sense of strangeness when suddenly transported to another context. Hence also the name's mixture of languages, which hints at the multilingualism of cultures and resists easy appropriation" (Ottinger, in *Presseheft*, 12).

Ottinger's dedication to cultural transfer is all aboard the Trans-Siberian Express, which also commemorates a certain origin of filmmaking. The shock of a railway accident led to the administration of one of the first inoculative shots given film audiences. The train was the first techno means of transport to travel the dotted line between trauma and entertainment. The roller-coaster thrill of transport placed us in a position of preparedness for a train wreck, which was, before World War I, the most common exciting cause of many brands of hysteria or traumatic neurosis (like "railway spine") for men and women alike. The early histories of cinema and of psychoanalysis wore training wheels. Freud suffered from train phobia that dated back to a train trip he took in early childhood (around the time of his younger brother Julius's departure), during which he shared a compartment with his mother (and with her body undressing at such close quarters). He looked out the window at the industrial landscape they were passing through and knew they were in the underworld. But the train also entered his work of analogy (together with the telephone) when it came time to describe the special kind of association and listening characteristic of the analytic session. Freud gives a demo of how to get the patient to free associate: "Act as though, for instance, you were a traveler sitting next to the window of a railway carriage and describing to someone inside the carriage the changing views which you see outside" ("On Beginning the Treatment," *SE* 12: 135). Thus the view of the rolling landscape through the window and via the train's motion let roll a certain techno vision shared by train passengers, moviegoers, and patients in analysis. They were now all in position to see relations between conscious thought and the unconscious. In other words, by taking their seat by the train window, which cuts and splices together frames of the passing view, what they see pass by passes through the different time zone or frame of media. *China: The Arts—Everyday Life,* which commences in a large train station, had already extended the invitation to see together with the camera the foreign spaces awaiting us once we were onboard. Together with the crowds waiting for transportation to distant places, we watch the trains pass by. The film's titles, the "stations" of our itinerary, are given in this setting of departure. Here too the reference to cinematic viewing as train-borne, in history and techno conditioning, is all aboard. The final station—remember, the film's self-reference, interiority, and its outer limit—is the outdoor screening of an epic film. "Perhaps one could say that *China* is the encounter with the foreign other and *Johanna* is the staging, the mise-en-scène of this encounter. But to the extent that both encounters actually take place, a 'new realism' arises, which has not been arbitrarily invented, but rather rests on extensive groundwork—on research, experiences, preliminary studies, all those procedures that the preparation of such a project entails. What I mean is: the freeing of enough spaces so the encounter really can take place" (Ottinger, in *Presseheft,* 21).

In *Johanna d'Arc of Mongolia* we begin our trip in Europe in a completely self-contained and artificial train interior. In the opening sequence, Lady Windermere is seated in her exclusive train compartment. As the camera pans over the props and accessories of chinoiserie adorning the traveling salon, the lady comments on the repetition and rehearsal marking the journey eastward:

> In 1581 Yermak Timofeyevich traverses the Urals with his ferocious Cossacks and sees for the first time . . . it's always the first time . . . things read—the imagination—the confrontation with reality . . . Must imagination shun the encounter with reality, or are they enamored of each other? Can they form an alliance? Does the encounter transform them? Do they exchange roles? It's always the first time . . . Yermak Timofeyevich crosses this border line dividing Europe and Asia and beholds for the first time the unending verdant expanses . . . the myth of the green void . . . Once only the bravest of the Chinese travelers and merchants ventured this far . . . into the utter void. With ingenious means they placed signs in the land of the void. An initial attempt to tame the wilderness with the aid of cultivated nature. They made clearings in the coniferous forests in the shape of huge written signs, which

Soviet station stop seen from the Trans-Siberian Express.

they then planted with oaks. The written signs altered their colors with the changing seasons and could be seen from a great distance . . . The attempt to place a sign in the void, a mark . . . here the fears of the travelers, whom the wind otherwise carried unchecked across the endless green plains of the taiga, were allayed for a moment . . . and now, much more than a sign, this line leading directly through the slumbering wilderness. As simply and easily as you can travel with your finger across the map from Europe to Asia, the Trans-Siberian follows this line.

Then, as we cross over into another compartment, the running commentary hands the baton to a German schoolteacher, who reads aloud the entry for the Trans-Siberian Express in her guidebook. These running, rolling transfers, through which the main figures continue to be introduced, comprise an overture to Europe as a total work of art on techno tracks. Ottinger describes this operatic opening setup of the train travelers for their first encounter with what lies beyond the constructed sets: "I play with many contexts and various narrative forms. The classic introduction of the four Western protagonists, who, as it were, sing their arias on the stage, observes the unities of place, time and action. The well-organized interior makes of nature an artificial exterior. But while the tundra rolls past the windows on a painted scroll, the people inside nevertheless hear its Siren call. Unaccustomed stories penetrate the familiar surroundings, which in the end are invaded by an exterior oblivious to all this domestication. In the grasslands, under the open sky, epic singers introduce Mongolian time" (in *Presseheft,* 26).

At one point, the German schoolteacher traveling across Siberia ponders, recites, remembers a line—"The steel worm crawled further and further along through the Siberian forests"—and the images contained in the motion-picture machine, the train, begin to derealize or surrealize. But the fantasy that begins to take over, to overflow the margins of its containment, is also the beginning of a new realism. Because the culture these travelers carry is not as assimilated as advertised. In this Schreberesque opera, the melting pot or plot spills over as an endlessly self-reflexive relay of unassimilable differences. If this film's consumption is "the occasion for a fabulous three-course blend of myth, spectacular visions of an ancient land and frisky song-and-dance routines" (Stone), then this mealtime, staggered as courses, also comes around the blend to encounter combos beamed back from another era, out of fashion, out of time. "It is a film that moves Eastward with figures we haven't seen on the screen since the 1930s. This

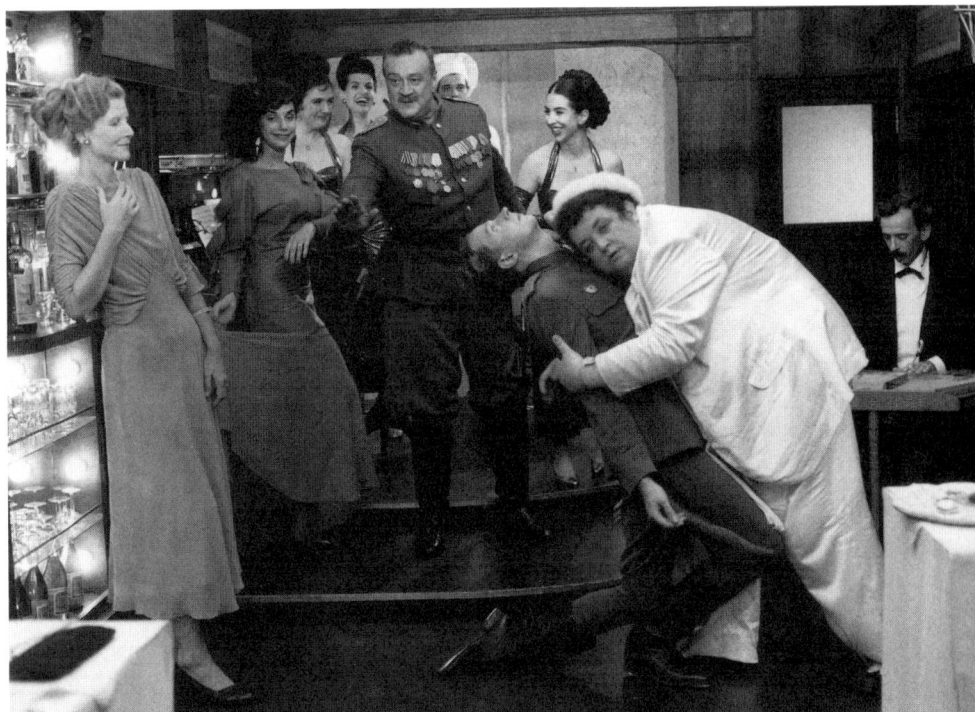

Micky Katz dancing with the Soviet general's aide: "Bei Mir Bist Du Schön."

The fiction film passengers join the documentary ensemble.

direction was taboo as image resource. Who dared to dress up a Soviet General with a Lermontovian or Pushkinian aura and focus on his medals as decorative ornament? No one thought of imagining an outdated musical group of Georgian ladies. No Broadway musical star has traveled on the Trans-Siberian since 1945, but this Fanny Ziegfeld is a fitting image, for the iron curtain is a theater term, and for a long time it was permeable only for cultural exchange" (Grafe, "Nomaden im Chattanooga choo-choo").

One of Ottinger's signature provocations is a certain inflationary performance of stereotypes of subcultural difference: "For people to know what you're up to, you have to exaggerate" (in "Piratinnen am Bodensee"). *Madame X: An Absolute Ruler* both addresses "all women" and dresses up the women in the film, strapped to the laugh track, as outrageous stereotypes either lifted or reclaimed from misogynist projections. In *Freak Orlando* Ottinger conflates the S-M look that gay subculture changes into (not only but also in the projection booth of the other) with the persecutory forces conjoining normative psychiatry, the Inquisition, and fascism. This fashionism association was described by one reviewer as evidence of the limitations of Ottinger's "historical memory." But then the critic gets the point: "There is no 'politically correct' space in these films. Ottinger's aesthetic is the grotesque; she pushes stereotypes to their limits—and then some." But then the critic projects onto the filmmaker the admission of a pleasure costing the "price of submission" (Dargis, 80). But one critic's concern is another critic's affirmation. Referring to a scene from *Johanna d'Arc of Mongolia,* in which Bronski too has to acknowledge that stereotypes could be seen as pushed to grotesque limits without political conscience, a second opinion can still be given: "Early in the film, Mickey Katz, the Kalinka Sisters, a Russian general and his aide and Fanny Ziegfeld all do renditions of 'Bei Mir Bist Du Schön'— each in their own musical dialect: Yiddish theater, Broadway musical, German beer hall, faux Andrews Sisters cum Balkan pop. The visual grace of the scene is complimented beautifully by its sheer musical elation; a cross-cultural meeting of the spirit and the voice that moves our minds as it stirs the senses. It is here that Ottinger sets the stage for the cultural meetings that are to happen later— and that concern the more profound issues of ethnic and national identity and love. *Joan of Arc* is a triumph not only of political filmmaking but of the idea that art and politics are not—cannot—be separated from the experience of pleasure" (Bronski, 11).

Even before the film opens wide for the documentary encounter with the foreign other, before the European travelers are held up by the Mongolian princess and her Amazon band, the travelers have already begun raising to consciousness the encounter with their own culture, from the museum in which they travel to the nomadic margins cutting across so-called Western civilization, which they end up sharing with their Mongolian captors. Again in an interview, Ottinger approaches this trans-, the big between, in the course of answering anticipated criticisms of exoticism or orientalism: "It was not my intention to create exotic images. The film is concerned, rather, with the transport of culture. If exoticisms arise in the process, they are never identified with 'the foreign' per se but rather with the unsuccessful encounter with the foreign other. I don't mean that only negatively, because the results are sometimes interesting. My film is devoted not to exoticism but rather to nomads. These can be Mongols, but also jobseekers, Jewish intellectuals and artists, refugees, those traveling for edification or adventure. I see the route of the Trans-Siberian . . . as a sort of guest-book of cultures, in which the most various influences leave their mark. The theme of the film is the infectiousness of nomadic ideas" (in *Presseheft,* 24).

Ottinger rejects the view mastery of her film as split down the middle. This split would be there only if she had in fact constructed a mirror to maintain background-foreground, margin-center distinctions. That is how the exotic other has been used—as foil for the main story, the story, say, of a group of European travelers. *Foil* covers mirror and duel in English (and in *Hamlet*); the cognate term in German, *Folie,* means mirror when it doesn't mean, in French, madness.

If her film belonged entirely to the line of the reading finger, laying tracks from point A to point B across the endless tundra, then, too, the train movie would end where the Mongolian docudrama took over. If the film does fall into two, it's not at one point or line, not once and for all time. Instead the breakup of a unity of vision or culture occurs moment by moment in each moment. The orient is always at its core caught up with the flux of orientation—for example, in the sense that the orient is always what provides projective orientation, whereby linear culture marks its progress. But all the wrong orientations can double as projective targets, whereby what falls apart in oneself is dumped as absolute difference from oneself (and one's kind) onto some marginalized other.

The traumatic break is also history. The old Europe that's all aboard was targeted as a goner in the course of national socialist all-out attempts to get it back on line, on the direct line to nothingness. Mickey Katz, the great collage and montage artist of consumer spectacle, was not once but a thousand times the wrong orientation in the midst of the linemen closing ranks. Ottinger thus also sets up the non-European Orient as portal to the outside chance of encountering the other in this life, and not only in the ghost appearances of old Europe replaying in the grooves or graves of the history of trauma's stuck record.

As with the train, which can be taken to an origin in trauma, so with the reference to Jeanne d'Arc, who for all her efforts and visions did, after all, get the torch, Ottinger manages to disencumber the legibility of these histories of the burden of traumatic or victim identifications, which can often block, as retraumatization, the encounter for which free spaces are needed, according to Ottinger. A sense of adventure draws her onward, but always on or in the same tracks of still-legible histories of violence. The Western women end up enchanted by the sojourn resulting from the disturbing event of their kidnapping. The German schoolteacher who remains behind, stuck on identificatory redemption in the foreign land, a mere reversal of her earlier projective rejection of the same setting, serves as a contrast figure that gives the measure of the film's overall circumvention of exoticism. Koch elaborates: "Every onset of exoticism is broken on the one hand through the documentary gesture, on the other hand through the reconstruction of the aesthetically autonomous aspects of the foreign culture. The trip into the past thus never leaves the modern era, but rather rescues it as way of seeing. The fascination with all that was seen abroad is taken along as new experience on the return trip. Of course the schoolteacher on an educational trip stays behind with her delusion of religious awakening, stuck in the tracks of mystical fascination" ("Auf Reisen gehen").

The fabulous story of the princess is finally undermined or rather folded back inside the frame of artifice by the end of the film, when all but one companion

Micky Katz gives instruction in culinary collage and montage.

(whose place is taken by surprise when the princess makes a belated arrival and dramatic boarding) take the return train trip back to Europe. The basic story—now "a delirious parody of 19th-century travel literature" (Hoberman, cited in Hartl), now a kind of road movie but this time for women only, which could also be read as a feminist lesbian fairy tale—mixes the Jeanne d'Arc myth of the heroic maiden with Mongolian epic celebrations of warrior women. According to a 1989 review in the *Bay Area Reporter*, it's not that the film ever gets to the "lesbian part": "There is a lesbian undercurrent—allusion—throughout the movie, which is never really overt. It can be described best as a sensibility that informs the work, that is part of its fabric, without being overt; standing out and being pointed to" (Barnes). Or in the most innocent terms: "What's fascinating in her often comic, West-meets-East clash of cultures is that the women performers eventually establish a common bond" (Warren). In Ottinger's films, same-sex relations, like any form of minority existence, are not scandalous, not a problem, but simply facts of life that are already in play. Her films thus open up a space that Ottinger doesn't find particularly available offscreen: "For me it is a highly contemporary theme, that on the one side society tries to exclude and push to the side whatever doesn't have majority status, and that on the other side there is the countermovement of the minorities to withdraw into a voluntary ghetto. I find this isolation problematic, because dialogue and exchange, outside the aspiration to bring about assimilation, remain next to impossible" (in Fischetti, "Ich glaube . . . ," 229).

Lady Windermere refers in name to Wilde's happy ending of coupling for the oedipal stage. But the triangulation represented by the lady in *Johanna d'Arc of Mongolia* guarantees instead that there is not a reproductive boner in this whole utopia to pick (utopia in the sense Herbert Marcuse developed, along the lines of Freud's theory of perversion). Instead we are presented the spectacular "couplings" of montage and collage. Mickey Katz asks the head waiter in the dining car before the assembled cast aboard (and directs his rhetorical question over the screen heads to the film audience): "Do you in fact command the techniques of collage, montage, mosaic, painting, sculpture, color composition, and taxidermy?" These are the birds and bees of the paradise on wheels, of the moving camera, which realizes itself as open wide and "on earth" in the Mongolian document.

The myth of the Amazon tells the story of the good and bad breasts of the pre-oedipal mother, the primal maternal relation, Freud says, to which a daughter, including the internal daughter, remains closely attached. In oedipal zones, one must melt down the distinction between good and bad into the background static of tolerable ambivalence. In the pre-oedipal zone, the bad breast must be cut off. This isn't castration, however. It's rather more about the maternal focus, pre the big pictures or ideas of Oedipus, on a particular life and body to be protected and preserved. The cut-away breast frees up space for the Amazon's encounter with what's out there within the taut span of her bow and arrow.

8
REAL TIME TRAVEL

I was pleased to welcome Ulrike Ottinger to the University of California, Santa Barbara, back in October 1992. She was appointed Regents' Lecturer and was in attendance at the screenings of seven of her films, beginning (out of chronological sync) with *Freak Orlando* and closing with the U.S. pre-premiere of her newest film, *Taiga*.

Between *Freak Orlando* and *Taiga* there are exemplary similarities that tell us something about the style or strategy of Ottinger's work. In both the freaks movie and the Mongolian-shaman-cult film, there's the interest in those traveling or nomadic cultures that to this day take us to the margin, which is the edge where reality begins.

A special relationship to reality, that is, to the other, that is, to the future, is what Ottinger's cinema is all about. And that's why with Ottinger's work we're at movies that take the time it takes to encounter the other. In other words: what gives *Taiga* its staying power is the real or epic time taken to record shamanistic séances and other rituals coming from no standard time zones and no received place.

The slow time Ottinger takes to approach the other (or, in other words, reality) can be followed as diplomacy already throughout *Freak Orlando*. A premise of this film is that the tolerant and integrationist manner in which we look past or overlook the freaks among us is way worse than what their former freak status gave them: even under the fire of persecution and exploitation, they had access, as sideshow attractions, to the center stage of visibility (and that means to some kind of inclusion of their otherness). So, in *Freak Orlando*, we watch the primal time combo of inquisition, fascism, and normative psychiatry working overtime to assimilate—that is, to efface—the freak, the other, reality, the future (you name it). But the film's resistance is the time it restores to us to read

(above) Scene inspired by Goya's Caprichos.
(below) Reindeer nomads.

complex combinations of images beamed up from many different time zones and levels of meaning.

Ottinger works the margins, which gives her the edge. The multiculturalism of her films is the kind that shoots up every identity, sexual or otherwise, with a megadose of difference. There is no other filmmaker.

LAURENCE RICKELS: So how did it come to this focus in your work (and I mean not only the Mongolian movies but also the China film and *Madame X*)? How did you start out on this journey to the other?

ULRIKE OTTINGER: I think the early childhood period I spent locked up in Germany instilled in me a love of travel, perhaps transferred over from my mother whose attempts to escape the Nazi terror failed. And so I threw myself into the reading of travelogues—which I really consumed rather than read—and in that pileup of texts there were many devoted to Asia, a far-off place that was truly foreign and other. That's one explanation. There's no doubt an unconscious motivation there too. But in any event there was a strong fascination that grew and developed: wherever I went on my travels, I devoted considerable time to the Asian collections in all the local museums, often in the company of my mother, which gave the foundation to my early fascination. There was a time when I wanted to become an ethnologist, and I wavered for a long while between the choice of an artistic or a scientific career. It has taken a long time to connect these two approaches in my work.

LR: Your claims to ethnology have been substantiated by your new documentary, *Taiga,* which went where no professional ethnologist or ethnographer had gone before. And I see your achievement in the extended contest of visibility versus invisibility: in *Freak Orlando* what is crucial is that something be made visible again. The other problem (it's really the same problem) is that others are reduced to sheer visibility, as so often happens in documentary films. So I'd be interested to hear a bit about the diplomacy you adopted in filming *Taiga* to make these others visible without reducing them to visibility, without making them disappear.

UO: You obviously can't just come out shooting. Rather lengthy greeting rituals must be observed because the guest, in an area where there are so few guests from very far away, has a completely different meaning. Only after you have provisionally satisfied their curiosity about where you come from do they ask what it is you're looking for or hoping to accomplish in their lands. I tried to explain my wish, which was to record a way of life that no longer exists in the place where I've come from, in order to show the document to the people back

Reindeer nomad in Mongolia.

home, who are very interested in nomadic ways. At first this puzzled them, but then they thought, yes, indeed, we too would be interested to know how your people live, and this brought up another wave of questions.

It's important that the guest contributes to the entertainment of the people there, and in this way one can even become quite popular. I was able to benefit from the Mongolians' fervent wish to be photographed. Photographs are sought after and are placed on the family altars along with the relics. Because I knew about all this from my many trips to Mongolia in preparation for *Taiga* and also for *Johanna d'Arc of Mongolia*, I brought along a Polaroid camera. Word got around to such an extent that I became something of an official family photographer for the Mongolians. When I visited one yurt, people came from all around by horse or motorcycle dressed up in their glorious festive costumes to get their pictures taken. It meant a great deal to them. And it made my work that much easier. At first, however, they did not quite understand why I wanted to film their everyday activities, and so I explained to them that our everyday life was different from theirs, and that this was why this record was of such interest for us. (They themselves prefer to be photographed during the ceremonial exchange of tobacco tins, when they are dressed up in their festive robes.) Once they realized that I was interested in their everyday life, they took it for granted that I would also be interested in their religious ways, since they don't separate the one from the other. I didn't even have to ask to film the shamanistic séances, they just told me to go ahead, and they were interested in seeing the sequence afterward because the shamaness, who goes into a trance during the séance, doesn't remember what was said; she has a recollection of whether the trip went well or not, but not of various details. Since we could not develop the films there, we were only able to let them listen to the soundtracks, which fascinated them. The shamaness helped us translate the Tuwinian parts, and this process gave me the opportunity to ask questions about otherwise unspeakable matters.

LR: The Polaroid as your special opener seems to have uncanny-proofed your techno presence for them.

UO: They have a very precise way of seeing. The Polaroid, which was indeed brand new to them, was given the description that everyone finally picked up and used as its name: "the camera that shits pictures."

LR: The so-called primitives in Freud's lineup of exemplary perspectives indeed have a precise way of picking up on the technological object and of receiving it within their own readiness for such long-distance relations. I wonder if there are examples of a Mongolian cultic reception of technology perhaps comparable to the Melanesian cargo cult. I'd imagine that shamanism would be a place where a techno reception was already in place.

UO: During the shooting of my first Mongolian film, I went to a little settlement in the middle of the grasslands, a few small houses where the Chinese lived and traded and to which the Mongolians traveled from far away—from the steppes or from the desert—to buy a few essential products. In this town, a tiny department store had recently been built. It was nothing more than two small rooms—one on top of the other. This two-floor house was such a hit with the Mongolians that they came from all over just to see it. The most important instrument for the Mongolians is the two-stringed horse-head fiddle, and on the resonators of these fiddles some of them built up tiny wooden replicas of this department store, which then became a part of their narrative store, their history. Another example: a shamaness fashioned out of wood a small pocket calculator, which she no doubt first saw in the so-called department store being used by a Chinese merchant. She would press the wooden keys, then look thoughtfully into the skies, then look at the calculator again, then type some more. Finally she would report an interesting answer, as though reading it off this instrument, in the course of performing prophecy.

Portrait of woman cooking in the yurt.

LR: I also remember the tour of the telegraph office in *Taiga*, which was less a technological site than it was, due to its complete lack of functionality, a cultic place.

UO: At some time in the beginning, surely, the telegraph did work. But over time what fell apart couldn't be repaired. But today one has the sense that the telegraph operator repeats the individual words a thousand times like prayers or litanies in the hope that they will arrive at their destination. It has the interesting side effect that everyone listens in on what the telegraph operator is repetitively trying to get across.

LR: In the United States, séance occultism arose or came back at the time of the telegraph's invention. So I wonder if the telegraph, for example, introduced any new improvements into shamanism.

UO: Shamanism is of course the oldest recorded religion and has, as such, a measure of stability, and yet it isn't ossified but vital. For the Mongolians every initiation must be marked by a séance. For example, when Mongolians were first drafted into the Chinese or Russian army, or now whenever a family member moves to the city or when any other important change occurs, it must be mediated by a séance.

LR: Were the Mongolian shamanesses herbal doctors and midwives, like the shamanskas in Europe?

UO: They seem to me to perform more of a psychic service: the healings are transmitted in a séance through the interrogation of the spirits. There's a great concern with the causes of the presenting disorder. That's why the whole family is also often present (though this of course depends on the nature of the complaint). Sometimes entire clans attend the largest séances. Séances always take place at night, start around midnight, but must end before daylight: otherwise the shamaness might not return from her journey. They see her as always at risk of remaining in the other world and of no longer being able to call the spirits. To this end they have developed interesting mechanisms for bringing back a shamaness in ecstasy. When one of the shamanesses I witnessed fell into a trance and then passed out, and the usual incense couldn't revive her, her assistant brought out a miniature bow and arrow and shot the arrow to bring her back from the trip. Sometimes regular-sized arrows wrapped in ceremonial veils are shot into the sky or simply stabbed upward to indicate they are being sent after her.

LR: In *Johanna d'Arc of Mongolia,* on the way from Europe to Mongolia, Yiddish plays a certain role, which brings us to your future project, "Diamond Dance," in which the diamond trade presents a kind of primal structuring of long distance. Will this film bring into ethnological focus a way in which the Jewish people have been rendered uncanny through their close association with what can already be called technology?

UO: In *Johanna d'Arc* I was concerned with the transfer of culture and the interesting pathways cultural ideas travel. There are only these mixtures and no separate and pure cultures. I've always been intrigued by this nomadization of cultural ideas—the obscure ways they take and flourish at one particular intersection and not at another. In my films I've often tried to re-create such a transfer. The project titled "Diamond Dance" will travel the old trade routes that were the precondition for this nomadization of all highly charged cultural ideas. The Jewish people in particular, who, by force, of course, nomadized over and over again along the trade routes, acquired a certain travel know-how. The diamond business is perhaps one of the oldest ones around; we know from Maimonides, the Talmud scholar and interpreter, that his brother was a diamond trader who at one point did not return from a business trip to India, where he presumably died. In the course of my research for this film project, it has become increasingly clear to me that the Jews, who have so often been nomadic because they had to be or for business reasons, nevertheless retained through their religion a strong long-distance connection, wherever they were in the diaspora. At each location or stopover in the long-distance network, there was a rabbi who was a person of trust; so, when the Colmar rabbi wrote the Constantinople rabbi to ask for help in some special mission, the assistance was granted and fulfilled in accordance with the ancient moral laws of the Old Testament and the Talmud. This incredibly correct, that is, efficient running of business across great distances was the occasion again and again, from the Middle Ages onward, of this defamation, this phantasm, of Judaism as the front for some international conspiracy. That's what is so interesting about the diamond business to this day, namely, that transactions involving millions are carried out against the collateral of a handshake—of a belief and trust—that still conforms to the moral codex of the Old Testament.

LR: The last scenes of this projected film show a condensation or intersection of diverse problems that might seem out of place together if it weren't for your having juxtaposed them. Everything involved in the diamond business over time comes into our time as a connection linking traumatic neurosis through Nazi persecution, psychoanalysis, and AIDS.

UO: The connections are clear, but at the same time the problem remains how to make them visible in an adequate artistic juxtaposition or form. One problem is that these connections have a long history of powerful connotations, including a long history of misunderstandings.

LR: My free association is that with AIDS it has become clear that we, together with our machines, form one body. There are no boundaries any longer; everything is given over to long-distance live transmissions. The whole world is no longer watching; now it's contracting AIDS.

UO: Yes, it drives home our utter unprotectedness. I've seen, for example, several AIDS films over the years and I found them sentimental; they were simply bad films that, in addition, did not do justice to the subject, one that does not tolerate sentimentality. So I tried to bring current fears together with the medieval ones in order to show the rhymes between the different anxieties that have plagued mankind under such diverse conditions over and over again. That's why Jewish history was important here: anti-Semitism has emerged everywhere again, and I thought this eternal return of persecution and distrust of the Jew needed to be brought into contact with the AIDS crisis, where all the medieval prejudices one assumed had long ago been overcome, remain virulent—are back—in the most evil and conventional manner imaginable. You can't do this work of juxtaposition in a Hollywood plot, which excludes everything that is really significant and not readily decidable.

LR: That's what thinking is: it means juxtaposing what comes your way without being phobic about it.

STATIONS

Unlike the determined narrative point of view the camera upheld in *China: The Arts—Everyday Life,* and unlike the movement out from a major city into the country and its margins that organized its travelogue, in *Taiga* the narrative perspective (which coincides with that of the camera and thus with that of the filmmaker behind the camera) is in flux, moving from one unknown wide-open space to yet another, because, precisely, the perspective is en route with the nomads. The "documentary" stay in Mongolia in *Johanna d'Arc* was, of course, already recollection and completely fictional. *Taiga* strays into this border zone: the personal identification between camera and filmmaker, between ethnographer and artist, blurs the boundary between document and fiction. *Taiga* follows the travels of two nomadic peoples and their journey to their own histories. Ottinger's own curiosity and the curiosity that her camera excites in her hosts lead to reflections on their history, the way things were, what has been lost, forgotten, changed. "Old shaman priestesses tell the story of their calling, shoemakers and metal workers talk willingly and proudly about their trade. Image and identity have come together again. Look over here, that's how we are, the Mongolians seem to be saying, in our everyday life and in our dreams, in the pictures and in reality" (Schifferle).

The nine hours, which in the logic of dream and fantasy translate into the nine months of pregnancy, for example, and which might thereby stand in for twenty-four hours, indeed for every measure of real time, mean quite simply that *Taiga* remains commensurate with dimensions of time and space. But as my formulation tries to underscore, the real time Ottinger traverses also makes room for the moment of time travel. "In the most effective scenes, conventional camera momentum simply halts and the camera dwells on the extended moment" (Holden).

In *Taiga*, Ottinger seeks therefore to realize the art form of stations, which she was up on through her research on nomadic cultures, in the nomadic setting not only of Mongolia itself but also of the Mongolian epic. (Even in the telling of time, we are after all not so far removed from *Freak Orlando*.) "One of the oldest dramaturgies is that of the stations. It is profoundly bound up with the earliest experiences of mankind. Nomads followed herds through grasslands, forests, mountains, chasms, steppes, deserts, seas, rivers, tundra and taiga. But not only the landscapes changed with their very different challenges, but also the seasons. . . . In the summer the epics were narrated out of joy in community and the well-supplied living conditions, and in winter in order to bear up better under hard times. These epics followed the laws of a very subtly thought-through and at the same time amazingly simple dramaturgy. It had a structural skeleton that could be filled with past—the history of the group as known by all—with future—the wishes, hopes, anxieties—and with present" (Ottinger, "Cinema of Stations," 56–57).

But this faraway other world's "utopian imperative" (Geldner) exists alongside the encroachment of modernization that has already preceded Ottinger's encounter. "We meet photographers, whose souvenir pictures already decorate the walls of the yurts, children who ride on carrousel animals, and finally a yurt made of cement in which a traveling singer performs as epic story-teller. What was authentic in earlier times is now already citation. . . . The journey through Mongolia shows a still vital ancient world that is already touched by decline, in which songs are sung which no one today knows how to translate" (Feldvoß). But regarding the closing station of her Mongolian journey, the rundown of towns that formerly were the coordinates of trade relations between Mongolia and Russia but which have in the meantime lost this significance, this function, Ottinger finds a transformation between the lines that she can still affirm: "The old ways don't apply here and the new exists in the form of phrases like 'new economy, new freedom, new era.' These are filled with wishes and dreams, which set them emphatically apart from the banality of what we understand by these words. They take on a mythic quality, and they are repeated and taken on faith as protective spells" (in *Produktionsmitteilung*).

Mongolian shamaness at the séance.

While Ottinger documents two actual shamanistic séances in Mongolia, the shamaness or woman as medium is a recurring figure, or condition, throughout her films. Caught in the tension span of doubling and in the separation of image and sound track, all onboard with Madame X develop mediumistic qualities before they are killed or doubled anew by the new crew. Another way to put

The client communicates to or through the shamaness.

it: Schreber, whose double charge of technologization and becoming woman is one of the legends to my mapping of technofeminism in *Madame X*, placed his memoirs, as Benjamin first pointed out and underscored, with a Leipzig press that specialized in spiritualist studies. It takes one to know one: the medium writes the autobiography of media.

The actual shamaness on the frontier of Western civilization marks the return of what stationary modernity trains out of us—call it a collage temporality and spatiality that doesn't observe linear notions of past and present or ontological categories of matter or spirit. In running contrast to the historical encounters between Western dominance and the exotic other as abject or monstrous outsiders (or regressed insiders), we find affinities spark with psychical contact that supports different formulations of possible responses to the bewilderments along the margin. Right from the start of the era of modern spiritualism, mediums often relied on figures from the margin—an Indian chief and a fourteenth-century Arabian princess, for example—as their spirit guides.

The modern history of Western spiritualism does not simply begin with the Fox sisters and their telegraph-like communication with spirits. A prior record of mesmerism, hypnotism, occultism was ready to make the doubly mediatic connection. Andrew Jackson Davis's "harmonial" call in 1847 for communication with spirits was most likely taken and then put through the next year by the sisters. Morse's description of the functioning of the telegraph most likely caused the delay in funding by members of Congress who scoffed at its supernatural qualities. Morse described his invention as conveying "an intelligence." First there were the raps that seemed to come from nowhere and no one. Then, after 1850, free-floating hands appeared to mediums at séances and were then revealed to others in photographs. Morse's model triumphed over earlier or alternate versions of telegraphy through its installation of the rapping soon-to-be-typing hand.

In 1874 Charles Darwin attended a séance. He was relieved when he was later able to convince himself that it was a hoax. Also seated at the same séance table was Frederic Myers, who would coin the term *telepathy* in 1882. One of Myers's hypnotic clairvoyants was a telegraph operator who read "telepathed" messages off hallucinated telegraph message slips. In 1884 Oscar Wilde was part of a group that a blindfolded "thought reader" led in and out of a newspaper office. When journalism covered séance activities, it never left the range of its own telegraphic and mediumistic medium. This other history of journalism, an inevitable undercurrent of haunting in the news media at large, is also summoned, cited, situated when Ottinger documents the two séances in Mongolia.

9
I WAS THERE

Berlin was set, document, and inspiration for allegorical metamorphoses in the trilogy of Ottinger's fictional films. In 1990 Ottinger turned her documentary camera on Berlin to follow and interpret historical events in the making, in transition. *Countdown* is the document of the ten days leading to unification of the two German currencies.

The American or global term *countdown* was first introduced in the 1950s in the United States. A 1969 American film about the space race already bore the title *Countdown,* which was advertised as "the motion picture that puts a man on the moon . . . and you follow him every terrifying second of the way." But in film history, the first countdown before takeoff of a rocket to the moon took place in Fritz Lang's *Woman in the Moon.* The technical precision of the rocket in Lang's film was guaranteed by the advisorship of Hermann Oberth, the Transylvania-born researcher and promoter of rocket flight in Germany. Four years later, Lang escaped to Hollywood, while Oberth, who stayed behind, found an outlet for his projection of space travel by joining the Wernher von Braun team that succeeded in launching the V1 and V2 rockets for Nazi Germany. This same team, parceled out between the two new superpowers, played a decisive role in subsequent developments in rocket science and space exploration during the Cold War. Ottinger's *Countdown* opens with the Einstein Tower in Potsdam. Built by Erich Mendelsohn in the era of Lang's German films and in a style that anticipates continuity with Lang's or Oberth's film rocket, the tower is the uncanny continuity shot called German history that could now be unearthed from under the rubble of the collapsed Cold War. Albert Einstein attended the Berlin premiere of *Woman in the Moon.*

What comes out in the wash or watch of this document of reunification is both the viewing of the spectral Jewish cemetery and the return of Sinti and Roma minorities. This return is marked by the phobic static already or still on the lines of their reception but also set aside, as the film closes with portrayals of everyday life in the outpost-towns of the former GDR. We are offered glimpses of an existence that will, for a historical change, be passed over and allowed to survive. One of the opening and one of the closing text inserts composed by Eva Meyer for *Countdown* summarizes between these two bookends Ottinger's documentary sensibility. First: "But what is being counted here, paid out or sold out? Is an entity being recombined or divided along new lines? What is being counted out and thus pushed to the margins? The arbitrariness of the beginning corresponds to the arbitrariness of the end. But in between there is so much to be recounted." Then, toward the end: "Why doesn't one wait until the ideological evacuation creates new contents? Why doesn't one take the time to react to realities now that one can no longer pursue politics with ideas? Why must every vacuum that could emerge undergo instant colonization by the old and familiar? Why does one never slow down and only always accelerate? Because slowing down could bring with it its own acceleration, one that does not always already count on being done with the next step."

Ottinger intervenes in the newsbreaking TV tempo assigned to history in the making. As Witte observes: "Ottinger . . . makes a case for thoughtful deferral in our perception, which would first create the precondition for that which is perceived. In a video clip desires are awakened, in a slowly panning camera movement thought pictures emerge. . . . *Countdown* doesn't so much tally up the gaps in the wall as in our historical consciousness" ("Grenzgänge und Mauersprünge"). Ottinger works the documentary medium with a sort of *caméra stylo*—a term she borrows from the 1940s French film director and critic Alexandre Astruc, and calls on already to characterize her camera-readiness for *China: The Arts—Everyday Life.* Her camera registers, for ten days leading up to the unification of German currencies, the political changes after 1989 in the everyday life of Berlin, in the margins at the center of the epoch-making ending of the Cold War. I was there when the allegorical status of the divided city began to be functionalized in the wake-up call of the reunified and opened-up metropolis, back on the map after all those years. Suddenly it mattered again that the Polish border was an hour's drive away. I remember attending Robert Wilson's *Orlando* at the Schaubühne in the Mendelsohn-designed theater on the Kurfürstendam. In the middle of a monologue, the German words for "all this" or "all these things," *"all dies,"* was not able to complete itself in a thought or sentence. The audience doubled over with loud laughter by the shock value of instant recognition of the double of that sound fragment. Only to Berliners at that time did Aldis, the supermarket chain name, supersede all sounds sounding like it. Lines and lines of one-stop shoppers from Poland had made "Aldis" the new grin-and-bear-it emblem and nick, in time, in the name of the city.

The Berlin Wall as condemned site in 1989.

The overall affirmative openness of Ottinger's document is notable because it cannot have been easy going. The allegorical status of the divided city, of what was once upon a time in the recent past the circumcised, displaced, cosmopolitan, ghostly capital of old Europe, was being functionalized literally with a vengeance, with a revenge Nietzsche defined as directed "against the 'It Was' of time." That no sizable portion of the wall—one of the great monuments in history—was left standing speaks volumes about the official plan for reunified Berlin, against which Ottinger's document can be seen to offer a stay of execution. Ottinger's camera records a soon-to-be repressed recent past as one more layering in the palimpsest of histories that made West and East Berlin, within the allegorical perspective, the most rewarding archaeological dig in Europe. In Ottinger's film, "Berlin is a foreign city in which the social work concept of multicultural appearances is not simply being documented but what gets shown is what's nearby and what is quite remote. . . . Not just the wall . . . is a place of adventure. Unwalled Berlin together with its environs as shown here is territory for adventure." Thus "the quiet, disquieting views of the marginal zones of the metropolis" are traversed, followed, affirmed (Witte, "Grenzgänge und Mauersprünge").

The encounters with Chinese minorities, from the Bai to the Mongolians, are on one receiving line with the minorities Ottinger encounters as they return to the site of their Cold War splitting in *Countdown*. In 1996 Ottinger returned her documentary attention to Chinese minorities, this time to the Jews of Shanghai, including the Austrian and German Jews who settled in exile in Shanghai during World War II. While filming in Shanghai in 1996, Ottinger experienced openly hidden forms of censorship under the cover of her cooperation with local officials and film-industry colleagues. In the course of filming, Ottinger didn't double-check everything with her local crew, although she might have done so if working with a German crew. Under the circumstances, she decided that it would be condescending if it looked like she didn't accept her foreign colleagues as professionals. But it was getting uncanny: the crew never got around to developing a sample bit of each reel, the customary test. One excuse led to another. But then it turned out that most of the film Ottinger shot with the Chinese crew was flawed, presumably because the camera was damaged. She had to start over again with a Berlin cameraman whom she called to the rescue. But even before the first round of filming, Ottinger made officially sanctioned and chaperoned visits to the locations where she planned to film. During these visits, she talked with Chinese citizens who remembered the time when Austrian and German Jewish refugees were crowded together with them in the Hongkew section of Shanghai. She visited former synagogues that were, as relics of times past, still recognizable down to details, still intact as historical evidence. When she returned to these same locations to make the filmic record, the spaces had been emptied out of all evidence, or the site was condemned, placed off-limits, and the people with whom she had spoken before couldn't be found, or, if met up with again, suddenly remembered nothing from back then, didn't know what she was talking about.

Only one shard of documentary evidence of Chinese testimony survived the censorship, a brief interview with the neighbor of Tonshan Lu: "I was very young at that time, maybe ten years old. We first moved here before the Jews arrived. They came later. We didn't know that they were Jews. For us they were just foreigners. Later on we became more familiar with them. My father worked as a carpenter. . . . As soon as they found this out, they frequently called on my father to work for them. They were very good to my father. To us children, too. Sometimes they gave us sweet rolls. . . . We empathized with each other. Later they departed. They came by and said goodbye to my father. We were all very sad, we knew each other very well after all. The adults told me that there were many of them, and that they were poor. Some people insulted them and persecuted them. Among them there was one tall man who was my father's good friend. We all called him 'Foreigner with huge feet.' After he left we often thought about him and were concerned about his fate." Ottinger's inclusion of this surviving shard of on-location interviewing in Shanghai, in contrast to the lengthy interviews with the former Shanghai dwellers living now in the San Francisco area, risked the misunderstanding, which I witnessed after screenings of the film, that her document was Eurocentric, that Shanghai was exoticized and denied a voice. But the shard or relic was served up as a placeholder for something Ottinger refused to comment on, for reasons of her own diplomatic relations with China. The documentation of the past largely denied her in Shanghai resonates via the relic or ruin of one surviving piece of Chinese testimony between the words of the survivors and the portrayal of Shanghai in 1996.

The background setting for the slapstick censorship routine to which Ottinger was subjected was the large-scale rapid-fire transformation of Shanghai into a modern megalopolis that would bear up under the comparison coming soon with Hong Kong. Hongkew in particular was being razed to make room for new highrises. That is why, when she was filming in Shanghai, she knew it was now or never: the old Hongkew, together with the traces of the history Ottinger was trying to document, kept on vanishing by the block on a daily basis. I visited Ottinger while she was finishing the on-location filming in Shanghai; at the end of my week there, the bad news of the damaged stock had broken; on the day of my departure, the German cameraman arrived from Berlin. But even during the happy lull before the catastrophe, the atmosphere surrounding us was right out of some spy thriller. When we sat together in the hotel bar, a gentleman with a briefcase always took the next table, the briefcase set down as close to us as possible. Our different hotel rooms (while I was there, the Ottinger group of foreigners occupied three rooms on the same floor) were always separated by one empty room that was currently out of circulation; for example, in order to make repairs. There was, however, a steady traffic of individuals in and out of these unused rooms situated between the rooms we occupied. Ottinger was reminded by these surveillance gestures of other frightening-to-eerie run-ins with authorities in Beijing, and near-miss deadlock disagreements, the kind that could have led to imprisonment, while she was making her first China documentary. While it unnerved her, what she also liked about all this excitement was that it demonstrated that the Chinese authorities still viewed film with interest and respect as a medium of highest ideological consequence, the status that film in our culture long ago ceded to TV.

TALE OF THREE OR MORE CITIES

Exil Shanghai (*Exile Shanghai*, 1997) is the document of two historically different Shanghais and of two distinct cities. The interviewees who recall their lives in Shanghai have all in the meantime settled in the San Francisco area. Inna Mink slips in her narration on her way to the "Garden Bridge" (which led to Hongkew, where the Austrian and German Jewish refugees were segregated after the Japanese occupied Shanghai) and stammers: "the Gold, the Golden Gate, the Garden

Bridge." Geoffrey Heller concludes his wartime story with his family's transfer from Shanghai to San Francisco, only to stumble first on a reversal: "we . . . took the trip to Shanghai, . . . to San Francisco, and that's where we landed."

One reviewer describes the relationship between the grim historical episode and the documentary portions (filmed in 1996), in which good looks at the arts and the everyday outnumber past-present juxtapositions: "Ulrike Ottinger would not be the film-ethnographer she lays claim to be in her most recent works if she had limited her film to the portraits of the fortunate survivors, enriched by countless family photos and historical documents. The camera glides over the scenes from the past which have by now been completely transformed, lingers over picturesque details like the fabrication of noodles, . . . and stares fascinated at the multicolored neon advertisements lining the main street, a sign of unbelievable Chinese prosperity. In general it can be said that this film composes against a gray background a shining symphony of color. Ulrike Ottinger's composition turns the biographical experience on the edge of crisis into an aesthetic experience, the beauty of which could alienate if it were not justified as a signal of joy and hope" (Rother).

The words given in an interview to conjure the past will at times guide the camera movement, as when the recollection of a lavish ball moves the camera to waltz around a relic from that time period, a chandelier in the Peace Hotel. The camera spends all the time in the "word" recording the interviewees as they speak. Long looks at the interviewees reminiscing (Ottinger asks next to no interview questions) became a new way for Ottinger to enable her audience to look and see. But the digressions that take off from the words in interview are not diversions. "When Mrs. Alexander shows her Chinese marriage certificate, which she was never able to decipher, the camera takes the audience to modern Shanghai where elaborate wedding pictures of young couples are being staged" ("Ein unbekanntes Kapitel").

"Shanghai is the starting point of the film. It is narrated and set in motion, however, by the Off-voices which, displaced in time, comment on the current cityscape" (Holz). "Ottinger shows the Shanghai of today as theatrical backdrop. The bright neon lights along the ocean promenade mix with the dark of the night into a ghostly twilight, in which one believes one can hear the whispering of the lost souls who once sought sanctuary here" (Simonoviescz). "Slowly and carefully the film approaches the city like a traveler on the sea, observes the harbor, stays with European-like facades, takes long looks at markets, city traffic, a soup kitchen. The film reports on a present absence, which left behind fragile traces—those of the Jews of Shanghai" (Rall).

The first reviewers of the film stepped back inside a pawnshop of traumatic histories to find, in exchange, their mournful relationship to the documentary materials. But as Eva Meyer demonstrates in a word, we should not pull up short before the possibility of pulling—via affirmative reversal—out of the dead ends of history.

> The chapters in the lives of the individuals reporting here appear torn into fragments, each of which seems to wrest its duration from time, as well as plunge into it. They lose their personal and collective unity to the extent that they mix with the outer world of their exile. It interrupts them in the form of ads, reports, documents, news items, catalogues, notes, and so on, and in doing so does not merely refer to diverse practical interests in time, but also embeds them in the course of the world which goes back 200 years before our time. It is no coincidence that the first German word on a Chinese shop sign is mentioned here, for this word—"Versatzamt"—not only seems to refer to the plight of the exile but also to reconstitute the fragmentedness of the tale, what it means to embrace the course rather than the ownership of things. ("Ulrike Ottinger's Chronicle of Time," 42)

The ghostly citation of *Versatzamt* (pawnshop) also adds, then, literally as "office of displacement," another piece of Ottinger's puzzling montage of mourning and affirmation in mourning.

Josef von Sternberg's *The Shanghai Gesture* gave an introduction to a place that is also a concept along lines Ottinger could cosign: "Years ago a speck was torn away from the mystery of China and became Shanghai. A distorted mirror of problems that beset the world today, it grew into a refuge for people who wished to live between the lines of laws and customs—a modern Tower of Babel. Neither Chinese, European, British nor American, it maintained itself for years in the ever increasing whirlpool of war. Its destiny, at present, is in the lap of the Gods—as is the destiny of all cities. Our story has nothing to do with the present." Ottinger's 1997 documentary, which excavates in the Shanghai of 1996, the Shanghai of the late 1930s and early 1940s, offers in this allegorical relay much ado about "nothing to do" with the present. Ottinger summarizes a "whirlpool" that was Shanghai, which she sought to grant continued exile, complete with the difference the present makes, in *Exile Shanghai*.

> Shanghai was an entirely artificial entity. It was extraterritorial. Everyone who was involved in World War II and who had political power in the years before was in Shanghai: the British, the Americans, the French, that is, not only followers of De Gaulle but also the Pétainists (there was an Avenue Pétain), the Germans were there—including lots of Nazis—and the Italians. Shanghai was a free trading zone. Each nation took a slice of this cake, each one maintained their own police force, their own jurisdiction. And then there

were the Chinese who had very different political views, i.e. the communists, the nationalists, the followers of Chiang Kai-Chek and many others who followed different reform movements. These were the last days of colonialism. Many Japanese lived in Shanghai, first as businessmen, then as conquerors. Sephardic Jews had lived in the city for more than one hundred years. They belonged to the colonial world. Russians, white Russians, but especially Jewish Russians who had come to Shanghai much earlier, fleeing pogroms, as a rule belonged to the poorer section of late colonial society. There was no other place in the world with as many contradictory interest groups as Shanghai. Shanghai itself was a mise-en-scène. . . . When Jewish emigrants from Germany and Austria arrived here they only owned ten Reichsmark. They had not been allowed to take along more. Jewelry and valuables had to be handed over to the authorities before departure. Unless they had relatives abroad who sent money they were dependent on local help and were sent to live in the poor city district of Hongkew. Those who still had access to extra money . . . were able to live in the "French Concession" or the "International Settlement" where they tried to establish new businesses. It is interesting to see how newspaper ads from this time refer to emigrants' countries of origin. Mr. Heinemann, for example, referred to his newly opened "Western Art Gallery" on elegant Avenue Joffre as "formerly bookshop Olivaer Platz Berlin." . . . In some way the emigrants fit well into this crazy scene, at the same time they were totally at odds with it. . . . You have to imagine people from Vienna, Frankfurt, Berlin or Breslau, stripped of their German citizenship, arriving in Shanghai and reproducing precisely what was typical for Vienna, Frankfurt or Berlin. They created the specialties of their home countries— that's something unbelievable. They lived in the midst of these Chinese quarters, in tiny rooms without running water, without toilets, in short: under very difficult circumstances to which Europeans were not accustomed. After a short while they had appropriated their new surroundings, turned it into a small European town. . . . The arrival of German and Austrian Jews brought a new aspect to life in Shanghai: not only did they introduce European flair, but also a different attitude towards the Chinese. When the Americans bombed the ghetto in 1945, for example, where Jews and Chinese lived side by side, Jewish physicians took care of the wounded Chinese population too. This had never happened during colonial times. (Ottinger, in Tax, "Interview mit Ulrike Ottinger")

The first Jews in Shanghai, Sephardic businessmen with prominent names like Sassoon, were the only Jews to come to Shanghai not seeking exile. A large number of Russian Jews in flight from pogroms settled in Shanghai in the early twentieth century. Three of the interviewees, Rena Krasno, Inna Mink, and

Former synagogue in the former French Concession in Shanghai (in 1996).

Georges Spunt, belong to this group (Spunt's mother came from Russia, but his father, who died in 1929, lived in Austria before he moved to Shanghai). Perhaps because Krasno had already written the history of her life in Shanghai before the interview, her testimony possesses a practiced and perfected overview or balance. Her interview opens *Exile Shanghai*'s narrative with great introductory poise: "Well, I am an old China hand, a member of a dying race, one could say. I belong to those who lived many years in China, in fact I was born and raised in China and belong to a Russian Jewish family."

The tale of cities is dedicated to parental figures of adventure and survival. Teenagers at world-war time, the interviewees in 1996 hand their history over to parental guidance. Krasno: "Among the Russian Jews in Shanghai there were many Russian Jews from Siberia, and that is quite interesting to know, because Siberia at that time was a kind of wild west in Russia and people who lived in Siberia had relatively more freedom than in other parts of Russia. So Siberian Jews were known to be very independent, especially the women were very independent." Krasno's mother was of this Siberian stock. Krasno balances her dependency between her strong mother and her poetry-writing, journal-founding father. Mink, by contrast, is under the refraining order to submit at all times to her mother's superior beauty. For example (she is showing off a photograph): "And here is my gorgeous and elegant mother, always posing, always beautiful." Spunt assigns his parents in equal measure to a past so golden he was spoiled for life. His father placed a bet on behalf of the servants when Spunt junior was born. Because it was the winning ticket, the baby was henceforth known as the "Dondinitse, which is the money child. And," George Spunt elaborates in interview, "it ruined my life, because my nanny used to say to me: 'You will never be poor because you are the Dondinitse,' so I felt, well, I don't have to turn a finger anymore. We're never going to be poor because I'm the Dondinitse. Of course I found out life doesn't work that way."

Spunt adds to the oral histories of Shanghai a sense of the gay life: "Park Hotel was a wonderful meeting place for everybody, but it was a place where a lot of gays used to go, and they used to go to the third floor bar [which] was the cruising bar. . . . You know, almost every night in Shanghai was unique, because you never knew where it was going to lead you and you never knew what kind of adventure you were going to have. . . . You could start out at an ambassador or a consul general's party and end up in the Honolulu Bar in Avenue Joffre." However, his awareness of the predicament of the refugees from Austria and

Typical back alley in Hongkew in 1996.

Germany during the Japanese occupation (Jewish refugees who were citizens of countries at war with the Third Reich were locked up separately together with gentile citizens of the United States or Britain) wears blinders (or gloves): "Back to the Germans and Austrians, they really had a very hard time, because they were then forced to go and live in a certain restricted area in Hongkew.... We would see them in the French concession, which is where we lived. But nobody wanted to go to the ghetto, and I'm not sure that you could." But you could, of course. Krasno went once with her mother to visit a German-refugee boyfriend: "When we came there we met Heinz, who was very happy to see us, and my mother insisted that we go somewhere out to a restaurant. I don't remember the name of the restaurant, but it was a tiny little coffee shop on a small roof. It was like a small roof garden, there were a couple of trees there and it was very pleasant.... I think that people's impressions are different according to their age and how they lived there. Heinz at this time was so happy to see us that I really don't know how he felt. Besides, he was just a very fine person and did not want to share his misery with other people." Mink gave up her protected or oblivious status when she married one of the refugees and joined him in Hongkew. She remembers "wonderful café houses" and restaurants that "were so European and . . . brought in a whole different flavor into our community."

The narrative also gives the story to three Jewish refugees from Nazi Germany, two German and one Austrian, including the only couple interviewed, Ted and Gertrude Alexander, who met and married in Hongkew, but who came from Berlin and Vienna, respectively. The European flavor that wartime refugees brought to Shanghai, their all-out attempts to reconstruct their home cultures, which had the closed-minded side effect of perpetuating prejudices and rivalries between, say, the Prussians and the Austrians, was supplemented by the openness of these Central European Jews to their Chinese environment, which in turn made the Alexander union possible. Geoffrey Heller, the other German Jewish refugee, captures this openness in flashback: "I ought to say that my experience in Shanghai is probably by no means a typical one. I don't think anybody's probably is. Shanghai is such a multifaceted city and the experience at that time during the early years of the war was extraordinary. It was sort of an island in time and a mirror of the times and yet in a strangely and almost exotic type of setting." Krasno recalls that at the *Volkshochschule* founded in Hongkew, a certain Professor Thon "gave courses on Chinese culture there." In contrast, "nobody among the Russian Jews that I knew was interested in Chinese culture."

The star of Ted Alexander's reminiscences is his mother, a strong woman with a Berlin accent. For example, when they arrived in Shanghai, she turned to her son and announced: "'Will you look at that already, they have skyscrapers here. No problem. You're going to be able to earn some change here, don't you worry about a thing.' And just as she said it, that's how it came to be." Before the surprise greeting of Shanghai's skyline, still en route by ship, the Alexander family was seated in the dining salon just when a storm hit: "Everyone jumped up and hurried out of the salon and my mother sits at the table and says: 'No one gets seasick at this table. We're eating well here and we don't know if we'll ever be so well-off again. We're going to eat our way through the menu, from top to bottom. Steward, bring us a bottle of Chianti!' We all felt queasy but we would never, never have had the courage to admit that to our mother." Gertrude Alexander expresses her strong ties with both parents (who were already in Shanghai awaiting her arrival) when she describes their reunion: "Everybody was crying and happy and I hardly noticed the city of Shanghai, because I was looking at my parents' faces all the time."

Heller, also originally a Berliner, was, like Gertrude Alexander, at first separated from his parents when the *Kindertransport* took him and his brother to Britain. His parents then succeeded in leaving Nazi Germany and took the Trans-Siberian Railway to Shanghai, where the family was later reunited. Heller's designated figure of identification and survival is his father, who flourished in business in Shanghai before the Japanese occupation, and who sought to remain in Shanghai after the war and to continue to conduct business together with his Chinese friends. Heller walks us through—and it was a walking cure—some of the changes brought on by segregation in Hongkew: "What my father and we particularly deplored when we were moved to the segregation area, was that the only piece of green land, of nature that existed in that part of the world, was skillfully cut out of the area that we were permitted to live and walk in. For my father that was a great tragedy, because he was a passionate walker. He had, when he lived in Berlin, known every inch of the Grunewald, and when he came to Shanghai it didn't take very long for him to buy this little book *The Shanghai Country Walks* written by a charming and very humorous, a very thoughtful Englishman, which described the walks that one could take about Shanghai."

Ottinger's camera perspective walks through Shanghai, both back then and in 1996, through the alternation between open vistas and the souvenir props originally introduced in the course and setting of the interviews. "The different eras mix in this film, past represents itself in the present: history doesn't simply die, it continues in people, buildings, streets. Ottinger's research project proves this. Formally strictly constructed, *Exile Shanghai* confronts the running documentary footage of the present with old objects, photos, and memories. Not a single strip of film is enlisted from the archives, but thousands of *stills,* newspaper articles and family photos. Memory freezes things, preserves them as snapshots, splinters of that which once moved, was animate: Ottinger's film is also a sort of exhibition of these memory splinters. . . . *Exile Shanghai* projects a substantial

Busy Hongkew intersection in 1996.

detail-obsessed image of the history of a period like hardly another documentary film before. 'Who never dreamed of happiness?' a song asks resoundingly at the end of the film, happiness—as we hear a few lines later—that goes around the world. Around the world: Ulrike Ottinger belongs to those filmmakers who film one location and at the same time can show us half the world" (Grissemann).

Heller's closing interview, a thoughtful and grateful account of his sojourn in China, in which one can make out a "melancholic connection with the country that took him in" (Depping), doubles Ottinger's own real-time affirmation in Shanghai in 1996 of the advent and adventure of the other. Heller seconded his father's emotion, wishing to "be part of the great rebirth of China" after the war. But the situation finally proved untenable, at the latest by the time of communist takeover, and it was California here we become. But Heller's respect for his hosts during the World War II years is the last and lasting document of *Exile Shanghai*: "What I was enormously impressed about my Chinese neighbors was how enormously civilized they were throughout the war. Remember, they were very, very poorly off, they were very poor. One would have assumed that we might have been exposed to all sorts of animosity. But most important is this: that when the war was over, and the Japanese surrendered, the Japanese forces of occupation actually retired, fled, disappeared, and left behind several days or maybe a week or a week and a half of an absolute void. Nobody was in charge, nobody enforced law and order, nobody policed anything. It's the time that you would have assumed tens of thousands of people to rampage in the streets, you know, ripping off property, since people were hungry, people were desperate, and yet nothing like that happened. A very civilized society. I'm very, very happy to have lived through these horrible years in China."

A PSYCHOANALYST IN SHANGHAI

In addition to the six Californians interviewed, it is the psychoanalyst A. J. Storfer who serves Ottinger as special guide: "Mr. Storfer is a fascinating personality. He was the publisher of the psychoanalytical press in Vienna that published the works of Sigmund Freud. He emigrated after the Third Reich annexed Austria. Later he founded a newspaper in Shanghai, *Die gelbe Post* ('The Yellow Post'), subtitled 'a bi-weekly East Asian magazine.' . . . It was an unusual magazine with an unusual mix of topics: an essay by Freud on anti-Semitism in Europe, another one about psychoanalysis in Japan, then an article about the Jews of Kai-Feng, a very early Jewish settlement in China. Furthermore there are some rather pragmatic texts by physicians about, for example, the timing for cholera injections. . . . There are a lot of articles about the cinema, especially about Chinese cinema. . . . Also a kind of introduction to Chinese culture—which was unusual and new for the colonial world. Articles about the Chinese script. . . . In his article, 'Hats Off to the Coolie,' he describes how he arrived in China in a state of depression, but nevertheless became immediately fascinated by what he saw: coolies loaded down with heavy burdens. I think that Storfer's attitude has a lot to do with the style of my film. I tried to bring together these different, contradictory issues surrounding Shanghai. It was important to me to find parallels and images in contemporary Shanghai to illustrate the stories the interviewees told me about the old Shanghai" (Ottinger, in Tax, "Interview mit Ulrike Ottinger").

Storfer was a psychoanalyst with overriding philological interests. The two books he finished before his flight from Europe testify to his "wordly" perspective: *Wörter und ihre Schicksale* (*Words and Their Fates*), which appeared in Berlin (still) in 1935, and *Im Dickicht der Sprache (In the Thicket of Language),* which was published in Vienna in 1937. In *Die gelbe Post,* Storfer published "a fragment" titled "'Jud' in der deutschen Volkssprache" ("'Jew' in German Folk Language"). He follows the bouncing *Jud* (a slang, folk, often derogatory contraction of *Jude,* or "Jew") across the German-language underworld: the word names now a spy, or, in general, a foreign presence, now a tear or glitch in tailoring (which may refer to the Jewish custom of making a tear in one's clothing to signal mourning), now the clitoris, now the penis, now the peas that are spilled and dispersed in the harvest, now pork, now a meatless meal. Like *freak* to this day in English, *Jud* in German in 1939 has the momentum of supreme repressibility, while enjoying a certain privilege that denial oddly bestows on whatever it at once rejects and names or touches.

In 1911 Storfer staked his claim to a name when he took interdisciplinary action against "The Special Significance of Patricide" ("Zur Sonderstellung des Vatermordes"). The original setting for right and wrong began, between hunger and love, in primal groupings like the family or hunting packs. The I is not bottom line. But it tears apart just like the bottom line when the group standard sets itself up against that egoic self-entitlement that never was. Storfer noted that when we transfer Freudian findings to the field of ethno-psychology *(Völkerpsychologie)* "we discover that ethno-psychological phenomena, like religion, myth, legend, fairy tale, serve not only the purpose of drive suppression but also at the same time, as accumulators of suppressed drive power, as meeting and gathering places for repressed wishes and fantasies" (5). Through the gods alone (and the exaggerated appetites attributed to them), human beings make unconscious confessions that too much sex and violence is not unknown to them.

Our enemies were economic and sexual rivals; only with the guest does a transitional category emerge between "us" and "the rest" (7). In determining the relationship between a murderer and the murdered, we began to differentiate between proper and improper killings. But there was one crime that demanded the reaction of the collective: high treason. In German, the word for treason *(Verrat)* is just a slip away from the word for father *(Vater)*. And thus it follows in Storfer's reading that patricide must have counted as the most grievous crime, as the highest treason (9). In his historical review of the status and punishment of patricide in past civilizations, Storfer arrives at an inspiring find that he raises as question: Why in the Roman Republic was every murderer legally stamped as patricide? (19). This reflects a certain mourning logic Freud set up, whereby the deceased you mourn is always (also) the dead father.

By the end of the Roman Republic the patricide (the murderer of father or relative) was sewn up into a body bag also containing a monkey, a rooster, a dog, and a snake, and then thrown into the sea. Storfer unpacks the meanings of each creature co-occupant in the sack throughout the history of legends and the history of each designating word. After several pages, he can conclude that the punishment of the patricide together with the creatures (that all bear illicit sexual associations) guaranteed that the contents of the bag thrown into the sea would never unite with mother earth. In this way restitution was made for the rage against patriarchal power, for the rebellion (not only in deed but also in thought) against the father's sexual omnipotence.

I submit Storfer's most famous essay as evidence for his own detail-obsessed investigation of what is essentially an image—the bagged patricide—and also for the all-important shift he introduces in the theory and history of violence: the guest enters the duo dynamic of us versus them as civilizing influence (as the creator at the same time of the host). Storfer promotes the good legacy of the host—hospitality, for example—and brackets out the residue of a more mixed reception of the advent of the guest/host (as evidenced in "hostile"). Because it brought him in proximity to filmmaking, one final incident deserves mention.

At a time when he was receiving proposals (from Hollywood and Berlin) that he consult on or supervise already-planned movies about or involving psychoanalysis, Freud argued in a letter to Karl Abraham, dated June 9, 1925, that cinema can present the abstract theoretical constructs of psychoanalysis only through cartoon literalizations of his own work with analogies. Though Freud accordingly withheld his endorsement, he did not discourage Abraham from supporting and supervising the UFA film *The Mystery of the Soul,* directed by G. W. Pabst, which was a critical and popular failure. Siegfried Bernfeld and Storfer thought they were coming to the rescue when they proposed another film on psychoanalysis. But Abraham nixed the project with the warning that the international press could not extend its authorization to a second film for several years yet.

I like to think that through Storfer's guidance or inspiration, *Exile Shanghai* is in part the film he was kept from producing or supervising.

10
CURTAINS

I attended Ottinger's production of J. Nestroy's *Das Verlobungsfest im Feenreich (oder Die Gleichheit der Jahre). Zauberposse in drey Aufzügen (The Engagement Party in the Fairy Realm)* for the 1999 Steierischer Herbst, the annual fall arts festival in Graz, Austria. As the sole theatrical project in Ottinger's extensive portfolio of directorial works for the stage that I had occasion to observe, including behind the scenes during the last week of dress rehearsals, the Graz production of *The Engagement Party in the Fairy Realm* provided a one-time opportunity to extrapolate Ottinger's relationship to theater, and the outside chance of assessing Ottinger's way of seeing and working in another medium.

Nestroy—one of Freud's fave authors, cited by the old guy with just as much gusto and know-how for trafficking with the unconscious as are Goethe, Heine, or Hoffmann—left a legacy that was in progress and in process, and therefore given over to quick decay. Written in 1833, *The Engagement Party in the Fairy Realm* was first printed in 1924. Its salvage operation was in large part held up in the censor's court because the original code for reversing the censorship had been lost, and because the loose-leaf inserts had gone the way of collectibles. A run of successes composed in a more naturalist style had interrupted its completion and propelled Nestroy away from his originally supernatural framing of this dramatic treatment of coupling. The success rate required the conversion of the *Feenreich* (fairy realm) into the earthbound common sense of what was beyond the *oder,* the "or," in the original: *Die Gleichheit der Jahre* ("The Equality of Years,") became the title of the desupernaturalized second version, which effectively buried the first version.

In the first version, the *Gleichheit* (equality) is ironically installed in couples between partners who must be peers, or even worse, perverse, or better yet, deceived and self-deceiving. Regina is forced to marry. Under this hetero-pressure, her wish emerges to open difference wider just the same and take a younger groom. In the second version, Regina is humbled when her certificate of baptism arrives. By the end, the two peer partners have their contracts to show. The show of force introduces "equality." Whereas the second version brings Regina to her senses and ends with the consensus of common sense, the first version makes Regina into the kind of villain with whom you, at least in your "perverse" part, sympathize. The consensus at the end, under Ottinger's direction, suggests in freeze-frame that Regina was just about to reintroduce her "but" of resistance to the new order of equality.

The supernatural frame of the rescued-from-consensus first version of Nestroy's peer revue serves as placeholder for Ottinger's designated juxtapositions: among the theatrical traditions of Japan, between isolated features of Japanese culture and matching details taken from alpine folkloric traditions, and the list goes on. "It is interesting how Nestroy . . . worked in this play with a plethora of elements. He is describing societal breaks. And the same problems existed and exist in Japan. The combination of all these breaks is made manifest in the performance: the aesthetic of early Nestroy in combination with the difference between the gestural canon of classical Kabuki theater and modern actors" (Ottinger, in "Die Hochzeit von Nestroy und Kabuki"). Ottinger stages a completely free and loose association, something that she would include as detail in her films, but never as the overriding frame or concept. Foreground and background could be seen as reversed: up front the theatricality of unfounded associations is supported by the background (notably the background supplied by Ottinger's oeuvre) of or in cinematic exploration of found juxtapositions. Onstage, Ottinger magnifies the miniaturist texture of her films and advances it to center stage as theatrical gesture that puts through connections via an entirely performative or deregulated common denominator. In keeping with the themes of Nestroy's play, we might say that the linking of "Austria" and "Japan" is a forced marriage that renders *Gleichheit* impossible.

The Japanese translation of the Nestroy play by author Yoko Tawada (who, though Japanese, writes in German) was performed by the Japanese players. The original text was "narrated" by Libgart Schwarz, veteran actress of the Schaubühne in Berlin, who in effect performed all parts in carefully choreographed sync with the Japanese players. "It is a very early play of his, one that still has a magic frame. Within this frame we alternate between the fairy realm and the world of mortals and experience in this way continual metamorphosis. This idea of transformation and constant change — for example from the realm of the dead into the world of the living — is fundamental to Japanese Kabuki theater. . . . Can you imagine how the combination of the strict, prescribed gestures of Kabuki with the witty discourse of Nestroy functions on stage? Then there's the tremendous feat performed by Libgart Schwarz as narrator who speaks all the parts with her highly stylized voice. Of course she also mimics the impudent, fresh manner and dialect of Schladriwuxerl. . . . And on the other side we have Mr. Hanayagi, a player of women's roles, whose gesture and mime are incredibly precise. The player of women's roles has, by the way, nothing to do with our current conception of transvestism. It is a specific role for which one trains in Japan" (Ottinger, in "Die Hochzeit von Nestroy und Kabuki").

Out West, the posse (that in fact goes back to the Middle Ages as a Latin word and concept) is the group of men on horseback that the sheriff deputizes for a stint of protecting the peace. The German word *Posse* means "farce, burlesque," but perhaps it too is just another formation summoned to the rescue (in an allegorical sense). This *Zauberposse* is a *Posse* with a supernatural frame (*Zauber* means "magic"), a hybrid and transitional artifact that was waiting for Ottinger's mix of "two" cultures, one identifiable via Kabuki and Bunraku elements as "Japanese" (although the mix of different Japanese dramaturgical traditions would be considered taboo in Japan), the other via yodeling and musical banding together of down-home alpine country voices and instruments, in folkloric outfits and masks, as "Austrian." In the nonhistorical association of the two cultures, similarities between artifacts, like the phonic doubling between words that flexes the pun power of the unconscious, put through new, at once uncanny and welcome, connections between them. "While I was showing the actors yesterday my extensive collection of materials, which aids in informing and inspiring us, one actor was quite taken by the picture of a grass coat, which he recognized as typically Japanese. . . . It was an old Styrian grass coat" (Ottinger, in "Die Hochzeit von Nestroy und Kabuki").

That year in Graz at the international arts festival, one showcase exhibition specialized in Australian art under the topic of trauma and memory. But what I could remember was that in the international language of the folks back home "Austria" and "Australia" were always being confused and used interchangeably, say in postal addresses. When I shared the free association with the local Austrian in charge of the festival, what snapped back in its place, beyond reservation or reserve, was the confirmation that this was the trauma one little country cannot forget. The anecdote is given as placeholder for countless examples of unconscious connection between "cultures" that, on Ottinger's stage, would have been assembled nonphobically rather than (as in the official exhibitionism in Graz in 1999) displaced with regard to the generalizing order form of a topic like trauma and memory.

When the interviewer tries out the guilt trap of a possible exoticism charge to be made to Ottinger's inclusion of Japanese theater traditions, Ottinger's comeback also covers the entirety of her work: "I would never find an actor in the German-language world who could supply the Nestroy text with this interesting gesture. And I don't have any concerns in regard to the issue you raise. You can see in all my work that I have great respect for different cultures and their traditions." If a marriage of the two cultures seems part of the stage celebration, then this is not because boundaries have been blended, assimilated. "Instead I piece together a mosaic in which every piece must be picked up and tried out five times before it fits. It is a highly complex process until every piece in the picture supports every other piece." Practically, this means that Ottinger cannot tell or model how she wants the actors to perform. "I must restrain myself since the Japanese dramatic gesture is in many ways different from ours. The difference must not be muddled. We constantly ask each other: What would you do in this situation? A gesture, which here in the folk drama would represent jealousy, would already signal in Japan hysteria. We must bring every detail into the form. . . . We work our way carefully through every word, through every meaning and every rhythm in both languages. In this compulsion to be precise we learn a great deal about each other." (All quotes in this paragraph are Ottinger, "Die Hochzeit von Nestroy und Kabuki.")

In a sense, we come full circle at this point of ensemble via a direct connection or flashback to Ottinger's first feature-length film, *Madame X: An Absolute Ruler*, her most improvised (and thus in an extended sense, perhaps also her most theatrical and most documentary) fiction film. Yvonne Rainer had her own good reasons to make manifesto her disenchantment with the art market. When a drive-by journalist interviews her, as Josephine Collage, about her motivation for joining Madame X, it's all her own text. "I liked very much her idea of quoting from Flaubert's *L'education sentimentale*. These experiences certainly aren't new, they were already made by artists and intellectuals, unfortunately, many centuries ago. . . . I simply used whatever I saw and so the project took on substance, the screenplay is in essence just a skeleton, and one works in all the fantasies and then one observes what qualities and abilities the individuals possess. . . . I find that very important that one not insist stubbornly on adherence to the screenplay or to one's own ideas, but rather that one can simply fold into the project the skills of the others. . . . I am not so fixated in this regard, I can view it all as a puzzle and then put it together out of all the existing pieces. And that works out because my figures are so stylized, almost like prototypes standing in for something else, otherwise my stories too wouldn't function" (Ottinger, in Treut, "Gespräch mit Ulrike Ottinger"). "When I make movies, I must find for each film the right form, whether it is a fictional film or a documentary. In the theater I am faced with the same task: every theme has a very specific form, and to find this form I view as my actual artistic labor. It is a very long process. It

Yvonne Rainer as Josephine Collage (in the context of Madame X: An Absolute Ruler).

involves language, music, costumes, light, and rhythm. It involves a certain relationship to time" (Ottinger, in "Die Hochzeit von Nestroy und Kabuki").

At the close of her essay "Correspondences," Ottinger refers to William Klein's documentary film on Little Richard, which is really a document of wide-open improvisation, transformation, and doubling—in the absence of the titular subject—as model for the way film realizes "the bizarre truth of wish dreams." "Little Richard, who had just become religious, only wanted to sing for Jesus. So William Klein put an ad in the paper, 'Seeking double for Little Richard.' Blacks, whites, women, men, children and the elderly applied. Klein decided to use them all."

11
MY LAST INTERVIEW WITH ULRIKE OTTINGER

The last time I interviewed Ulrike Ottinger (in 1992), the receiving area of her films was pressing to divide, as Before and After, Ottinger's dual—and in every filmic-moment double—investment in fictional art cinema and documentary film. A series of films that could be identified as documentary led first to a sense of changed direction in Ottinger's work in progress; second, to a massive repression of her recent art-cinema past; and third, to a projection of Ottinger's exclusively documentary filmmaking in place of the other cinema that had been lost. But back then, as the interview underscored, the movie Ottinger was looking forward to making was a new fiction film, "Diamond Dance." That project spent the interim in the Hollywood from development hell. In the 1990s, Hollywood set a spell with so-called independent films, inoculated itself with a shot of what's "new," and doubled and contained all "other worlds." As the protracted near-miss of the "Diamond Dance" project documented, European art cinema was over and out with Hollywood's declaration of independents. Consequently, in 2000 Ottinger went on relocation in the international art world. Her photographic work began to be shown in prominent art scenes and venues, rather than, for example, in ethnological museums. In 2002, when the Goetz collection was selectively presented in Munich, Ottinger's photographs "in the context of *Freak Orlando*," which had been only recently acquired, nevertheless made the cut and were prominently displayed alongside works by Matthew Barney, Robert Gober, Yayoi Kusama, Tony Oursler, and Cindy Sherman, among others. Her film *Southeast Passage,* while identifiably documentary in nature and budget, was at the same time commissioned for the 2002 Documenta in Kassel, the international art extravaganza where the film had its premiere.

A document of a trip along historical trade routes through the forgotten half of Europe, *Southeast Passage* was Ottinger's most highly edited film to that date.

In fact, it was her first film that could be said to have taken shape only in the course of editing. In particular, the inclusion or installation of her photographs within the film was a striking feature of the editing process. With *Southeast Passage*, her photographic work—which until 2002 inhabited a parallel universal in her artistic production, hovering mainly in the context of her films—entered her film work as a montage element.

I saw the rough cut of *Southeast Passage* in the winter of 2001, and the final cut late in the summer of 2002. While the structure of the film and of each part had already been in place in the rough cut, the final version revealed a highly encrusted and intrawoven product. In addition to photographs, *Southeast Passage* also incorporates black-and-white sequences, including one extended insert based on Valentine Katajev's short story of 1926, "The Exemplar," which actors perform with a silent-film mannerism that draws from both Eastern European traditions of the grotesque and German expressionist film (this sequence was also released as a short, titled *The Exemplar*). While the actors mouth the air or mime speech, Hans Zischler narrates the text: an Odessa official who falls asleep in 1905 wakes up years later in the Soviet Union. By the time he understands the new situation, he withdraws from the series of his comic encounters with the new order into the anonymous crowd. The story thus glosses another reversal in the fortunes of Odessa that is not part of its own plot but that we witness (by turning up the contrast) in the film document. Now the people wake up to find themselves no longer merged or missing in collectivism: they struggle to make the new crowd of individuals in which they in turn must disappear. But the film (*as* film, as a projective medium that both historically and technically is at the peak of its development and refinement) also admits continuity shots lifted from its own history. At one point in the Odessa portion of *Southeast Passage,* the pressure is on—it's ready made—to include a more direct citation of one of cinema's most famous scenes. Raymond Wolff comments on this self-reflexive moment: "This viewer's favorite scene in the film concerns a child. All film buffs will recall the famous baby carriage scene in Sergei Eisenstein's 1925 classic *Battleship Potemkin*. The steps shown were in Odessa and are still there. They lead down to the harbor and are known as 'The Potemkin Steps.' In the Eisenstein version a mother with a baby carriage is shot, and there is great drama as the carriage heads down the steps on its own. In the Ottinger film, a four-year-old boy and his father are seen heading down the steps hand-in-hand. Because of the differences in their gait, the child seems to trip more than walk. The viewer has that Potemkin feeling all over again."

Before her journey, Ottinger was acquainted with the places in her documentary trip mainly through books. In *Southeast Passage,* she selected quotations from Isaak Babel, Walter Benjamin, Elias Canetti, and Joseph Roth, among others, that run by the document of contemporary settings—that everywhere admit historical remnants and fragments—now audible, now legible commentary from a past that only the dead know as (more or less) whole. As is typical for Ottinger's approach to filmmaking, the musical score represents a profoundly archival montage that meets the visuals more than halfway. But it is photography that made the grand entry at the art of her film work, with a layering effect that at the same time stages and staggers the motion in or passage through the picture titled *Southeast Passage*.

Southeast Passage has a subtitle: *A Journey to the New Blank Spaces on the Map of Europe*. In German they are literally "the white spots" on the map, which, cartographically speaking, is how empty or undescribed (or uncathected) spaces appear. As form and in content, Ottinger's film explores the dislocation of Eastern and Oriental Europe with regard to a once-interrelated Europe. This dislocation and this missingness circumscribe the (white) spot her film was in with the recent past. In presenting Europe as the emperor's new closure, Ottinger offered an alternative to the long-standing coordinates of projection. Everyone was talking about Europe. But how could we have overlooked it? Half of it was missing.

A sign advertising the services and address of an insurance firm named Veritas opens the relay and delay of still images (including a photograph of the director herself on-location). The first part of *Southeast Passage* concludes in Varna, the turning point in another journey or quest that is legend to the map of Ottinger's project. It was in Varna, in Stoker's novel, that the Western European and American vampire hunters (and gadget lovers) began to double and contain Count Dracula's Oriental challenge to systems of circulation and orientation as new and improved: our mass-media culture of long-distance connections—or, in the terms of Freud's second system, the security or insurance drive—first emerged over the doubly dead embodiment of this challenge from the east of Europe. The uncanny zone was thus mapped and tourist-trapped, registered, or identified and forgotten.

An absence right next door is the place setting of what Adorno identified as the recent past, conceived, that is, as the most remote or primal past, a past that can be received only as catastrophe or return. The "white spot" of the recent past and the culture next door is thus—in Veritas—a "reality" effect (beyond the media of projection) of our TV era of "liveness," in which, for security reasons, the present tense (and ongoing tension)—the seeing I of our media sensorium—is dislocated within the fantasy arc of past (perfect) and a future of wish fulfillment.

Accompanied by stirring music of the lost era, the titles also rise with the photographs in the opening moments of *Southeast Passage*. Then text from Ilja Ilf and Jevgeni Petrov's *The Twelve Chairs* commands the frame. With the commencement of "Part 1 (Wroclaw to Varna)," the motion pictures for the first time let roll. But photographs continue to punctuate the movement.

By and large, photographs are pressed into the service of ironic self-reflexivity at the blended boundary between documentary real time travel and the advent of the other. For example, in filmed images we watch three girls shyly resist being portrayed. The sequence ends with a photo portrait of the beaming threesome proudly looking at the camera (and ultimately at themselves). In passing, a Hungarian mimics Ottinger's camera with a bottle. Then two old women are caught in the act of commenting on being filmed. One says: "It is not permitted." But the second assuages her friend's anxious sense of decorum: "But it doesn't really matter." Someone asks: "Will you send me a photo?" Another subject comments: "I am being filmed now." We're told that the goats she helps herd are often used as extras for Italian TV movies. Then we see the shepherdess's photo portrait. Ottinger also films the goatherds. Then we see the still-photo images of the animals. Halfway to Varna, the camera looks out from the driving minibus giving the digital gadget the frame of automobilic, analogic technology and apparatus, and thus another twist of self-reflection or self-historicization in this affirmation of the medium of film. A digital camera is not (yet) a movie camera. But it synthetically gets around the former divide between video and film that Ottinger would otherwise never have crossed. "The automobile becomes an extended camera casing that manifests itself in the movement blur in the pictures. The situations passing quickly by have to be recognized at lightning speed and caught like a Ping-Pong ball in flight—exact observations of the everyday surrounded by the blur of the fleeting passage" (Ottinger, "Südostpassage"). This is how Ottinger characterizes the photographs she took during the trip and the photographic moments in the film. Other moments in the film generate out of close encounters with people and their locale's "filmic miniatures. These compare almost imperceptibly the new with the old, are allusions and become clear *[deuten an und werden deutlich]*" (ibid.). Allegorical rescue must underscore that the blanks to which vast territories can be reduced cannot in turn be filled in, not even by their own (being) history.

LAURENCE RICKELS: I understand you are working on two new projects, a short here in Berlin to premiere fall 2002, and a feature-length film, between documentary and fiction, that will take you back to the former Soviet Union.

ULRIKE OTTINGER: In Berlin we have the "Jewish Culture Weeks" and the organizers had the idea to commission several short films for the November 2002 celebrations. Since the budget is very small, it will cover only a digital production. They were thinking mainly of documentary films. The guidelines were left open. But they were looking for a Berlin theme that, however freely or flexibly, stands in some relation to Judaism. The Esther story plays a very big role in "Diamond Dance," and in the course of my research I became more and more interested in the Esther story and in the Purim games and plays. The Esther story is so interesting because there are so many of them, there are Babylonian and Jewish variants, for example, and simply the most diverse interpretations, and in addition there are so many local versions. In recent years the Jewish community in Berlin has grown unbelievably, more than doubled. For the most part the newcomers are Russian Jews. Many of them had very little contact with Judaism, but then perhaps because their immigration here was made possible by their being "Jewish," since otherwise they never would have gained entry into the European fortress, a form of contact was renewed after all. What interests me about this group are the many new fascinating faces. I thought it would be lovely to perform an Esther story with these older people, who speak in altogether different languages: some still speak Yiddish, others a heavily accented German, yet others only Russian, are just starting to learn German. I would like to keep it simple. They would wear their everyday clothes (I would probably still help make the selections). Then, as it was in former times in the Purim plays of the children (as one knows from photographs or oral histories from the turn of the century through the 1920s), I would have them put on hats, crowns, the diadem of Esther painted on papier-mâché or made with gold lamé. They can play the different roles, possibly argue about the competing versions. I have to wait and see a bit what will happen. In any event, that is my plan, a sort of Esther story performed and followed through with these people. They have been through so much already. I expect they will bring a new relationship to or experience of the Esther story through their memories, or that through the Esther story they are able once more to face certain fundamental threats. For the Esther story is associated in particular with the overcoming of threatening events.

LR: And the larger Russian project?

UO: In the course of my research for *Southeast Passage*, I became enchanted by the literary works of several Odessa authors. The novel I would like to use as the basis for the new film is a kind of travelogue that traverses the entirety of the Soviet Empire, and at every way station one encounters the madness of bureaucratic administration. The narrative is written with an unbelievable joy in fabulation, and yet at the same time discloses a certain Russian reality that one can only convey with the formal means of the grotesque. There is in Central and Eastern Europe, also in Russia, an ancient tradition of the grotesque. I would like to take up and follow out this travel route again with a troupe of actors, encountering the realities of today that are no less grotesque.

I will start by building a scaffold in the manner of the Mongolian dramaturgy that allows me the freedom to insert and build up inside it all manner of details. I love the form of travel and the cinema of way stations that corresponds to it.

LR: Russia played a role in your earlier film work as backdrop, as part of the background of certain characters, as part of history. But a documentary encounter seems to have been reserved for the new millennium. How did this newer documentary interest come into focus?

UO: It was already very interesting in Mongolia, the differences arising from the two competing administrations, the Chinese and the Russian. You can recognize the different influences right away. I was interested to see these different influences in Mongolian culture. In *Taiga* I showed settlements in the north that look like Siberian villages. In the Chinese part, in the south, it looks different. And you can follow the history of these influences by comparison of a current setting with old photographs and even fiction films from the 1920s and '30s.

LR: But in the year 2000 you traveled through Eastern Europe with a digital camera. How had this region come closer? You no longer had to take the detour via Mongolia.

UO: The fall of the wall introduced rapid changes that were immediately perceptible. Suddenly you could hear so many Eastern European languages in Berlin. I'm always fascinated when places that were off-limits for so long are opened up for travel. Odessa was always for me a magical place, like Samarkand or Timbuktu, places that extend into our fantasies.

I have good friends here who speak excellent Russian, Ada and Boris. Boris is Bulgarian and speaks several Balkan languages, or at least understands them well. He studied in Moscow. As did his wife Ada, who is a scholar of the 1920s, an unusual topic of study back then in the Soviet Union. It was surely considered inappropriate to specialize in that period. And so I would ask them how one goes about traveling there. And one day they said, why don't we go together? And so we began to plan the trip. The most difficult thing we faced was the car rental. Because we were apparently going to be driving beyond the Europcar universe. The rental agency is called Europcar, and it is significant that one cannot travel to Eastern Europe with one of their cars.

Up until World War II there was one Europe, it all belonged to Europe. The opera house in Odessa is up to the standards of Vienna or Paris. Beautiful old hotels, arcades, and streetcars, everything you would expect to find in a major European city. That is one thing I tried to show. Old Europe is entirely there still in the cities, intact, right down to the clothes of the people who, no matter how poor they are and even if they have to piece together their outfits out of rags, are clearly determined to look fantastic. The same old European atmosphere pervades the arcades of Istanbul. In this spirit I explored and used

Merchants of Odessa.

the music of the 1920s, tangos from Odessa and Istanbul, music that counted as modern back then, elegant and chic, and the music in turn bore a unique local stamp. Bucharest was famous for its tango bars with famous female tango singers. Ataturk was involved with a famous tango singer who stood by him at political gatherings, especially when he was promoting change in the social standing of women. The relics of old Europe, which are still manifest in these cities, I showed them in the architecture, music, streetcars, in the arcades, in the countless details, even in the cuisine, but always with a focus fixed on the local variation and alteration.

LR: It seems that while Berlin changed from being an allegorical site in its divided and split-off state, and started functionalizing, these Eastern European cities lost their functioning and took on the allegorical format of memorial relics.

UO: Yes. They are relics, memory fragments, but at the same time I have the feeling that they are parts of something, parts that in some form, perhaps psychically, save the people in all their poverty. Certainly that is true for the older people. Then I documented all the new developments that can also be seen on the street. I think that what distinguishes my films is that I look around the streets to see what is different, what has remained.

I also used a great many literary quotations in the film. But from different eras. I quoted, for example, from Joseph Roth, who traveled a great deal through the Soviet Union. Back then all the utopians visited the Soviet Union and invariably published glowing reports of their travels in the West. They were themselves so enthusiastic about their utopian ideals that they were often too uncritical. Joseph Roth was an exception. He traveled in the countryside too, through the villages, and he documents his travels in a mode that is thoughtfully and critically observant. He posits very interesting contexts. I also quoted Walter Benjamin, Isaac Babel, and Elias Canetti. Canetti writes about his place of birth, a small town in Moldavia, almost at the mouth of the Danube, and he related how when one traveled up the Danube toward Vienna, one would then say that one was going to Europe. He came from a Sephardic family that had lived a long time in Turkey. When the Spanish Jews were cast out, many landed in the Balkans and in the Ottoman Empire, especially in Istanbul, where they were prized for their skills.

I structured the film in a differentiated way. The part dedicated to Istanbul is structured according to the story of the seven princesses, which I transposed to the seven hills of Istanbul and the seven days of the week. The first part passes through Poland, the Chechen Republic, Hungary, Rumania, Bulgaria, and stops in Varna. The second part is dedicated to Odessa but includes an outing into the countryside, and in this section I reflected on the past with literary citations. The film as a whole is a permanent exchange among old Europe, the Ottoman Empire, and the new Europe—including all the desolate conditions of life in Eastern Europe. In the Ukraine, the only remaining export, the country's only sellable raw material, are the women.

LR: It seems that your documentary works resist globalization now by inhabiting the ruinscape of a former cosmopolitanism, now by entering the bazaar of foreign languages as yet unidentified in their provenance and mixture. With *Johanna d'Arc of Mongolia* you created a work that even in title invites a mix of languages that proves difficult to translate into one language. Untranslatability appears among the phenomena you "document" in *Taiga*.

UO: I don't introduce myself into the film like many documentary filmmakers prefer to do, showing us how they cross the desert in the jeep or how it gets stuck in the river. I don't show that sort of thing because it doesn't interest me. Just the same I am present in the reactions of the people I encounter. And that does interest me. I never edit out the moments in which people address me. For example, I was with tribesmen living together with reindeer. These animals have the special characteristic that two small bones at their heels click like castanets when they walk. And when a herd arrives or the people are bringing a caravan—they ride the reindeer there—one hears the clicking, and they of course hear it more acutely and know the sounds better and hear them before we would. And so they said, watch out now, get the camera ready, soon you can take pictures, soon the reindeer will be here. Moments like that I leave in my films. And I translate them. I don't want to keep anything from the viewer.

But it is of course a false conception to believe that one can experience a culture by translating word for word. One must also know the significance of the word, its context; it's all so much more complicated. We too have our own social codes and know when something is said in one moment that something else is also meant in addition. What was meant and said in a polite way can also imply criticism. All these codes must be taken into consideration. One can't just imagine that one has grasped something completely by translating it one-to-one. This is a misunderstanding or perhaps a widespread fantasy that one can immediately and completely comprehend anything at all that comes from another culture. It is a long process. Even with cultures that one has studied and with which one has concerned oneself intensively there are always again surprises, and that is a good thing.

I find it interesting to ask What is foreign? What is other? in particular in film. To give an example, while I was making *Exile Shanghai* I occupied myself intensively with the programs of Chinese films in Shanghai in the 1920s and 1930s. American, British, and French movements in cinema were all represented. But it was in the first place American movies that influenced Shanghai cinema, and there was a development just as there was with photography in the United States to document what was happening in the streets. I don't know if this is the case, but I ask myself if this isn't an influence, I mean those American films that were made outside, no longer in the studio, already on the streets, whether these films didn't have a certain influence on Chinese filmmakers who began to make films in the streets. Much of what is foreign is reworked in the new setting and interpreted so that it is understood. This process tended usually to stimulate the development of interesting new forms, including the adaptation of other things, also of foreign things from other cultures. Something very interesting in culture is the adaptation, which can indeed be a misunderstanding, but one that takes on a brand-new sense in its new cultural setting. Adaptation, perhaps assimilation, certainly alteration describe a creative process. But while I have always affirmed this, it seems today under the conditions of film business, conditions of monopoly, strictly economically speaking, conditions of the so-called global, something quite other than adaptation is happening, namely a certain production of sameness is what is promoted or allowed. The last time I was in Beijing, I had a hotel room with a television set and I watched

American shows with recognizable stars speaking perfect Chinese. They could speak Armenian too, I'm sure. And I wonder what this could lead to.

LR: A Korean artist who lives and works in New York told me that when he first came to the United States as a young man he expected everyone to speak Korean because that's what the Americans always spoke on Korean television.

UO: Of course. It seems to me that this no longer has anything in common with the creative alteration, the adaptation of the encounter with the foreign or with the other.

LR: But maybe after the fact, through this shock of recognition that the world is not peopled by Americans who speak Korean. That changes everything.

UO: Yes, that changes everything. But really only for the weaker partner in the exchange.

When I titled the interview I conducted with Ottinger in 1992 (in which we looked back at *Freak Orlando* and greeted, made contact with the then brand-new *Taiga*) "Real Time Travel," I was hoping to address in this way the connection between the earlier films that invoked metamorphosis (in *Freak Orlando*, that of sex change and time travel) and the documentary encounter with Mongolian nomads in all the time it takes in a world of difference to encounter the other. But as "My Last Interview" documented a decade or so later, between the two former sites of Ottinger's "real time travels"—the allegorical mourning pageant that Berlin once was, and the Far East that afforded first contacts with unhistoricized nomadic cultures, as well as the recent history of cultural transfer and rescue—it was now the former Eastern Block that invited Ottinger to record, rescue, or render legible in the allegorical state of transition otherwise uncathected spaces and histories.

Following the opening relay of photographs (and the titles) in *Southeast Passage*, the first text piece makes extended reference to the novel *Twelve Chairs* (by Ilya Ilf and Yevgenii Petrov), asking the viewers/readers if they in fact know this crucial work. In the interview above, Ottinger discusses *Southeast Passage* in its planning stages. To make the new film, Ottinger took up and followed out a travel route with a troupe of actors on documentary location in the former Soviet Union, encountering contemporary realities as grotesque in genre as many scenes described in the novel *Twelve Chairs*. Ottinger centers her version of the narrative and journey in Odessa (rather than Moscow, the novel's hub), making the main characters citizens of Odessa as were, in fact, the authors of the novel. In *Southeast Passage* one of the three parts comprising its documentary encounter was devoted to Odessa. *Twelve Chairs* thus mixes the literary text and screenplay with the attributes of documentary filmmaking—improvisation, site specificity, chance encounter, and juxtaposition—in a context (demarcated by the two films) of rehearsal or repetition. Christine N. Brinckmann responds to these diverse directional signals at the intersection of the film's composition: "Ottinger gives the actors ample room for spontaneity, but masters the narration in expert style. Each vignette is a surprising, accurately applied tableau, every shot an opulent painting. The narrative rhythm is generated by a static composition that invites the eye to linger and a lively performance that could almost burst out of its structure. Overall, this corresponds to the twin movement of completing a numerical task (that of searching for the twelve chairs, piece by piece and beyond) and unfolding within the autonomy of the individual episodes. Such structures take a lot of composing."

The relationship between *Southeast Passage* and *Twelve Chairs* repeats the duo dynamic of the earlier major turn in Ottinger's oeuvre: her first documentary film, *China: The Arts—Everyday Life,* turned out to be the exploration, the encounter, to which her subsequent film, *Johanna d'Arc of Mongolia,* gave an art-cinematic form. If in *Southeast Passage* Ottinger documented what old Europe there is or is still there, albeit in stately ruination, in the cities of the former Eastern Block, then in *Twelve Chairs* she drew from these ruins, remainders, and reminders a continuity shot, administered by the documentary encounter, that kept her art cinema going, going, but not gone.

Ottinger's 2004 film *Twelve Chairs* summarizes, summons, looks back upon, and builds on her collected feature-film work up through this point. As in Federico Fellini's *8½* or in Franz Kafka's story "Elf Söhne" ("Eleven Sons"), *Twelve Chairs* counts Ottinger's twelve films. This countdown takes the liberty of including "Diamond Dance," which could, should, and would have been made in the 1990s but for the loss of art cinema's marketability cornered by Hollywood's self-made alternative, independent film. In the course of the 1990s, the original allegorical compatibility and interchange between Berlin-based art cinema and the encounters with China and Mongolia seemed to double back as a one-way trip without return. Like Berlin, art cinema was withdrawn from what began as an alliance with certain possibilities afforded by the documentary genre.

In the novel *Twelve Chairs,* three treasure hunters seek to track down jewels hidden away at the time of the revolution in one of a suite of twelve chairs. At the end, the treasure inside the twelfth chair was, it turns out, already accidentally discovered and put to good communal use. The well-appointed clubhouse in which the chair still stands reflects the treasure's purchase power. In the last chapter of the novel we are reassured (as the last of the three hunters goes insane on the spot): "The treasure remained; it had been preserved and had even grown. It could be touched with the hand, though not taken away. It had

(above) Russian mannequins in Istanbul (in the context of Southeast Passage).
(below) The cleric, Father Fjodor, with the (wrong) twelve chairs.

(above) The rascal marries for money.
(below) Waiting in the Hall of Records.

gone into the service of new people" (Ilf and Petrov, 394). Throughout the novel, we pass through corridors of bureaucratic administration and writing (including journalism) that represent the manically upbeat version of or alternation with Kafka's uncanny or melancholic writing apparatuses and bureaucratic organisms. As such, the world or word of screed saturating the novel is the internal simulacrum and affirmation of the fact of life of writing. In the final station, that of the twelfth chair, we witness a comparatively successful rendition of administered community space. Thus the mere treasure inside the chair has yielded the greater "wealth" of another public, published space, the narrative *Twelve Chairs,* or, in the case of Ottinger's film, the investment, cathexis, and gift of both this twelfth film, which the title counts down to and becomes, and of all twelve feature-length films.

12
TOTEM TABOO

Ottinger's exhibition, Totem, at the Salzburg Kunstverein (summer 2005) assembled work Ottinger made during her residency at Artpace in San Antonio, Texas (fall 2004), alongside earlier and regular explorations of the settings of animal sacrifice (beginning with photographs taken in the context of her 1977 film *Madame X: An Absolute Ruler*) and around a tepee-like installation from 1986–87 titled *Europa and the Bull*.

Via a loopy network of association represented by knickknacks from the Mexican holiday of the dead, which she set up as her own alter-altars, Ottinger invited us to recognize in the photo-portraits of Mexican Americans not only the face-to-face outlines of Aztec or Mayan ancestors, but also the resonance between the sombrero, for example, and more primal forms and artifacts. The Europa tent was decked out with Ottinger's remakes of notable artistic renditions of *The Rape of Europa,* with one panel set aside for a bull's hide and topped off with antlers bearing a disc reminiscent of Isis's sun accessory.

Ottinger gives form to juxtapositions that are out there. That can mean both that they are really "out there," as in wonderfully bizarre, *and* that they are grounded, founded, and found in reality. While these juxtapositions or encounters cannot but draw support from our dream states and the unconscious, they at the same time cannot be reduced to free or rather not-so-free associations. Carl Jung explored a collective unconscious that he originally derived from the hallucinatory hypnagogic figures one is liable to witness in the liminal state of awakening; for example, figures that reveal the subliminal thought processes that double or shadow conscious thinking, but in a symbolic mode at once more general and archaic than conscious thought.

But how does that differ, for example, from the subliminal suggestions of mass-media advertising? Benjamin, in contrast, selected the hypnagogic state of

Suerte.

awakening from dream as the defective cornerstone where his approach overlapped with and then went beyond such dialectical constructs as the collective unconscious: "There is one completely unique experience of dialectics. The determining, drastic experience that contradicts all makeshift universality of becoming and proves all apparent development to be its eminently composed dialectical reversal is the moment of awakening from the dream state" (*Das Passagen-Werk*,

5/2, 1006). Based on this vulnerable phase of transition between dreaming and waking states, Benjamin sought "to break through into the heart of discarded things in order to interpret the contours of the banal as picture puzzles *[Vexierbilder]*. . . . Psychoanalysis has already uncovered picture puzzles as schemata of the dream work. We however are with such certainty on the track less of the soul than of the things. We seek the totem tree of objects in the thicket of primal history" (*Das Passagen-Werk,* 5/1, 281). Benjamin thus allegorically rematerializes Freud's science in terms of its own original tracks and tracking systems that were never really replaced by the oral histories of the personal cure. Also inspired by the scene of writing in Freud's science, Derrida reinscribed in terms of trace structure all philosophical concepts or conditions based, often verbatim, on human speech, precisely in order to admit all forms and modes of existence into the ethical and ontological understanding or staging area of life.

British psychoanalyst Ella Freeman Sharpe explored the 1877 discovery in Spain of prehistoric cave drawings of bison and men in animal masks as the always-renewable encounter with the primal bottom-line of artistic mediation and meaning. In her 1930 essay "Certain Aspects of Sublimation and Delusion," Freeman Sharpe folded out of this primal scene a psychohistory of the arts in which film served as her own most up-to-date and successful example of artistic mediation: "A Spaniard, interested in problems of the evolution of culture, was exploring a cave on his estate at Altamira, in Northern Spain. He was searching for new examples of flint and carved bone of which he had already found specimens. His little daughter was with him. . . . The child was scrambling over the rocks and suddenly called out 'Bulls, bulls!' She pointed to the ceiling, so low that he could touch it with his hand. He lifted the lamp and saw on the uneven surface numbers of bison and other animals drawn with great realism and painted in bright colors. . . . At that dramatic moment of recognition in the bowel of the cave a common impulse unites the ancient hunter artist and modern man. Between them lies the whole evolution of civilization, but the evolution that separates them springs from the impulse that unites them" (125). The hunter-artists of the reindeer age and the Spaniard in search of more bric-a-brac for his hobbyist scholarship meet across 17,000 years on the common ground of an impulse "to reconstruct, to make a representation of, life that has passed away" (125). "Behind the animal we have the man. So I see in the drawings of primitive man, in the animals, and men with animal masks, the first attempt in art to resolve a conflict raging around the problem of food and death" (127).

In her 1937 book *Dream Analysis,* film is integrated by Freeman Sharpe (as by her patients in the case material she presents) as the contemporary and appropriate analogue or symbol for the so-called "internal dream picture mechanism," specifically that of dream dramatization. But before addressing the movies in or as dreams, she interprets a movie reference brought to session:

> About half-way through the hour she "chanced" on the theme of a cinema entertainment she had seen the night before. She became enthusiastic about "Mickey Mouse" and described how Mickey Mouse jumped into the giraffe's mouth. She said: "The long neck had a series of windows down it, and one could see Mickey all the time, you didn't lose sight of him, you saw him go in, and come out." My realization was that there is a moment when a child sees a train for the first time, a time when it is a new and exciting phenomenon. People get out whom the child never saw get in. At such a moment a train can become the symbol of the human body. (57)

With these mediatized and mutating or metamorphosing animals all aboard, Freeman Sharpe performs a genealogical condensation in her own writing. The early histories of cinema and of psychoanalysis overlap in these tracks. The train was the first technological means of transport to travel the fine line between trauma and entertainment. The roller-coaster thrill of simulated transport placed us in a position of preparedness for train wreck, which was, before World War I, the most common exciting cause of many new brands of hysteria or traumatic neurosis.

When the film camera was mounted on moving trains, the "traveling shot" was introduced. In turn, the frontal shot of the train advancing steadily toward the audience to arrive somewhere just behind the last row in the theater was another early or primal example of film's administration of thrill shocks or inoculative shots of otherwise traumatizing catastrophe.

In her essay on sublimation and delusion, Freeman Sharpe turned to incorporation to answer the question: What stands behind the hunted, haunting animal? Or, in other words, behind the crowded intersection between food and death? It is ultimately a figure of parental guidance that can be raised to the power to haunt. "Art, I suggest, is a sublimation rooted in the primal identification with the parents. That identification is a magical incorporation of the parents, a psychical happening which runs parallel to what has been for long ages repressed, i.e., actual cannibalism." (135). Freeman Sharpe's understanding of artistic sublimation as exploring a universe or history that runs parallel to the repression it is rooted in finds resounding confirmation in cinema: "Of all arts, the last, the moving picture, is destined for the widest human appeal. The resources of science and art have converged in answer to man's deepest necessity and will consummate the most satisfying illusion the world has known" (136). As in Freeman Sharpe's interpretation of the Mickey Mouse movie as projecting a child's need-to-know view of the inside-out body strapped to train tracks, Benjamin situates Mickey Mouse's therapeutic value at the bursting point of group laughter within the introjective field. According to Benjamin (in the first version of "The Work of Art in the Age of Mechanical Reproducibility"), the release of laughter occasioned by Mickey Mouse films was cover for the injection of shocks or shots of inoculation that defended audience members against their own destructiveness (or self-destructiveness), which had become intensified by the double impact of technologization and massification.

In *Laughter: An Essay on the Meaning of the Comic,* Henri Bergson considered the example of the laughable animal from the other end of the techno transmission that Benjamin saw going through Mickey Mouse. You may indeed find yourself laughing at an animal, Bergson advises, but only because you recognized in it the reflection of some human attitude or expression. Thus, more important than the definition of man as the animal that laughs would be a definition of man as the animal that gets laughed at. It is not, however, the recognition of anthropomorphism that makes us laugh at animals. What is laughable is the imitation or caricature of ourselves we become in the course of rigidly stamping out our character (at once effacing it and fixing its debased remainder in place) along the assembly lines of mechanization or automatization. If laughter is triggered by the imitable automatic behavior and language thus assembled, then laughter itself (which is always group laughter) does not so much lube this machine as loosen its riveting interest in ill-fitting solitude or alienation, which resists and hinders the inclusive flexibility of the group dynamic. Man is ever in danger of becoming something mechanical encrusted on the living. (The other ambiguous form of relationality that is inherently or instantly groupified is suicide.)

Elias Canetti argued that the human capacity for laughter was the placeholder for cannibalistic incorporation as its nonconsummation: "Man alone has learned to replace the complete process of incorporation with a symbolic act. It appears that the movements that start out in the diaphragm and are characteristic of laughing replace and summarize a series of internal bodily swallowing motions" (*Gesammelte Werke* 3, 262f.). However, he ends with an exception that need not prove but could indeed break the rule: the hyena, he admits, is another laughing animal. Canetti's many remarks on animals scattered across his theoretical and literary oeuvre inhabit a primal world in which, as Freud too emphasized, the relationship to the totem animal, for example, wasn't simply that of symbolic substitute for a human figure. Canetti emphasizes that the so-called kangaroo ancestors of the Australian aborigines were at the same time kangaroo *and* human. But it is with regard to the "monstrous life" of dogs, in all their shapes and sizes, that Canetti considers a mode of interspecies existence that cannot be reduced to the slow-motion linearity of certain mainstream receptions of the theory of evolution: "It often seems that the whole religious essence that we composed with devils, dwarves, spirits, angels, and gods stems from the real existence of dogs. Whether it could be that we modelled our representation of our manifold beliefs on them, or whether it rather might be that we have existed as humans only since we started keeping dogs—in any case, in them, through them, we can read and review what we are actually doing, and it can be assumed that the majority of dog owners feel more gratitude for this knowledge than for the gods who get their lip service" (*Gesammelte Werke* 4, 13).

In his 1972 study *Wohin der Stier Europa trug (Where the Bull Carried Europa)*, Hans Georg Wunderlich called into question the archaeological reconstruction of Minoan civilization by Sir Arthur Evans. Whereas Evans celebrated an advanced bungalow and pool culture, Wunderlich saw everywhere the evidence of mortuary palaces: everyday life had been reproduced rather than lived, reconstructed in materials more flimsy than functional, even at a slightly reduced scale, and around a trajectory displaced westward, the orientation of the dead. But when Wunderlich next concluded that Greek drama, for example, led to a new and improved mode of disposal or commemoration of the deceased whereby the elaborate constructions of funerary cities for the dead could be replaced as overcome, he missed the ancillary element of repression that accompanies this shift into antiquity, or into neoclassicism, or into our own gadget-loving mass mediatization and globalization. Benjamin saw it otherwise: "One indicated in ancient Greece places where it went down into the underworld. Our waking existence is also a land where hidden places lead down into the underworld, full of inconspicuous sites into which dreams flow. During the day we pass by them, sensing nothing out of the ordinary, but as soon as we sleep, we reach rapidly back to those sites and lose ourselves in the dark passages" (*Das Passagen-Werk,* 1046). In *Totem*, the art installation, Ottinger deciphers and marks the repression of the underworld subtending our mediation and transmission of life and shows that the effects of its return can be everywhere recognized—even in the very word "Totem," which in its German-language setting is also the dative form of "that which is dead." Long before we pull up from behind the totem animal the interpersonal relationship to our own parents, we owe a debt to Totem, to that which is dead, and to the underworld.

13
GOING APE

At the 2007 Academy Awards ceremony, clips representing the camera work of each of the nominees for the Oscar in cinematography were screened. But what could also be seen was the interchangeability of cinematography and art direction in movies that Hollywood prizes. With her 2007 film *Prater,* Ottinger took the opportunity its documentary status afforded her—in documentary work, cinematography always has the upper hand, if only because there is no set construction to fall back on—to explore along a self-reflexive trajectory (with references to her collected work in progress) what it means to render something cinematic.

While as document *Prater* admits that the destruction of the amusement park at the end of World War II (the SS turned the Prater into Vienna's outlying line of defense, and then turned it into a wall of fire when the line could not be held) injected a shot of discontinuity between the before and the after, Ottinger's cinematic work of affirmation in mourning nevertheless insists that a tradition or transmission not only passes on but also still passes through. While affirmation is afforded when the camera sweeps up the Prater night in which the bright lights are outnumbered into jewelry, the task of mourning is heralded and guarded by the countless puppets, mechanical figures, mannequins, and ventriloquist dummies. The opening of *Prater* conjoins both tendencies. In front of the ghost ride, the huge dark demon sweeps up and down, but now in a rhythm dictated by the camera movement. The mechanical bowing before the weight of the past is reanimated by camera work that doesn't so much meet the artificial figure's movement halfway as dissolve its creaking fixity. The camera establishes its power to redefine every moving artificial image as cinematic motion picture. However, as the photographs taken in the context of this film attest, like signatures, the cinematography we watch pass before our eyes is about composition as much as movement.

The Prater.

I've been to the Prater, the first time in the late 1970s, and it right away reminded me of the many dead-in-the-water ghost parks dotting the New Jersey shore at that same time. What Ottinger explores as the turnstile of multiculturalism, the photographic studios that put you into 1900 set and costume, would strike me as more continuous with ye-olde-gift-shoppe amusements so typical (at least in the United States) of life on the tacky edge of the new frontier of urban blight since the 1970s, than with the pageants of transport and travel we watch in the historical footage Ottinger intercuts from films of the old Prater before the world wars.

By the 1970s, Disney represented the state of the art in amusement-park entertainment by virtue of its new and improved ways of administering thrills in all the cardio rides. The Disney ride internalizes and mediatizes the experience of risk, now by analogy with cinema, now with TV. The other genre of thrill park, to which the Prater manifestly belongs, has continued to explore risk through rides that pack all the unmitigated dangers of really fast transportation. The Disney decision for mediatization is not in itself all bad. But Ottinger's camera has the last word.

In the course of writing her vampire screenplay "The Blood Countess," Ottinger had already researched the Prater as the concluding station in the series of nineteenth-century Viennese institutions on which her film would be set. In these museums, archives, and infotainment centers, Ottinger recognized the archivization of the macabre along the rock-bottom line of the city's profoundly baroque heritage. Rumors that the Prater was going to be renovated and revalorized along the streamlines of the Disney amusement parks prompted Ottinger's own archivizing impulse, which led first to a research document and proposal titled "Prater ABC," which thus announces itself as another primer from which one learns the basics. *Prater* redoubles the projective machinery of the amusement park, which, technically and historically, is continuous with the materialization of the film medium, back upon the primer medium of the printing press, which via the literacy requirements for socialization it introduced is directly linked to the invention of childhood (which in each lifetime must be reinvented). Poet Elfriede Gerstl and author Elfriede Jelinek composed and read texts for Ottinger's film dedicated to the Prater as the machinery of childhood impressions (which led, in Jelinek's case, to their regular erasure by her mother, who feared the independence that gadget-love as a sense of control through and inside machines might inspire).

Within the opening of the section devoted to the backrooms of the Prater's repair and storage, the camera passes through a funky version of "It's a Small World," in which we count among the now-archaic, now-makeshift fantasy figures one Donald Duck, one Mickey Mouse, and several of the 101 dalmatians. Two gangly clown figures hold up the one and only sign: "I Like You." But here, in this musty underworld, the Californian casting or cattle call of assimilation is counterintuitive as intervention. This is not, after all, the small world revolving around only likeable figures that like and would like to be like all the other cute critters. In *Prater* the primal park subsumes the Disney effects within the ongoing pileup of its own detritus. Or again, going back to Frankfurt School, one might argue that in *Prater* the Prater is the primal memory of the Disney commodity that the Disney forget-together suppresses or loses and has already exchanged for a very particular brand of loser-friendliness.

There is another happy face, however, which Ottinger conjures up from the archival materials. A Nazi propaganda film that was pitched in the first place to Ukrainian audiences celebrates the Prater as the sanitized version of Eastern European multiculturalism. The cinematography has the same sweeping assuredness we associate with the work of Leni Riefenstahl. Everything moves and is proportioned along the lines of a ride in a Mercedes. Slavic peasant faces are scrubbed-down reflections of trust in a future—of entrusting themselves to a future—that the Prater advertises as marvels of technology protected and projected through war. Most of the visitors to the park are soldiers on leave from a front that is either so secure that their efforts can be spared or so challenged that losses must be cut through their special assignment as extras for propaganda films. Since we're at the point when the German army started refilling its ranks with non-German soldiers, you were right if you selected the "or" choice. This was at the same time the phase of heightening of Nazi violence in sync with the suicide drive. Certain multicultural others could be used or recycled before they too, like the other others, would be destroyed.

The clean machine fun of the Disney amusement park, at once the friendliest and most efficient place on earth, revalorizes seekers of a leave of their senses as extras in the media record of their imitation contact with risk or violence. According to Karl Kraus's reading of the press of violence between the lines that immunize the inquiring mind against the very risk of violence and thus against direct contact with word or world, the lay of the land of Disney would be only one degree of simulation removed from the film packaging of the Prater for Ukrainian self-consumption.

That *Twelve Chairs* could be seen as self-reflexively contemplating the twelve films that comprised Ottinger's oeuvre up to and including her 2003 feature was largely an effect of reading or interpretation. *Prater* openly reflects itself and its objects through a relay of references to Ottinger's earlier films. There are even several citations from *Freak Orlando* intercut with sequences involving the sideshow attractions of the Prater. Veruschka as Barbarella is encrusted with references to Ottinger's cinematic and photographic oeuvre. While her own return to the Ottinger screen of course trails reference to her earlier starring role as Dorian Gray, her Barbarella outfit together with her silent-movie-style animation of and around its mirroring and commanding outlines spans two figures: Madame X and the upper-class drinker in *Ticket of No Return*. After winning a toy chimp at the shooting range, Barbarella enters the funhouse interior of mirror distortion. Ottinger organized several photographic shoots around this sort of mirror relationship to metamorphosis, notably with Tabea Blumenschein in preparation for *The Ticket of No Return*, and with Magdalena Montezuma in the context of *Freak Orlando*.

Barbarella also plays a role specific to *Prater* in the assemblage of one of its guiding themes. She is the blonde object of ape desire. She gestures toward some passion play with the caged artificial gorilla appended to the exterior of the ghost ride. Once inside the mirroring funhouse, however, the baby chimp doubles as primal prop in the mirror show of disappearing and reappearing, which resembles both a mirror staging of the origin of life and the *fort-da* game of death and, on the rebound, haunting. At times, woman and chimp are in the game together fading in and out via distortion. But then we see the chimp as her bobbin or baby swinging into view and out of sight between the blonde woman's legs.

The Barbarella sequence is introduced right after the shooting galleries have been set up against the historical background of the Prater as hunting preserve. The consumerism of violence thus begins with our relationship to animals over the double problem of food and death. Since prehistory, hunting has been tied to haunting. The evil eye was first projected onto the dying look the animal could still give the hunter. The relationship between gorilla and blonde woman is spread across the entire film. But in the Barbarella sequence, the tendentious tale of passion is staged as intimate relationship. Immediately following the scene in which Barbarella gives interspecies birth with mirrors, we attend a funky puppet sideshow. The blonde girl from Austria is on a visit to New York. She's writing a letter to Daddy. New York is peaceful, not the way they talk about it back home. Suddenly a large ape doll appears between the skyscraper outlines. "You are so completely different [or other, *anders*] than back home," the blonde doll notes, unafraid. But then the ape grabs her, takes her to the top of the outline, and when he drops her, it appears she's dead.

King Kong is only the screen memory of a longer-term preoccupation with the beast and the blonde. The motif was introduced into the Prater in the late nineteenth century as syndication of the latest Paris fad surrounding Emmanuel Frémiet's gorilla sculptures. Everyone was carried away via misinterpretation of the French artist's first sculpture, which was of a female gorilla carrying off a woman, presumably to eat her, as the woman's rape by a male gorilla. But even that showstopper served as stopgap novelty in lieu of its prehistorical reception. The line that needs to be redrawn (or withdrawn) begins—and ends—with our relationship to animals. Reflecting on Adorno's identification of the tight spot we are in with racism and specism as each the other's rationalization for radical intolerance, Derrida takes us back to the basics: "Here there are premises that need to be deployed with great prudence, the gleams at least of a revolution in thought and action that we need, a revolution in our dwelling together with these other living things that we call animals" ("*Fichus*: Frankfurt Address").

Ottinger sets up the blender of these projections earlier in the film. The camera encounters and follows a group of men in folkloric outfits visiting the Prater. The first intercut is to a band of mechanical chimps playing windup music. The next intercut tells the story of the African tribe that was transplanted to the Prater as a natural history display, which Ottinger situates within a confetti parade of "orientalist" images and anecdotes. But the distinguishing mark of Ottinger's way of seeing is that she doesn't stop there. It is not so much that *Prater* doesn't get the charge out of what's so blatant, but it is more to the point of this film to be interested in the details of the members of the tribe circulating among the Viennese, going to the movies, and engaging in intimate relations with the locals.

In 2006 Eva Meyer addressed Ottinger's *Exile Shanghai* as specifically exemplary of Ottinger's work of montage. For the exile that is historically grounded also stages a loss of the inherited viewing subject position, which can only be found missing in every one of Ottinger's productions. Meyer views the displacement subtending the perspective of (or in) exile not as a form of blindness but as the inclusion of a blind spot that lets one see better:

> This blind spot does not rob the eye of its gaze. To the contrary, it effects an opening for the gaze and exerts pressure on it. Yet this is not a gaze that captures; rather the gaze itself is captured and set in motion. It is in the position of a swaying, suspended, fluctuating splinter of a people whose footing is constantly uncertain. It may well change its place in space, though it does not really come from any one place. It has lost the position of a viewer and so goes deeper than recollection, which for its part is placed in the past. It is in the course of this continual displacement that a gap widens and widens, and takes over the position of a viewer who no longer jumps the gap. He or she literally plunges into it. (42–43)

Montage articulates the perspectival displacement as that of the missed connection in time. To view "in exile" is to be at a loss of steady relations with the times of remembering. Instead, montage binds memories into a course of time that, at once discontinuous and retentive, is its melancholic or allegorical model and medium. Thus time becomes a discrete perception that can enter and exit the montage and pass through, to, between fiction and the present (without undergoing the separation of before and after). "By doing so we by no means attain a reality that exists independently of the montage but a chronicle of time that co-exists with it" (44).

Exile thus thematizes as loss the very perspective that is constitutive for Ottinger's way of seeing as adventure. The reversal of exclusion as adventure aligns the Shanghai exiles with all the other cast (or outcast) members of Ottinger's cinema. Whether pirates of feminism, the lady drinker who tours the Berlin sights as the sites of her own narcissistic disturbance, sideshow freaks across the ages and stages of the theater of the world, new nomads in Eastern Europe, or Russian actors by profession taking up roles within the timely improvisational settings and site-specificities of documentary film—each designated outsider perspective in Ottinger's films also rises to the occasion of affirmation as inside view along a new frontier of vision and understanding. The final viewer "in exile" turns out to be the ghost of Prater past seeing itself full length in the mirror not of the present (or of history) but in that of the film medium itself.

WORKS CITED

"O-Graphy," which I originally assembled for this study, has in the meantime been made part of the Ulrike Ottinger Web site. I refer you to www.ulrikeottinger.com for its thorough documentation of her films, art exhibitions (group and solo), theater and radio work, and publications. In the text, I refer to original versions of published texts (like "Stationenkino"), unpublished texts (like "Südostpassage"), and printed texts that served as press releases or program notes that were no doubt at least in part written by Ottinger but not in the same sense of authorship that she associates with her published work. These latter texts are identified in the main text as *Presseheft, Produktionsmitteilung,* or Edition Bischoff (Brochure of World Sales Export film, Munich). I do not include these preliminary, transitional, or loose-leaf promotional texts in this listing. I also do not list here Ottinger's unpublished screenplays (only two screenplay albums have been published in facsimile), to which I also had access. Many of the articles and reviews listed below have been reprinted in *Ulrike Ottinger. Texte und Dokumente,* ed. Freunde der Deutschen Kinemathek Berlin. *Kinemathek* 86 (October 1995); 2d ed., 2001. Finally, a number of published and unpublished texts are available on the Ulrike Ottinger Web site.

Barnes, Noreen C. "Ottinger's Mongolia, Fascinating, Funny." *Bay Area Reporter,* June 15, 1989.
Barthes, Roland. *Camera Lucida,* trans. Richard Howard. New York: Hill & Wang, 1980.
Benjamin, Walter. *Berliner Kindheit um Neunzehnhundert. Gesammelte Schriften,* ed. Rolf Tiedemann and Hermann Schweppenhäuser. 4, 1. Frankfurt am Main: Suhrkamp Verlag, 1980.

———. "Books by the Mentally Ill. From My Collection." In *Selected Writings,* ed. Michael W. Jennings, Howard Eiland, and Gary Smith. 2, 1. Cambridge, Mass.: Belknap Press, 1999.

———. "Critique of Violence." In *Reflections: Essays, Aphorisms, Autobiographical Writings,* ed. Peter Demetz. Trans. Edmund Jephcott. New York: Schocken Books, 1978.

———. "On Some Motifs in Baudelaire." In *Illuminations: Essays and Reflections,* ed. Hannah Arendt. Trans. Harry Zohn. New York: Shocken Books, 1968.

———. "Paris, the Capital of the Nineteenth Century." In *Selected Writings,* ed. Michael W. Jennings, Howard Eiland, and Gary Smith. Vol. 3. Cambridge, Mass.: Belknap Press, 2002.

———. *Das Passagen-Werk. Gesammelte Schriften.* 5, 1982.

———. *Ursprung des deutschen Trauerspiels. Gesammelte Schriften.* 1, 1. 1980.

———. "The Work of Art in the Age of Mechanical Reproduction." In *Illuminations: Essays and Reflections,* ed. Hannah Arendt. Trans. Harry Zohn. New York: Shocken Books, 1968.

Benker, Gertrud. *Der Gasthof.* Munich: Verlag Georg D. W. Callwey, 1974.

Benson, Sheila. "Women in Film Festival Draws Innovative European Entries." *Los Angeles Times,* October 18, 1989.

Berg-Ganschow, Uta. "Tausend Tode unterwegs." *Die Zeit,* November 12, 1981.

Bergius, Hanne. "Freak Orlando—Orlando Freak." In *Freak Orlando. Eine künstlerische Gesamtkonzeption.* Exhibition catalog, DAAD, Berlin, 1981.

Bergson, Henri. *Laughter: An Essay on the Meaning of the Comic.* New York: Cosimo, 2005 [1901].

Bergstrom, Janet. "The Theater of Everyday Life: Ulrike Ottinger's *China: The Arts—Everyday Life.*" *camera obscura* 18 (1988): 42–51.

Bondeson, Jan. *A Cabinet of Medical Curiosities.* New York: W. W. Norton & Company, 1999.

Brinckmann, Christine N. "Ulrike Ottinger's Picaresque Universe." Catalog of the Thirty-fourth International Forum of New Cinema, 2004.

Bronski, Michael. "Two Other Ottinger Highlights." *Gay Community News,* January 21–27, 1991.

Brunow, Jochen. "Kreuzfahrt der Phantasie." *TIP* 7, no. 5 (March 3–16, 1978).

Canetti, Elias. *Gesammelte Werke.* Munich: Carl Hanser, 1993.

———. *Masse und Macht.* Hamburg: Fischer Verlag, 2006.

Conrads, Bernd. "Grusel zum Abschied. Am 9. 12. wird Elfriede Jelinekes Abrechnung mit Jörg Haider uraufgeführt. Ulrike Ottinger über das Polit-Stück." *Welt am Sonntag,* December 3, 2000.

Cordingly, David. *Under the Black Flag: The Romance and the Reality of Life among the Pirates.* San Diego: Harcourt Brace, 1995.

Crowley, Aleister. *The Confessions of Aleister Crowley. An Autohagiography,* ed. John Symonds and Kenneth Grant. New York: Bantam Books, 1971.

Dargis, Manohla. "Price of Submission." *Film* (1991).

Depping, Iris. "Fluchtpunkt Shanghai." *TIP* 20 (1997).

Dermutz, Klaus. "Hermeneutischer Blindenhund in den Alpen. Elfriede Jelineks Haidermonolog 'Das Lebewohl' in der Uraufführung am Berliner Ensemble." *Süddeutsche Zeitung,* December 12, 2000.

Derrida, Jacques. "Above All, No Journalists!" In *Religion and Media,* ed. Hent De Vries and Samuel Weber, 56–93. Trans. Samuel Weber. Stanford: Stanford University Press, 2001.

———. "Droit de regards." In Marie-Françoise Plissart, *Droit de regards.* Paris: Editions de minuit, 1985.

———. "*Fichus*: Frankfurt Address." In *Paper Machine,* trans. Rachel Bowlby. Stanford: Stanford University Press, 2005.

Dignam, Virginia. "Johanna d'Arc of Mongolia." *Morning Star* (London), 1989.

Dunn, Katherine. "Introduction." In *Freak Like Me,* by Jim Rose, 9–17. London: Indigo, 1996.

Dyer, Richard. *Now You See It: Studies on Lesbian and Gay Film.* New York: Routledge, 1990.

"Ein unbekanntes Kapitel. 'Exil Shanghai'—Ulrike Ottinger über jüdische Flüchtlinge." *Süddeutsche Zeitung,* February 19, 1997.

Elbin, Cora. "Film und Frau. Wie die Düsseldorfer den letzten Film der Ulrike Ottinger verpaßten . . ." *Überblick* 40 (May 1984).

Ellis, Bret Easton. *American Psycho.* New York: Vintage, 1991.

"Entretien avec Ulrike Ottinger." Festival d'Automne a Paris, November 21 to December 15, 1990.

Feldvoß, Marli. "Ulrike Ottinger, ein Porträt anläßlich ihres neuen Films 'Taiga.'" Radio broadcast, HR and Deutsche Welle, March 1992.

Field, Syd. *Screenplay: The Foundations of Screenwriting.* New York: Dell, 1984.

Fischetti, Renate. "Écriture féminine in the New German Cinema: Ulrike Ottinger's *Portrait of a Woman Drinker.*" *Women in German Yearbook* 4 (1988): 47–67.

———. "'Ich glaube, daß Kunst ganz anders rezipiert würde, wenn man erst schaute und staunte. . .' Gespräch mit Ulrike Ottinger." In *Das Neue Kino.* Münster: Verlag Tende, 1992.

———. "In der Tradition der Avantgarde—Ulrike Ottingers Kino der Imagination." In *Das Neue Kino.* Münster: Verlag Tende, 1992.

Flusser, Vilém. *Die Geschichte des Teufels*. Göttingen: European Photography, 1993.

Focus. "(R)echte Verkaufsargumente. Ulrike Ottinger bringt Jelineks Haider-Stück 'Das Lebewohl' auf die Bühne des Berliner Ensembles." *Focus* 49 (2000).

Foucault, Michel. "Introduction." Trans. Donald F. Bouchard and Sherry Simon. In Gustave Flaubert, *The Temptation of Saint Anthony*, trans. Lafcadio Hearn, xxiii–xliv. New York: Modern Library, 2001.

Franke, Anselm. "Realitäten Formen." *KW Magazine* (January 2001): 51–52.

Freeman Sharpe, Ella. "Certain Aspects of Sublimation and Delusion." In *Collected Papers on Psychoanalysis*, ed. Marjorie Brierly. London: Hogarth Press, 1950 [1930].

———. *Dream Analysis. A Practical Handbook for Psychoanalysts*. London: Hogarth Press, 1961 [1937].

———. "The Impatience of Hamlet." In *Collected Papers of Psychoanalysis*, ed. Marjorie Brierly, 203–13. London: Hogarth Press, 1950 [1929].

Freud, Sigmund. *The Standard Edition of the Complete Psychological Works*, ed. and trans. James Strachey. 24 vols. London: Hogarth Press, 1953–74. Cited in the text as *SE*.

Frey, Reiner. "Unterwegs mit Ketzern und Freaks. Ein Interview mit Ulrike Ottinger über ihren Film *Freak Orlando*." *Filmfaust* 25 (1981): 41–47.

Gardiner, Robin, and Dan van der Vat. *The Titanic Conspiracy: Cover-ups and Mysteries of the World's Most Famous Sea Disaster*. Secaucus, N.J.: Citadel Press/Carol Publishing Group, 1997.

Geldner, Wilfried. "Penner werden Prinzen. Zum Abschluß des 22. Internationalen Forums des Jungen Films." *FAZ* (February 25, 1992).

Grafe, Frieda. "Mythen auf dem Mist des Alltags." *Süddeutsche Zeitung*, November 8, 1981.

———. "Nomaden im Chattanooga choo-choo." *Süddeutsche Zeitung*, April 3, 1989.

———. "Der Spiegel ist kein Medium." *Süddeutsche Zeitung*, May 5, 1984.

Grissemann, Stefan. "Um die Welt: Erinnerungen an die Emigration, ans Glück." *Die Presse*, February 7, 1998.

Grob, Norbert. "Die Lust am Schauen. Ulrike Ottinger's 'China. Die Künste—Der Alltag.'" *Die Zeit*, May 30, 1986.

Großklaus, Goetz. "Produktive Rätsel." *Filmfaust* (May–June 1984).

Habernoll, Kurt. Untitled. *Berliner Morgenpost*, September 30, 1983.

Hake, Sabine. "'And with Favorable Winds They Sailed Away': *Madame X* and Femininity." In *Gender and German Cinema: Feminist Interventions*, ed. San-

dra Frieden, Richard McCormick, Vibeke R. Peterson, and Laurie Vogelsang, 179–88. Vol. 1. Providence: Berg Publishers, 1993.
Hallwylska Museet. Historiska Myheter 42 (1995).
Hansen, Miriam. "Visual Pleasure, Fetishism, and the Problem of Feminine/Feminist Discourse: Ulrike Ottinger's Ticket of No Return." *New German Critique* 31 (winter 1984): 95–108.
Harris, Frank. *Oscar Wilde*. New York: Carroll & Graf Publishers, 1997 [1916].
Hartl, John. "Female Directors Have the Spotlight at Film Fest." *Seattle Times,* October 12, 1989.
Heimgärtner, Sabine. "Doppelbödige Konstruktion." *FAZ* (April 28, 1984).
Highsmith, Patricia. "Ich rufe auf zu der geistreichen, sarkastischen und irgendwie doch romantischen MADAME X!" In *Ulrike Ottinger. Texte und Dokumente,* ed. Freunde der Deutschen Kinemathek Berlin. *Kinemathek* 32, no. 86 (October 1995): 65.
"Die Hochzeit von Nestroy und Kabuki. Ulrike Ottinger über die universale Sprache der Kultur, das Lachen und was der Jodler mit Japan zu tun hat." *Kleine Zeitung* (Graz), September–October 1999, 10–11.
Hoff, Claudia. "Träume aus spitzem Glas. Bildnis einer Trinkerin." *medien praktisch* 2 (1980): 49–51.
Hoffman, Gerhard. Untitled. *Cinema* (November 1979).
Holden, Stephen. Untitled. *New York Times,* March 4, 1993.
Holz, Gudrun. "Urbaner Rundumschlag. Ein volles Forum: Geschichte, Erinnern, Dokus, Hongkong, Brasilien usw." *Junge Welt,* February 13, 1997.
Idel, Moshe. *Golem: Jewish Magical and Mystical Traditions on the Artificial Anthropoid.* Albany: SUNY Press, 1990.
Ilf, Ilya, and Yevgenii Petrov. *The Twelve Chairs,* trans. John H. C. Richardson. Evanston, Ill.: Northwestern University Press, 1997 [1928].
Jochum, Norbert. "Berlin ohne Rückfahrkarte. 'Bildnis einer Trinkerin' — exzentrische Visionen aus einer fremden Stadt." *Die Zeit,* November 23, 1979.
Kemetmüller, Klaus. Untitled. *Neue Zeit,* November 1977.
Kilb, Andreas. Untitled. *Die Zeit,* January 23, 1987.
King, Viki. *How to Write a Movie in 21 Days.* New York: Collins, 1993.
Kittler, Friedrich A. "Draculas Vermächtnis." *Zeta* 02 (1982).
———. "Weltatem. Über Wagners Medientechnologie." In *Diskursanalysen 1: Medien,* ed. F. A. Kittler, M. Schneider, and S. Weber. Opladen: Westdeutscher Verlag, 1987.
Klein, Melanie. *The Psychoanalysis of Children,* trans. Alix Strachey. London: Hogarth, 1932.
Knode, Helen. "Joan of Arc of Mongolia." *LA Weekly,* October 20–26, 1989.

Koch, Gertrud. "Arabesques and Intrigues. The Gaze of the Grotesque." In *Ulrike Ottinger: Image Archive*, 237–41. Nürnberg: Verlag für moderne Kunst, 2006.

———. "Auf Reisen gehen. Sehenswertes von Chantal Akerman und Ulrike Ottinger bei den Berliner Filmfestspielen." *Frankfurter Rundschau*, February 16, 1989.

———. "Demokratisierung des ästhetischen Blicks. Neue Filme von Jonas Mekas und Ulrike Ottinger auf dem Forum." *Frankfurter Rundschau*, February 27, 1986.

———. "Kino der Attraktionen." *Emma* (April 1984).

———. "Von der blendenden Schönheit des Häßlichen." *Frankfurter Rundschau*, November 14, 1981.

Kranz, Oliver. "Half Pipe von Loge zu Loge. Das Publikum am Berliner Ensemble freute sich über Sportliches mehr als über die Botschaften des Textes." *Münchener Abendzeitung*, December 11, 2000.

Kremski, Peter. "Postmoderne Collagen. Ulrike Ottingers Welt der Bilder." *Filmbulletin* 4 (1996): 56–57.

Kuhn, Annette. "Encounter between Two Cultures. A Discussion with Ulrike Ottinger." *Screen* 28, no. 24 (1987): 74–79.

Kuzniar, Alice. "Allegory, Androgyny, Anamorphosis: Ulrike Ottinger's Dorian Gray." In *The Queer German Cinema*. Stanford: Stanford University Press, 2000.

Lau, Mariam. "Pariaballade." *tageszeitung* (Berlin), September 19, 1997.

Liebl, Waltraut. "'Biete Welt!' Die Filme der Ulrike Ottinger." *Bodensee-Hefte* 3 (1988): 28–35.

Liese, Kirsten. "Ulrike Ottinger probt im Berliner Ensemble die Uraufführung von 'Das Lebewohl,' Elfriede Jelineks Abrechnung mit Jörg Haider." *Berliner Morgenpost*, December 6, 2000.

Longfellow, Brenda. "Lesbian Phantasy and the Other Woman in Ottinger's *Johanna d'Arc of Mongolia*." *Screen* 34 (1993): 124–36.

Luckhurst, Roger. *The Invention of Telepathy*. Oxford: Oxford University Press, 2002.

Luzina, Sandra. "Ulrike Ottinger inszeniert 'Das Lebewohl' von Elfriede Jelinek am Berliner Ensemble." *Der Tagesspiegel*, December 11, 2000.

Mannix, Daniel P. *Freaks: We Who Are Not As Others*. San Francisco: Re/Search Publications, 1990 [1976].

Marx, Leo. "The American Ideology of Space." In *Denatured Visions: Landscapes and Culture in the Twentieth Century*, ed. Stuart Wrede and William H. Adams. New York: Museum of Modern Art, 1991.

Mayne, Judith. *The Woman at the Keyhole: Feminism and Women's Cinema.* Bloomington: Indiana University Press, 1990.

Meyer, Eva. *Die Autobiographie der Schrift.* Frankfurt am Main: Stroemfeld/Roter Stern, 1990.

———. "Ottingers Artefakt." *Ulrike Ottinger. Texte und Dokumente,* ed. Freunde der Deutschen Kinemathek Berlin. *Kinemathek* 86, no. 32 (October 1995): 7–8.

———. "Ulrike Ottinger's Chronicle of Time." Trans. Catherine Kerkhoff-Saxon and Wilfried Prantner. *Afterall. A Journal of Art, Context, and Enquiry* (Autumn–Winter 2007).

Midding, Gerhard. "Das kritische Alter, mein Lieber! Ein Gespräch mit der französischen Schauspielerin Delphine Seyrig." *taz* (April 13, 1989): 14.

Möhrmann, Renate. *Die Frau mit der Kamera. Filmemacherinnen in der Bundesrepublik Deutschland. Situation, Perspektiven. Zehn exemplarische Lebensläufe.* Munich: Carl Hanser, 1980.

Mueller, Roswitha. Catalog text for *Ulrike Ottinger: A Retrospective.* USA and Canada Goethe-Institutes, 1990.

———. "Interview with Ulrike Ottinger." *Discourse* 6 (1983): 108–25.

———. "The Mirror and the Vamp." *New German Critique* 34 (winter 1985): 176–93.

Olivienza-Vostell, Mercedes Guardado, ed. *El Enigma Vostell.* Barcelona: Tipografia Emporium, 1982.

Ottinger, Ulrike. "Bon Voyage, Delphine." *Kameradschaft—Querelle. Kino zwischen Deutschland und Frankreich.* Munich, 1991.

———. "East-South-East. A Journey to the Blind Spots on the European Map." *Die Tageszeitung* (Berlin), October 12, 2000.

———. "Freak Orlando." *Eine künstlerische Gesamtkonzeption.* Berlin: DAAD Catalog, 1981.

———. "Korrespondenzen." *Kino, Movie, Cinema—100 Jahre Film—24 Bilder einer Ausstellung.* Berlin: Argon Verlag, 1995.

———. "Last Passages: Von Odessa nach Istanbul und zurück nach Nordwest." *Die Tageszeitung* (Berlin), December 21, 2000.

———. "Madame X—Eine absolute Herrscherin." *Drehbuch.* Frankfurt am Main: Stroemfeld/Roter Stern, 1978.

———. "Peter Lorre: Der Verlorene." In *European Coordination of Film Festivals.* Brussels: European Film Heritage, 2000.

———. "Stationenkino" ("Cinema of Stations"). In *Bildarchive.* Berlin: Kunst-Werke Catalog, 2001.

———. "Zum Film Ticket of No Return." *Trignon 79: masculin feminin.* Neue Galerie am Landesmuseum Johanneum, Biennale 1979.

———. "Der Zwang zum Genrekino." *Augenzeugen. 100 Texte neuer deutscher Filmemacher,* ed. Hans Helmut Prinzler and Eric Rentschler, 201–7. Frankfurt a/M: Verlag der Autoren: 1988.

———. "Zwei deutsche Patriarchen in Paris." In *Friedrich Wilhelm Murnau: Ein Melancholiker des Films.* Berlin: Bertz, 2003.

Ottinger, Ulrike/Blumenschein, Tabea/Bergius, Hanne. "Fazit ans einem Gespräch." *Kinemathek* 86 (2001): 56–58.

Perlmutter, Ruth. "German Grotesque: Two Films By Sander and Ottinger." In *Gender and German Cinema: Feminist Interventions,* ed. Sandra Frieden et al., 167–78. Vol. 1. Providence: Berg, 1993.

Perthold, Sabine. "Die maßlose Titanin—zwischen Stereotyp und Monomanie. 'Dorian Gray im Spiegel der Boulevardpresse,' 'Madame X' und andere Filme von Ulrike Ottinger." In *Mörderinnen im Film,* 106–9. Frauen Film Initiative. Berlin: Elefanten Press, 1982.

Pflaum, H. G. "Abstieg zum Bahnhof Zoo. Ulrike Ottingers Film 'Bildnis einer Trinkerin.'" *Süddeutsche Zeitung,* February 12, 1980.

———. "Gegen filmische Konventionen. Ulrike Ottingers 'China. Die Künste—Der Alltag.'" *Süddeutsche Zeitung,* July 19, 1986.

Pidduck, Julianne. "Freaks Amour." *Mirror* (Montreal), November 15, 1990.

"Piratinnen am Bodensee." *Emma. Zeitschrift für Frauen von Frauen* 8 (August 1977): 11–13.

Rall, Veronika. "Das Exil in den großen Städten. Dokumentar-Exkursionen im Forum von Ulrike Ottinger und Johan van der Keuken." *Frankfurter Rundschau,* February 20, 1997.

Rocamora, Carol. "The Germans Call It 'Vergangenheitsbewältigung.'" *New York Times,* May 13, 2001.

Rosenbaum, Jonathan. *Film: The Front Line / 1983.* Denver: Arden Press, 1983.

Ross, Robert. "Introduction." In Oscar Wilde, *Salomé,* trans. Lord Alfred Douglas. New York: Dover Publications, 1967 (facsimile 1930 London edition).

Rother, Hans-Jörg. "Satanstango im Forum. Die Berlinale zählt die Tage des analytischen Dokumentarfilms." *Frankfurter Allgemeine Zeitung,* February 15, 1997.

Russo, Mary. "Freaks, Freak Orlando, Orlando." In *The Female Grotesque: Risk, Excess, and Modernity,* 75–106. New York: Routledge, 1994.

Sachs, Hanns. "The Delay of the Machine Age." Trans. Margaret J. Powers. *Psychoanalytic Quarterly* 11, nos. 3–4 (1933): 404–24.

Sade, Marquis de. *Philosophy in the Boudoir,* trans. Julian Jones. London: Creation, 2000.

Sawicki, Diethard. *Leben mit den Toten. Geisterglauben und die Entstehung des Spiritismus in Deutschland* 1770–1900. Paderborn: Schöningh, 2002.

Schaper, Michael. Untitled. *Stern,* February 23, 1984.
Schifferle, Hans. "Von Partygästen und Schamanen. Deutsche Frauenfilme im Forum und im Panorama." *Süddeutsche Zeitung,* February 26, 1992.
Schmidgall, Gary. *The Stranger Wilde. Interpreting Oscar.* New York: Dutton, 1994.
Scholem, Gershom. *On the Kabbalah and Its Symbolism,* trans. Ralph Manheim. New York: Schocken Books, 1997 [1960].
Schreber, Daniel Paul. *Memoirs of My Nervous Illness,* ed and trans. Ida Macalpine and Richard A. Hunter. Cambridge, Mass.: Harvard University Press, 1988. [*Denkwürdigkeiten eines Nervenkranken nebst Nachträgen und einem Anhang über die Frage: "Unter welchen Voraussetzungen darf eine für geisteskrank erachtete Person gegen ihren erklärten Willen in einer Heilanstalt festgehalten werden?"* Leipzig: Oswald Mutze, 1903.]
Schreck, Nikolas. *The Satanic Screen: An Illustrated Guide to the Devil in Cinema 1896–1999.* Los Angeles: Creation Books, 2001.
Schütte, Wolfram. "Kleine Komödien des Low-Budgets samt Freaks, Wahnwelten und Endspielen. Auf den 15. Hofer Filmtagen gesehen." *Frankfurter Rundschau* (Feuilleton), November 7, 1981.
Silberman, Marc. "Interview with Ulrike Ottinger: Surreal Images." *Jump Cut* 29 (1984).
Silverman, Kaja. "From the Ideal-Ego to the Active Gift of Love." In *The Threshold of the Visible World,* 39–81. New York: Routledge, 1996.
Simonoviescz, Andre. "Letzte Zuflucht." *Berlinale-tip,* February 5, 1997.
Sitwell, Edith. "Pride." In *The Seven Deadly Sins,* 14–22. New York: William Morrow & Co., 1966.
Spies, Hansjörg. Untitled. *Kleine Zeitung,* November 1977.
Steinwachs, Ginka. "Ein Versuch zur Archäologie der Subjektivität von Ulrike Ottinger und Tabea Blumenschein." *Die Schwarze Botin* (January 1978).
Stern, Harold. *The Couch: Its Use and Meaning in Psychotherapy.* New York: Human Sciences Press, 1978.
Stoker, Bram. *Dracula.* Toronto: Bantam Books, 1981 [1897].
Stone, Judy. "Westerners Kidnapped by Warrior Women in Mongolia." *San Francisco Chronicle,* June 23, 1989.
Storfer, A. J., ed. *Die Gelbe Post* 1–7 (May–November 1939).
———. "Zur Sonderstellung des Vatermords." *Schriften zur angewandten Seelenkunde* 12 (1911).
Straayer, Chris. *Deviant Eyes, Deviant Bodies: Sexual Re-Orientations in Film and Video.* New York: Columbia University Press, 1996.
Strempel, Gesine. "Interview mit Ulrike Ottinger." *Courage. Aktuelle Frauenzeitung* 3 (1979).

Sykora, Katharina. "China. Die Künste—Der Alltag." *epd Film* 9 (1986).
———. "Stills und Sessions." In *Ulrike Ottinger. Sessions*. Berlin: Contemporary Fine Arts, 2001. English translation is on errata insert.
Tax, Sissi. ". . . la forza / power / le pouvoir . . ." *Konkursbuch* 12 (1984): 23–35.
———. "Interview mit Ulrike Ottinger." Program for *Exil Shanghai*. 27. Internationales Forum des Jungen Films, 47. Internationale Filmfestspiele Berlin, 1997.
"TIP-Interview mit U. Ottinger." *TIP* (November 16–27, 1979): 16–18.
Treut, Monika. "Ein Nachtrag zu Ulrike Ottinger's Film Madame X." *Frauen und Film* 28 (1981): 15-20.
———. "Gespräch mit Ulrike Ottinger." In *Ulrike Ottinger. Texte und Dokumente,* ed. Freunde der Deutschen Kinemathek Berlin. *Kinemathek* 32, no. 86 (October 1995). The interview was conducted on July 8, 1982, and was not published before 1995.
Ulrike Ottinger. Texte und Dokumente, ed. Freunde der Deutschen Kinemathek Berlin. *Kinemathek* 86 (October 1995). 2d ed., 2001.
Visarius, Karsten. "Sündenregister." *Frankfurter Allgemeine Zeitung,* January 27, 1987.
Warren, Ina. "Women's Film Lineup Offers Lively Panorama." *Gazette* (Montreal), June 14, 1989.
Weiss, Andrea. *Vampires and Violets. Lesbians in Film*. New York: Penguin Books, 1992.
White, Patricia. "Madame X of the China Seas." *Screen* 28, no. 4 (autumn 1987): 80–95.
Wiener, Norbert. *God and Golem, Inc.—A Comment on Certain Points Where Cybernetics Impinges on Religion*. Cambridge, Mass.: M.I.T. Press, 1964.
Wilde, Oscar. *The Picture of Dorian Gray*. In *The Picture of Dorian Gray and Other Writings,* ed. Richard Ellmann, 3–193. New York: Bantam Books, 1982 [1891].
———. *Salomé*. Trans. Richard Ellmann. In *The Picture of Dorian Gray and Other Writings,* ed. Richard Ellmann, 261–95. New York: Bantam Books, 1982 [1896].
Witte, Karsten. "Der Dandy als Dame." *Frankfurter Rundschau,* November 13, 1979.
———. "Gespräch mit Ulrike Ottinger." In *Ulrike Ottinger. Texte und Dokumente,* ed. Freunde der Deutschen Kinemathek Berlin. *Kinemathek* 32, no. 86 (October 1995): 185–93.
———. "Grenzgänge und Mauersprünge. Berliner Dokumentarfilme von Jürgen Böttcher, Ulrike Ottinger u.a. über ein geschleiftes Monument von Weltruhm." *Frankfurter Rundschau,* March 7, 1991.

———. "Die Spielerin." *Frankfurter Rundschau,* April 27, 1984.

———. "Weiblicher Piratenakt." *Die Zeit,* April 14, 1978.

Wolff, Raymond. "Ulrike Ottinger Takes On Europe's 'Blank Spaces': Her New Documentary Premieres at Documenta." *Aufbau,* June 27, 2002.

Woolf, Virginia. *Orlando. A Biography.* New York: Signet Classic, 1960 [1928].

Wunderlich, Hans Georg. *Wohin der Stier Europa trug.* Reinbek bei Hamburg: Rowohlt, 1991 [1972].

Youens, Rachel. "'Ulrike Ottinger' Stills." *NY Arts* (international edition), June 2000.

LAURENCE A. RICKELS is professor of German and comparative literature, as well as adjunct professor in the departments of art and film and media studies, at the University of California, Santa Barbara. He is also Sigmund Freud Professor of Media and Philosophy at the European Graduate School in Saas Fee, Switzerland. His writing is renowned for its stylistic experimentation, and as a theorist he takes seriously the task of finding form for thought.